Slamming Spam

Slamming Spam

A GUIDE FOR SYSTEM ADMINISTRATORS

Robert Haskins
Dale Nielsen

♦♦Addison-Wesley

Upper Saddle River, NJ • Boston • Indianapolis • San Francisco •
New York • Toronto • Montreal • London • Munich • Paris • Madrid
Capetown • Sydney • Tokyo • Singapore • Mexico City

The publisher offers excellent discounts on this book when ordered in quantity for bulk purchases or special sales, which may include electronic versions and/or custom covers and content particular to your business, training goals, marketing focus, and branding interests. For more information, please contact:

U. S. Corporate and Government Sales
(800) 382-3419
corpsales@pearsontechgroup.com

For sales outside the U. S., please contact:

International Sales
international@pearsoned.com

Visit us on the Web: www.awprofessional.com

Library of Congress Cataloging-in-Publication Data:

2004112840

ISBN 0-13-146716-6
Text composed in Minion and Lucida Sans Typewriter using FrameMaker 7.1 and printed in the United States on 45# Lynx Recycled paper at Phoenix Book Tech in Hagerstown, MD.
First printing, December 2004

WE DEDICATE THIS BOOK TO OUR WIVES, MARY AND JANICE,
FOR THEIR SUPPORT AND ENCOURAGEMENT.
—ROBERT AND DALE

Contents

About the Authors

ROBERT HASKINS works for Renesys Corporation, a leader in real-time Internet connectivity monitoring and reporting. He has been a Unix system administrator since graduating from the University of Maine with a degree in Computer Science. After an initial stint working at a nuclear power plant, Robert has fought spam in many environments, including enterprises, cable modem ISP, network equipment manufacturer, wholesale dialup ISP, competitive local exchange carrier, and traditional ISP. He has presented on the topic of fighting spam at NANOG, FBI Boston Infragard, and LISA. Robert writes a regular technical column called ISPadmin on service provider topics for Usenix's *;login:*. He is a member of Usenix, SAGE, and IEEE.

DALE NIELSEN is a partner in Avacoda, LLC, a consulting company specializing in systems administration and software development. He has worked as a systems administrator since receiving his degree in Computer Science from the University of Massachusetts. He has more than twenty years experience administering Unix- and Linux-based mail servers, firewalls, and workstations. He has worked in a variety of engineering and software development environments and has taught courses in systems administration at Sun Microsystems. Recently he's done consulting work for clients including Nortel Networks and Ziplink. He has written about Linux-based firewalls for the *Linux Journal*.

Robert and Dale have also developed a patent-pending method to reduce spam for Ziplink, Inc.

Preface

This book is meant to be a reference for the email system administrator who has been asked to implement an anti-spam solution for their organization. This is an administrator's "how to" stop spam book. It is very hands on, with none of the "why people spam" or other topics which are usually only peripherally interesting or useful to a mail administrator.

Fighting spam is a complex problem, with many potential technical, legislative, and social solutions. No book could ever hope to cover them all in a reasonable amount of space. In fact, when considering only the possible technical spam-fighting solutions, it isn't possible to give them all the coverage they require. Our focus in this book is on the widely used open source anti-spam solutions available for major mail transfer agents (email servers).

Check out the web site for this book at *http://www.slammingspam.com*. It has all the latest information on the book, including updated URLs, errata, and other useful information in the fight against spam.

WHO THIS BOOK IS FOR

The reader is assumed to have a limited knowledge of Linux/Unix. In most cases, step-by-step instructions are provided for the covered package or approach. These "cookbook" examples are meant to work for most installations, with minimal changes and/or customizations. While some knowledge is assumed of the mail-transfer agent software used (such as Sendmail), the administrator doesn't need to be a mail server expert or Linux guru to implement the solutions outlined here.

You will learn about the best current anti-spam methods and software available. Most of the methods are open source and freely available (as in free beer). These open source solutions offer the "best of breed" anti-spam solutions available today. Implementing open source solutions requires more work than commercial solutions, but often the administrator ends up with a more flexible, better solution than is otherwise available.

We initially thought we would discuss anti-spam services such as Postini and Symantec's Brightmail in the book. However, we found that most of the commercial anti-spam solutions (such as anti-spam firewalls) and services were documented quite well and didn't require additional coverage. As a result, most commercial solutions are only mentioned in the Introduction. The only non-open source anti-spam solution covered here (McAfee SpamKiller) is directly related to the commercial mail servers covered—IBM/Lotus Notes/Domino and Microsoft Exchange.

The IBM Lotus Domino and Microsoft Exchange administrator has a choice. An anti-spam solution can be implemented directly as part of the mail server, since both IBM Lotus and Microsoft Exchange support plug-ins. To supplement or as an alternative to a tightly integrated solution (like McAfee SpamKiller), additional open source email servers can be deployed specifically to perform spam filtering or virus checking. These anti-spam/virus servers would process the message before sending it on to the Domino/Exchange server for delivery to the recipient.

While adding to the "box count" an administrator needs to manage, this approach does enable an open source best-of-breed solution to these otherwise "closed" commercial email servers. A hybrid approach can reduce the out-of-pocket cost while giving the administrator much flexibility in tweaking the anti-spam solution.

WHAT YOU WILL NEED

The solutions in this book focus on Linux, on the server side. There is some coverage of the client side, but primarily the client coverage is meant to complement the server implementations we examine. Although the solutions presented here have been tested on Debian and/or Fedora Core Linux, they should work on almost every version of Linux available without too many modifications.

The covered mail transfer agents (MTAs) are Sendmail, Postfix, qmail, IBM Lotus Domino, and Microsoft Exchange. We assume the reader has a previously installed and working MTA, as the task of installing and configuring a single MTA can be a book unto itself. SMTP authentication support for Postfix, Sendmail, and qmail may require the recompilation of the MTAs in order to implement. Having a previously installed compiled and working MTA makes SMTP AUTH much easier.

We assume the reader has root access to the machine(s) they want to implement the anti-spam solutions covered here. Although many of the solutions do not require root access and can be installed and run as a "regular" user (though sometimes this requires configuration changes), we assume root access in our examples. You will see the use of root only when absolutely necessary. You won't see us compiling or installing anything as the root user, unless there is no other way to do it.

Often, we use the sudo command in order to run privileged commands which otherwise would require the root password. sudo is potentially a better way of giving out root access, without disclosing the root password. The commands prefixed by sudo could just as easily be run as root, assuming the root user's path is identical to the unprivileged user's path. For many examples, we assume the user performing the installation tasks has write access to /usr/local.

A few notes regarding other Linux/Unix command assumptions. We presume the reader has access to and knowledge of the following Linux utilities:

- tar for tar formatted archives
- gzip for GNU zip formatted archives
- zip for the Info-zip formatted archives
- bzip2 for bzip2 formatted archives
- wget, lynx and/or ftp for retrieving source archives

We presume you have a recent version of gcc on the system to build the anti-spam utilities outlined here. Some of the packages covered here specifically require GNU make. Most Linux distributions come with GNU make. If you are building these solutions on a BSD derivative such as FreeBSD, or another platform such Sun Solaris or HP-UX, you may need to install GNU make for the spam-fighting utilities that require it.

In this book, we often mention maildir and mbox (or mailbox) formatted files. You should be aware which type of mailbox your email server software uses. The configuration for many anti-spam utilities covered in this book will vary depending upon which mailbox format is used. (Lotus Domino and Microsoft Exchange use their own internal format, so the mailbox format doesn't apply to those email servers.)

The mbox format stores the messages for a particular user in one file per folder. Because mbox was the original (and at one time only) mailbox format, it has wide support. Sendmail and Postfix use mbox formatted mailboxes by default. Mailboxes in the mbox format work fine in many installations, but can pose problems for some administrators in some cases. For example, mbox formatted mailboxes on NFS-mounted filesystems have locking issues that can result in mailbox corruption.

Maildir stores each message as individual files, with unique names in a directory structure with a directory for each folder. In many cases, a "/" after a filename parameter will indicate maildir formatted message directory, and the lack of a "/" will indicate that a mailbox is in mbox format. qmail uses maildir formatted mailboxes by default. Postfix can be configured easily to use maildir formatted mailboxes. If Procmail is used as the mail delivery agent, Procmail can easily be configured to use maildir format by specifying the folder name with a trailing "/".

HOW THIS BOOK IS ORGANIZED

This book can be read cover to cover in order to give the reader a hands-on view of the many methods to fight spam. However, the individual chapters are self-contained, so if there are specific anti-spam solutions you want to implement, you can just skip to those particular chapters.

Chapter 1, "Introduction," is an overview of some of the currently available major anti-spam technologies. It is useful for putting the solutions provided in the rest of the book in context. The focus is designing an anti-spam infrastructure for an organization's network, walking through policy, information gathering, design questions, and goals. If you are interested in designing an anti-spam architecture from scratch, Chapter 1 is an excellent starting point.

Chapter 2, "Procmail, " is a tool often used as a mail-delivery agent by anti-spam software to complete the job of fighting spam. For example, many statistical analysis tools depend upon procmail to perform the filtering of messages into the spam or non-spam folders. If the anti-spam tools of interest require the use of procmail, this chapter should be read if the reader is not familiar with the procmail utility.

Chapter 3, "SpamAssassin," covers the widely known and used spam classifier program. This chapter contains a treatment of the popular anti-spam scoring program, from installing the required packages to configuring SpamAssassin, and ruleset (scoring) creation. If the reader is planning to utilize a general purpose anti-spam filter, SpamAssassin is an excellent choice.

Chapter 4, "Native MTA Anti-Spam Features," covers the native anti-spam capabilities included with the covered open source MTAs. Topics covered here include whitelisting/blacklisting, blackhole listing services, tweaking the MTA to help block spam, and other functions native to the modern MTA. If you wonder what the access database is, or how to tweak Postfix's configuration to block the PIPELINE command, then this is a good chapter for you.

Chapter 5, "SMTP AUTH and STARTTLS," shows how to secure the covered MTA's from sending unwanted outbound spam. Cyrus SASL is used as the basis of SMTP AUTH and STARTTLS functionality for the Sendmail and Postfix MTAs. Installation and configuration of Cyrus SASL for Sendmail and Postfix is covered, as well as the netqmail-1.05 distribution of qmail, which includes patches providing SMTP AUTH and STARTTLS functionality.

Chapter 6, "Distributed Checksum Filtering," covers the Distributed Checksum Clearinghouse (DCC) and Vipul's Razor protocols for exchanging email checksums to identify bulk emailings. Distributed Collaborative (or Checksum) Filtering is an excellent way to help determine whether a message is spam by querying other servers and seeing the number of times a particular message has been processed by other servers.

Chapter 7, "Introduction to Bayesian Filtering," gives the reader a working knowledge behind the most efficient spam-fighting technology to date, Bayesian analysis. Written by Rob Kolstad, it gives an accessible treatment of how the Bayesian analysis algorithms are implemented in the covered applications as well.

Chapter 8, "Bayesian Filtering," covers installation and configuration of a number of the more popular Bayesian filters available, including bogofilter, ASSP, and CRM114.

Chapter 9, "Email Client Filtering," walks the reader through the built-in anti-spam capabilities in Microsoft Outlook, Microsoft Outlook Express, and Mozilla Messenger. It also covers POPFile, one of the Bayesian filters available for any POP3-compliant email client platform.

Chapter 10, "Microsoft Exchange," covers the basic anti-spam capabilities in this popular email server, including the Intelligent Message Filter, Microsoft's anti-spam solution based upon its Smartscreen technology. Chapter 10 also covers McAfee SpamKiller for Exchange 2.1.1, which is an implementation of SpamAssassin tightly integrated into Exchange.

Chapter11, " Lotus Domino and Lotus Notes," walks the reader through the built-in anti-spam capabilities in this popular enterprise email server, Domino, and associated email client, Notes. McAfee SpamKiller for Domino 2.1, a Spam-

Assassin-based implementation tightly integrated into Domino, is also covered. In addition, how to set up Lotus Domino for use with SMTP AUTH/STARTTLS is detailed.

Chapter 12, "Sender Verification," covers some of the lesser known open source products available in the areas of challenge response and one-time use email accounts (Active Spam Killer and Tagged Message Delivery Agent). Also covered is a sender compute implementation with very nice CRM114 integration known as Camram.

Appendix A covers Sender Policy Framework, a relatively new method for determining the validity of sending email messages by domains publishing "reverse mail exchanger" (MX) records, and recipient email servers enforcing those SPF records published by domain owners.

Appendix B shows the reader how to read email headers, and covers tools associated with spam fighting including SpamCop. It uses an example spam message to show how spammers try to obfuscate their intentions.

Appendix C explains the SpamAssassin default ruleset as it is shown on the SpamAssassin web site.

Appendix D covers SpamAssassin utilities command line interface options.

Appendix E shows SpamAssassin configuration file keywords.

Appendix F covers DSPAM, a Bayesian classifier designed for speed and accuracy, aimed squarely at the organization with thousands of email boxes.

Appendix G contains a list of resources the spam fighting reader should find useful.

CONVENTIONS USED IN THIS BOOK

The following conventions are used in this book:

http://www.slammingspam.com	URLs are in italic and preceded with http: or ftp:
`$AddWarningsInline = 1;`	Anything output from a program, or input into a file, is in a monospace font
`bash$ mkdir spam`	Any non-privileged input the reader must type in is in a monospace font and preceded by `bash$`

`bash$ mkdir ~/spam`	~ indicates the current user's home directory
`bash$ mkdir ~/`*`dirname`*	Any variable input the reader must change in input lines is in a monospace italic font
`# mkdir /var/quarantine`	Any command that requires privilege is in monospace and preceded with #
`bash$ sudo mkdir /var/amavis`	Lines in monospace prefixed with `bash$ sudo` also indicates a command requires privilege
`bash$ cp amavisd.conf \` `/etc/`	The \ character at the end of a monospace input line indicates that the line continues from the preceding line.
`FEATURE( `dnsbl', `rbl.example.com'` `➥)dnl`	The ➥ character at the beginning of a monospaced line indicates a continuation of the previous line in certain cases where line exceeds the printed page width.

ACKNOWLEDGMENTS

No project like this occurs without the assistance of numerous people, some of who are listed here.

First of all, we would like to thank Rob Kolstad for contributing Chapter 7, "Introduction to Bayesian Analysis". This is an accessible and thorough treatment of the theory behind what we consider *the* most important spam-fighting technique available today.

We owe a great debt of gratitude to all the people from Pearson: Mary Franz, Noreen Regina, Jim Markham, and Lori Lyons.

The following people reviewed the entire manuscript, for which we are greatly indebted: Fredrick M. Avolio, Eric S. Johannson, and Sarah Ratta. The following individuals reviewed pieces of the manuscript under very short notice, for which we are very grateful: Tim Speed, Henrik Walther, Lars Powers, and Pete Moulton.

We would like to thank all the authors of open source packages used in this book, along with the many people who have devised (and shared) their anti-spam solutions through web sites, email lists, and other avenues. Without people like you, our inboxes would be even **more** flooded with spam! We truly stand on the shoulders of giants.

The Resources appendix lists many of the URLs we used in building the software components listed in this book. In particular we would like to thank the following people for allowing us to use portions of their web sites in parts our coverage. For pieces of the SpamAssassin (*http://spamassassin.apache.org*) coverage in Chapter 3 and Appendixes C, D, and E, Justin Mason; for parts of the Vipul's Razor (*http://razor.sourceforge.net*) coverage in Chapter 6, Vipul Ved Prakash; for portions of the Tagged Message Delivery Agent (TMDA) (*http://tmda.net*) coverage in Chapter 12, Jason R. Mastaler.

From Microsoft's public-relations firm of Waggener Edstrom, we would like to thank Tina Austinson and Amy Petty. From IBM/Lotus, we thank Erica Topolski and Edmund "Ted" Stanton. From McAfee Inc., we thank Tracy Ross, Zoe Lowther, Tim Smithson, and Brian Barnes. From Microsoft support, we thank Fred Wander.

Robert Haskins thanks: Jim Markham of Pearson for his very able assistance in manuscript preparation; my employer, Renesys Corporation (especially Todd Underwood, Andy Ogielski, Jim Cowie, BJ Premore, Rob Bushell, Eric Smith, and Joe Edelman) for their ideas, feedback, and support; David Webster of Computer Net Works for his support and the use of CNW facilities; and most importantly, to my spouse Mary and children Claire and Peter for their encouragement, patience, and understanding during this project.

Dale Nielsen thanks: My partners at Avacoda, LLC, Daniel Dee and Scott Reed, for the use of the Avacoda computing lab facilities as test beds for the software described herein; and especially my wife Janice and my daughter Crystal, for their willingness to have their email put through experimental anti-spam configurations, but most of all for their patience and support over the months that were spent on this project.

Introduction

The problem of spam is largely based upon your perspective. If you are a marketer who sends information via electronic means, you might be of the opinion that "there is no such thing as spam." If you are a service provider or a large enterprise, you know spam by the complaints you receive in the call center. As an individual, you probably "know spam when you see it."

Unfortunately, the problem of spam is here to stay, at least until the proper social, legislative, and technical controls are in place to stop it. No book on the topic of spam can really address the social and legislative aspects of the problem. The only realistic means we have to control spam today is technical. The ultimate technical solution to the problem of spam is to redefine the protocol that standardizes it, namely RFC2821/2822 (and others). Unfortunately, a protocol-level solution to the problem of spam will likely not be available for some time and will be difficult to implement, so technical solutions to the problem must be put together piecemeal.

As a result, we are left with technical processes that are largely inadequate but must be used because they are the best methods available today. These methods vary widely in their approach, scope, and difficulty to implement, among other factors. In this book, we cover the most common methods used to fight spam.

EMAIL TERMINOLOGY

We use many electronic mail terms and acronyms throughout this book. In this section, we briefly cover some of the basic terminology that you'll encounter.

Mail Transfer Agent (or Server)

A mail transfer agent (MTA) is a program that transmits messages from one machine to another. We use MTA interchangeably with "email server" throughout this book. Examples of MTAs include Sendmail, Postfix, qmail, MS Exchange, and Lotus Domino.

Mail Delivery Agent

A mail delivery agent (MDA) is a program that delivers messages to users' mailboxes. Sendmail ships with the `mail.local` utility, which writes messages to users' mailboxes. You can also use Procmail as an MDA. Some MDAs are incorporated directly into the MTA, such as Lotus Domino and MS Exchange.

Mail Client

A mail client is a program that enables a user to read his or her email messages. Some mail clients (such as mutt) are based on a command line interface (CLI) and require the user to log in to a Unix interactive session and view messages in a text mode. CLI mail clients often require direct access to the user's mailbox.

Other mail clients (such as Mozilla Messenger, Microsoft Outlook, and Microsoft Outlook Express) are graphical in nature. These programs require the use of POP3 or IMAP protocols to display the messages in an easy-to-read format for the end user.

INBOUND VERSUS OUTBOUND SPAM

Throughout this book, we use inbound and outbound to describe the direction of messages that your users receive and send, respectively. *Inbound* refers to messages (and spam) that end up in mailboxes on machines that you, as an administrator, manage. For example, these messages end up in IMAP or POP3 servers and are downloaded to an email client such as Mozilla or Microsoft Outlook. *Outbound* refers to messages that your users send from email clients, such as Microsoft Outlook Express or Lotus Notes, to remote users hosted on other mail systems. These messages (which hopefully are not spam!) pass through your mail systems on their way to their ultimate destination in some system not (necessarily) administrated by you.

This book focuses on inbound spam, or messages received by your users. Although Chapter 5, "SMTP AUTH and STARTTLS," is dedicated to stopping outbound spam, preventing your users from sending spam is usually a much easier problem to solve than managing the spam your users receive (inbound spam). The much more difficult problem to solve is inbound spam. Of course, you do not want to run email systems that are considered "open relays," which allow anyone on the Internet to send spam through them, so you must take steps to secure all mail servers appropriately against open relay access.

(MIS)CLASSIFICATIONS AND SIDELINING

Before we go any further, we should talk about misclassified messages. In a perfect world, spam wouldn't exist, and no legitimate messages would be misclassified as spam. However, we live in an imperfect world, so we must deal with spam and messages that get routed to our spam folder incorrectly.

A *false positive* is a legitimate message that is incorrectly identified as spam. Most anti-spam implementations try to minimize false positives because they are messages that recipients may not see if they don't check their junk email folder often enough. A *false negative* is a spam message that ends up in a user's regular inbox. These are usually more acceptable because the recipient won't be as likely to miss a message sitting in his or her inbox.

Besides just tagging a message and sending it along, another way to handle spam messages is called *sidelining* or *quarantining*. This involves placing the suspected spam message in a separate repository for the user to look at later. The anti-virus companies refer to this as "quarantining" a message. The user (or administrator) will then inspect the message and either delete it (if it was correctly identified as spam) or move it to the user's inbox for later disposition if it is a legitimate message. Anti-spam services such as Brightmail and Postini often use this approach. Sidelining is also available in certain MTAs such as Microsoft Exchange.

FUNDAMENTAL ANTI-SPAM TECHNIQUES

In this section, we cover some of the common methods used to defeat spam. These techniques show up many times throughout this book and are the basis of the ongoing fight against spam.

WHITELISTS AND BLACKLISTS

These are lists of senders who are always allowed (whitelisted) or always denied (blacklisted) the ability to deliver messages. These whitelists/blacklists are less useful now than they were when spam first became a problem, but they can be helpful in some circumstances. Depending upon how they are implemented, whitelist/blacklist checks can happen at one or more points along a message's journey. For example, list checks can happen at the edge of the network, at the POP/IMAP server, or at the email client.

Whitelists or blacklists can be enforced within most MTAs at different times in the transfer of the message. Such times include prior to the connection being accepted by the server, after the connection has been accepted but before delivery to the recipient, and at email recipient delivery time. Some of the more common fields that can be whitelisted/blacklisted include

- From/To username or domain
- Server name, domain, or IP address

All modern MTAs have good support of whitelisting and blacklisting. Many of the anti-spam packages covered in this book have their own whitelist/blacklist support. McAfee SpamKiller for Mail Servers even has hierarchical whitelists/blacklists, allowing the administrator to override certain client-listed items.

Whitelists/blacklists are an integral part of many anti-spam solutions and are an added feature of others. For example, POPFile's "magnet" feature is a whitelist/blacklist. In a challenge/response system, after an email address is "known" to the system, it is whitelisted so that the sender needn't go through the authentication process on subsequent messages. SpamAssassin gives you the ability to whitelist senders automatically.

HEADER CHECKING

Another common method of determining a message's legitimacy is to perform header checks when the MTA accepts the message. Some of the tests that can be done here include

- Valid From address
- DNS checks
- Strict header checking
- Blacklists/whitelists (static or dynamic)

Valid From Address

One way spammers conceal their true identity is by forging their From address. You can defeat this trick by requiring your mail server to check the validity of the From address's domain. Of course, spammers can counter this technique by using valid From addresses, but many do not bother.

Sender Policy Framework (or SPF) is an attempt to standardize the process by which a From address is considered legitimate. This is accomplished by publishing special DNS TXT records indicating that mail with a particular From address should be coming from a certain set of email servers. More information on SPF is available in Appendix A and at *http://spf.pobox.com.*

DNS Checks

Similar in nature to the valid From address, many spammers use servers with no forward or reverse DNS entries or servers whose forward entry does not match the reverse. Mail originating from servers with incorrect DNS setups like this can be stopped with the appropriate setup in most MTAs. Be aware that strict DNS checking may stop some legitimate email from getting through to users, though.

Strict Header Checking

Email standards are defined by Request for Comments, or RFCs. RFCs are the basis for how the entire Internet interoperates at a low level. Email-specific RFCs specify how sending email servers connect to recipient servers in order to transfer their messages. Older versions of Sendmail are lax in interpreting RFCs. For example, Sendmail version 8.8 and earlier are very lenient in their default acceptance of parameters to the MAIL FROM: and RCPT TO: commands. Other rigorous header checking techniques include requiring HELO/EHLO, accurate parameters to HELO/EHLO, etc. Many MTAs can control how strict the server should be when accepting inbound messages. Making these sorts of changes may reduce spam but can also cause problems for legitimate email delivery from misconfigured systems.

Blacklists and Whitelists

Blacklists and whitelists can be defined in all modern MTAs. These lists can take the form of servers, domains, or IP address ranges and can be static (defined locally on the server in a text file or database) or dynamic (for example, domain name system block lists or DNSBLs). When used at mail transfer time, DNSBLs can reduce the amount of spam coming into a mail system. However, use these lists with caution because they can end up blocking legitimate messages if the block lists are too strict.

CONTENT FILTERING

The ability to scan email for certain spam-identifying characteristics is an excellent method to reduce spam. Content filters often generate a score for a message that helps the end user decide how to handle the message, rather than automatically rejecting or sidelining the message. The user utilizes the email client filtering capability to move messages identified by the content filter to a junk email folder.

The downside of content filters is the effort required to keep them current. Spammers constantly tweak their messages to get past content (and other) filters.

Bayesian Analysis

Bayesian analysis is a special form of content filtering, in which statistical analysis of the message components (including headers) takes place. Bayesian analysis is a particularly accurate way of identifying whether a message is spam. Refer to Chapter 7, "Introduction to Bayesian Filtering," for an introduction to Bayesian analysis and Chapter 8, "Bayesian Filtering," for Bayesian solutions. Chapter 9, "Email Client Filtering," has a section on POPFile, which is usually implemented on email clients such as Microsoft Outlook Express. The Bayesian analysis can actually work as a complex filtering mechanism to replace the filtering capability typically included in the email client itself.

Email Client Filtering

The capability to filter in the end user email client software is a method used throughout this book to help identify the modifications that anti-spam software makes to messages. The changes to email messages are usually either the addition of a header or headers indicating a spam score and other information or modifications to the subject line of the message. Chapter 9 includes coverage of how to configure popular email clients for use with the server-side solutions outlined in this book.

DISTRIBUTED COLLABORATIVE FILTERING

These systems calculate checksums of every message processed and place the result into a database. Then, each time a particular checksum is encountered, a counter is incremented. If the count for a particular checksum (email) is high, then the message is probably either a legitimate mailing list message to a large number of recipients or a spam message. In the case of a mailing list message, the sender can be whitelisted so that the message does not get misclassified as spam.

It is important to understand that Distributed Collaborative Filtering (also called Distributed Checksum Filtering, or DCF) systems do not identify messages as spam or non-spam. They simply count the number of times a message has been seen by a particular set of email systems and report that count appropriately. The DCF method is very good at what it does, but the system needs to be deployed as part of a larger anti-spam solution, or else a high rate of false positives will likely be encountered. Mailing messages will often be treated as spam unless some sort of whitelist is used with a DCF solution. Chapter 6, "Distributed Checksum Filtering," contains coverage of two common distributed collaborative filtering systems: DCC and Vipul's Razor.

SENDER VERIFICATION

Sender verification is a broad category of techniques that require some action on the part of the sender in order to prove that the sender is not a spammer and that the message is not otherwise undesirable (such as an electronic virus). Numerous types of sender verification systems are available; we cover the following types in Chapter 12, "Sender Verification."

Challenge/Response

This method requires the receiver to send some sort of an acknowledgement back to the sender before the sender is able to view the message. Many email recipients won't respond to challenge/response systems. Another issue is the "chicken and the egg" problem, where two people who use challenge/response systems want to communicate with each other for the first time without any other method of communication. This is a difficult, if not impossible, situation to address with the challenge response solution.

Tagged Message Delivery Agent, Active Spam Killer, and Camram all have support for challenge response. They are covered in Chapter 12.

Special Use Email Addresses

One way to reduce the amount of spam is to generate special-purpose email addresses. Some MTAs (qmail in particular) make it very easy to generate email addresses on the fly that effectively can be one time (or special) use. Tagged Message Delivery Agent also has support for special-purpose email addresses.

Sender Compute

In the sender compute model, a recipient requires the sender to calculate an algorithm and send the result back to the recipient, usually in the form of a web page or special email header in the original email. This method is often called "proof of work" or "Internet postage," although the latter term implies money transferral, which doesn't happen in the sender compute model. Camram (covered in Chapter 12) contains support for the sender compute model, as well as challenge/response and a GUI interface to CRM114 (a highly accurate Bayesian classifier).

OTHER ANTI-SPAM METHODS

The following methods are less effective in general and therefore less useful for most organizations. However, they may be useful for some people in some cases. They are not covered elsewhere in this book, except peripherally or in an appendix.

REPORTING SPAM

For the benefit of all who use email, it is a good idea to report spam. Although this is an after-the-fact method, it can reduce the amount of spam that everyone receives in the future. One of the best-known sites for reporting spam is *http://spamcop.net*. This and other ways of reporting spam are covered in Appendix B.

CHARGING PER EMAIL

Some people have suggested charging all senders per email message sent. This would require significant changes to the underlying email transfer protocol and would have to be addressed by a change in the SMTP protocol itself. Also, this idea brings up all of the usual issues related to handling money—determining who handles transferring funds from one party to another, settlement, escrow, and so on.

THIRD-PARTY ANTI-SPAM SOLUTIONS

A number of commercial anti-spam solutions are available on the market. Unfortunately, we can only cover a couple of types and solutions here.

Anti-Spam Services

Symantec Brightmail and Postini are anti-spam services where a subscribing organization's mail streams are "washed" of spam by the vendor's service. The resultant "cleaned" email stream is forwarded to your regular email infrastructure for delivery to the end user. Any messages identified as spam end up in a quarantined area on the vendor's infrastructure. Both Symantec and Postini claim patents on their respective solutions, which makes them unique. The benefits of using an anti-spam service like these include

- No hassle for the IT department
- No infrastructure to manage
- No impact on the email infrastructure for blocked messages

The negatives of using anti-spam services include

- Quoted accuracy rates of both products are below CRM114 and other Bayesian-based analysis programs, although this likely is due to the conservative marketing approach rather than the actual accuracy of the anti-spam services
- Most services require "sidelining," where the email user must go to a web site to view spam and potential false positives.

For some organizations, a service-based solution is precisely what is needed. They are certainly worth considering when shopping for anti-spam solutions.

Anti-Spam Appliances

These devices are similar in nature to firewalls—they are standalone single-purpose devices that, instead of protecting your network from security events as firewalls do, protect your network from spam. McAfee, Inc. makes its SpamKiller anti-spam product available in an appliance product that can be extended to include its anti-virus products. Also, some firewalls have built-in anti-spam capability as well.

Some examples of products in this area include Ciphertrust Ironmail and Mirapoint. Benefits of anti-spam appliances include

- One platform for managing anti-spam functions
- Less headache for IT staff

Additional benefits of combining anti-spam with other security functions such as anti-virus or firewall include

- Reduced box count and management overhead
- Improved security policy enforcement

Of course, the downside to such devices is their potentially lower spam identification accuracy, flexibility, and cost. A big negative to anti-spam firewalls is the fact that it is much more difficult to swap out individual anti-spam components and replace them with higher accuracy techniques.

DESIGNING AN ANTI-SPAM ARCHITECTURE

Designing a solution to the problem of spam for an organization is a complicated task. Many design parameters are similar, if not identical, to designing an email infrastructure itself. Because this is not a book on designing email systems in general, we focus on the area of spam.

Often, the first step in a design process is to gather data. Once the appropriate data has been gathered, a policy can be developed around how the organization should deal with the problem of spam. This policy can be as simple or as complex as needed.

After an anti-spam policy is defined, the next step is to plan and implement it. When implemented, statistics such as identified spam, false positive rates, and other data can be calculated for management and others.

GATHERING DATA

Information can be collected in various ways to help determine what type of solution should be used in the fight against spam. Some of these methods include

- Inspecting the setup of existing email-related systems
- Gathering policies, procedures, and other similar documentation from within the organization
- Talking to other IT professionals inside or outside the organization regarding their thoughts on spam best practices

Perhaps one of the best methods is to ask questions, which is covered next.

QUESTIONS

A large part of the data to be gathered can be obtained by asking questions of knowledge-able people in the organization. These questions should include how the email system is configured and working currently, the user community's attitude toward spam, and management's take on the problem of spam.

Some areas to think about when coming up with a plan to address spam include

How well does the organization's existing email infrastructure work?
- How many email boxes exist?
- What is the rate of growth of mailboxes?
- What is the spare capacity of the current email system?

- What types of protocols are used?
- Are there any existing issues such as dropped messages?
- How long has the email system been in production?

How complex is the existing email infrastructure?
- What is the staff skill level?
- Is the email system tied to a particular vendor (Microsoft, IBM/Lotus, McAfee, etc.)?
- What email clients are used within the organization?

What do the users think of spam?
- Are users willing to put up with false positives?
- How sophisticated is the user base?
- How tolerant are users to email problems in general?

What is management's position on spam?
- Is management willing to pay for a commercial solution?
- What level of support exists within the organization and executive management for solving the problem of spam?
- How does the company's line of business(es) relate to the problem of spam (if at all)?

Of course, you should adjust the questions to suit your organization. Bear in mind that most administrators will not have the luxury of designing a mail infrastructure from scratch, which includes support for fighting spam. This makes the design and implementation more difficult because a solution must be inserted into the existing mix of systems and networks.

POLICY

After the spam-related questions are defined and the answers are obtained, your spam-fighting policy must be developed. This policy can be as formal or informal as your organization dictates. Ideally, it would simply be part of a larger email policy. Some small organizations might have an email from an administrator to the IT manager outlining their policy. Others may set up formal committees and processes to handle an anti-spam policy definition.

The spam-related policy should attempt to answer at least the following questions:

- How are users expected to deal with spam?
- What is the acceptable false positive rate?

- How does the spam policy fit in with your other malware defenses (such as anti-virus)?
- How aggressive should the organization be toward the problem of spam?

Any other details deemed necessary should be added to the policy. The policy should be as simple or complicated as needed, and should reflect the needs of the organization.

DEFENSE IN DEPTH

As with many things, a multiple tiered strategy has many benefits. The idea is to block as much known spam at the edge of the network with as few false positives as possible.

If the organization's infrastructure includes Microsoft Exchange or Lotus Domino, a few options are available to the administrator. You can

- Implement an anti-spam solution specific to Exchange or Domino such as McAfee, Inc. SpamKiller directly on the Exchange or Domino server.
- Deploy a Sendmail/Postfix/qmail machine with the desired anti-spam features implemented on it.
- Purchase and install a third-party spam firewall and/or anti-spam service from companies such as Brightmail or Postini.

What you use in a Lotus or Exchange site will depend upon the policies, goals, and budget of the organization.

MX Host

At the mail server that collects the inbound mail from Internet hosts (the machine that handles the mail exchange services (MX) for the domain), you might consider using one or more of the following anti-spam solutions:

- Blackhole Listing Service—Dynamic list of IPs that are known to be spammers
- Static whitelist/blacklist
- Static lists of known senders or recipients to accept and reject mail

If your organization doesn't care about false positives, any of the following could be implemented:

- Strict controls outlined in the "Strict Header Checking" section
- Distributed Collaborative Filtering (DCF) checks

The content filtering checks can be run on the MX host, depending upon the load of the mailbox server. Otherwise, unless messages need to be rejected at the border on the basis of content or Bayesian checks, any nondestructive checks are normally run on the mailbox server.

Sidelining/Quarantining

Deciding whether to sideline messages can be difficult. Most anti-spam services such as Brightmail and Postini utilize quarantining as an integral part of their solution, so a user of those types of services has no choice.

In other cases, you may have the option of implementing the sidelining of messages. However, this does add another decision—whether to quarantine the potential spam. Much of this decision rides on the quality of the user interface for processing quarantined email and the willingness of the user base to check the sidelined message repository on a regular basis.

Mailbox Server(s)

For the purposes of the discussion here, the mailbox host is the machine that runs IMAP and/or POP3 and hosts user mailboxes. This could be one machine or many, depending upon the organization's mail setup.

Normally, content type checks are done on the mailbox server. These would include

- Bayesian analysis
- Heuristics (scoring)
- DCF checks

A tool like SpamAssassin can be run on the mailbox server in order to perform these checks. However, bear in mind that SpamAssassin is essentially a Perl script with lots of overhead.

If you want to use native Bayesian filtering, you may want something more than the SpamAssassin scoring aggregation type of analysis. If this is the case, you have at least two choices:

- Run a Bayesian analyzer (such as POPFile) on the email client.
- Use a native Bayesian classifier (such as bogofilter or CRM114) on the mailbox server.

If both a Bayesian classifier and SpamAssassin are utilized, you may want to adjust (or even eliminate) the scores assigned by the Bayesian classifier within SpamAssassin. Otherwise, messages may be weighted with too much emphasis on Bayesian analysis.

CLIENT

Mozilla Messenger is one of the few email clients with embedded anti-spam support. Messenger includes a rudimentary Bayesian-style classifier that works quite well, although it is still under development. We believe that over time, other popular email clients such as Microsoft Outlook will begin to have a much higher degree of spam fighting within the application itself. As a result, third-party plugins will be the exception in the future, not the rule as they are today.

Most of the third-party applications for email clients like Microsoft Outlook are based upon some type of content analysis or Bayesian statistical analysis. Many of these applications that assist the email client in determining message legitimacy are available on the market. There are also specialized email client plugins (for example, Cloudmark) that implement Vipul's Razor signature (distributed checksum filtering) style of spam checking.

A number of client-side Bayesian analyzers also are available. One, POPFile, works with any POP-capable email client and does an excellent job of filtering spam. One author has a 99.31% accuracy rate with 15,000 messages using POPFile. Bayesian analyzer plugins for Outlook are available, which provide a seamless interface for fighting spam. Chapter 9 covers email client filtering and POPFile.

ANTI-SPAM DESIGN NOTES

This section covers "rules" you may want to consider when designing an anti-spam solution. They are by no means "hard and fast," but you should think about them when designing an anti-spam system.

GENERAL RULES

There are as many different ways to architect an anti-spam solution as there are people who run mail systems. Each organization's computing environment is different, and every organization has different goals, so it is very difficult to generalize. However, it is worthwhile mentioning some common themes when setting up an anti-spam solution.

- **Reject spam at edges of the network whenever possible**—In order to lessen the amount of spam your infrastructure has to deal with, it is always best to reject known spam as early in the process as possible. Of course, this may lead to lost messages, which may or may not be an acceptable risk. A possible compromise is to use blackhole listing services that are very careful about the IP addresses that are placed into them. In this way, only the well-known spam will be rejected at the edges, and the spam that slips through can easily be identified.

- **Bayesian analysis should be performed as close to the end user as possible**—The Bayesian method works best if the filters can be trained to understand what each user considers to be spam. The closer the Bayesian analysis is to the end user, the easier this retraining will be.
- **Utilize additional headers when identifying spam**—If the email client supports filtering on arbitrary headers, and the server-side tools support adding spam headers, always try to use the additional header mechanism. Adding headers reduces inconvenience for your email clients.
- **Score messages for spam when closest to the end users mailbox**—The closer the message is to the recipient, the less likely it will be rejected outright and the more likely it will be scored for spam probability and delivered to the end user for final disposition.

DOMINO/EXCHANGE CONSIDERATIONS

Lotus Domino and Microsoft Exchange present a unique problem for fighting spam. Basic anti-spam functionality in Domino and Exchange is covered in Chapters 10, "Microsoft Exchange," and 11, "Lotus Domino and Lotus Notes." Due to the nature of commercial software, the limitations will take more time, effort, and money to correct.

Many of the open source solutions outlined here will not work directly with a Domino/Exchange server. Most of the open source solutions are designed to work on an open source MTA such as Sendmail, qmail, and Postfix. The only way to deploy many of the open source anti-spam solutions outlined in this book is to put up a separate machine with an MTA of choice and run the anti-spam checks on that new machine. An alternative to this would be to use a commercial spam appliance of some sort in place of an open source solution. However, many commercial solutions have a lower spam identification rate than available open source anti-spam solutions.

Many commercial anti-spam plugins for Exchange and Domino exist. These programs insert directly into the Exchange/Domino application programming interface (API) and help block spam. We have chosen to cover McAfee Spamkiller for Exchange 2.1.1 and McAfee Spamkiller for Domino 2.1. Both are based upon the open source SpamAssassin package and include integrated Bayesian analysis (although without training capability).

EXAMPLE CONFIGURATIONS

You can add anti-spam capability to an email infrastructure in many ways. In this section, we show two hypothetical examples. We start off with a simple configuration that a small enterprise might use. This system contains a single overloaded machine running all mail services for the organization. We finish the chapter by showing how a larger organization might deploy an open source anti-spam solution on its network.

SMALL ENTERPRISE

In a case where the existing email infrastructure is overloaded, it is usually best to add a dedicated machine that handles anti-spam and mail relay functions. The addition of a resource-intensive application such as SpamAssassin will simply put too much load on the existing servers.

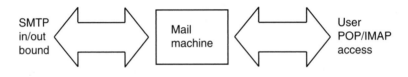

Figure 1.1 Small enterprise.

Also, it may make sense to move the mail (SMTP) relay functionality off of the server that provides POP services to the end user. Of course, the mail relay must have the proper SMTP authentication functionality put on it, along with the authentication data itself. If an LDAP-based system were used, setup and integration would be relatively straightforward. Otherwise, static authentication data could be used by `saslauthd`. This is covered in Chapter 5.

Moving outbound SMTP services may require some work on each client if the organization hasn't set up named aliases such as SMTP and POP for providing those services to the end users. In any case, it is usually easy to migrate SMTP services from the old machine to the new machine as staff time allows.

On the new server, we will run SpamAssassin in order to perform a first-level classification of the inbound messages as spam or not. The administrator might adjust the Bayesian points scored to be lower than their defaults because Bayesian analysis will be performed at the email client as a final step.

On each email client machine, a native Bayesian classifier program such as POPFile will be installed to analyze all of the information within the message (including the

SpamAssassin score) and end up with a final assessment of whether each message is spam or not via POPFile scoring. Finally, the email client on each user's desktop will be configured to filter messages according to POPFile and SpamAssassin headers.

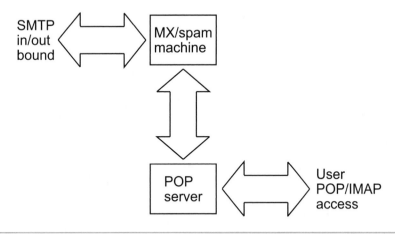

Figure 1.2 Small enterprise final configuration.

Any additional anti-spam methods such as challenge/response, limited use From: addresses, or sender compute could be added, as policy or desire dictates.

MEDIUM/LARGE ENTERPRISE

For the enterprise with a larger infrastructure that isn't using a commercial email server such as Domino or Exchange, we will assume that multiple mail exchange (MX or relay) machines are configured with spare capacity that can be utilized for fighting spam. If spare capacity doesn't exist, we can add additional MX machines or put dedicated spam fighting machines in place, which would become the MX machines.

In a larger environment with more email client desktops, we don't want to take the additional time of visiting everyone's desktop. As a result, we will forego the end user email client Bayesian filter. However, Bayesian filtering at the email client is easily added if desired.

Our setup is somewhat easier here because our company has a defined email policy stating many of the requirements that must be implemented. For example, the policy states that email systems connecting to ours must use strict interpretation of the SMTP protocol. This results in additional (potentially spam) messages being blocked before they have a huge impact on the company's IT infrastructure. Of course, being a larger

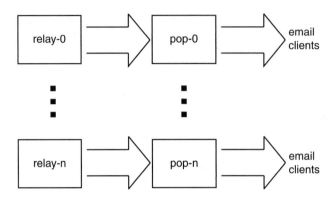

Figure 1.3 Large enterprise email configuration.

company, there is a help desk that can handle the complaints when employees are unable to receive email from certain senders.

Rather than running a Bayesian style filter on the client, we choose to run them on the mailbox (POP) machines. Although the Bayesian filters could run on the mail relay machines, we have spare capacity on the POP servers and decided to run the filters there. We choose to run CRM114 because of the high accuracy rate and low overhead. Additional protection measures such as anti-virus or challenge response systems can be added to the mix as necessary.

CONCLUSION

Spam is a problem that is not going to be solved by technical means alone. The best that can be done right now is to make the problem "less bad." Many methods to fight spam are currently in use, of which the most promising to date is the Bayesian statistical analysis approach. Another useful method in wide use is the content analysis approach taken by programs like SpamAssassin. Using a "defense in depth" strategy with a number of anti-spam solutions working together results in the best spam catch rate with the lowest false positive rate.

Designing an anti-spam architecture can be a complex task, given the wide variety of hardware and software in existing mail systems today. The most important step is to analyze the organization's needs and come up with a coherent anti-spam policy. After the policy is decided upon, the design of the solution can take shape. It is often best to reject as much spam at the edge of the network as possible while minimizing false positives. As messages get closer to the end user, scoring the message for its spam potential works best.

Procmail

This chapter introduces the Procmail mail delivery agent (MDA). The MDA is called by the mail transport agent (or MTA, such as Sendmail) as the final step in the mail delivery process. A call to the MDA delivers email to each end user's home directory for Maildir-style mailboxes or `/var/spool/mail` for other MTAs such as Sendmail. The MDA can also perform other checks such as anti-spam, anti-virus, filtering, and many other functions too numerous to list here.

Under the default Sendmail MTA installation, the default MDA is `mail.local`. `mail.local` is very limited in its capabilities. For example, many `mail.local` implementations in use today cannot perform a disk usage check (quota) prior to delivery or filter messages based on From:, To:, headers etc. This lack of functionality in `mail.local` led to Procmail's development and widespread use.

Procmail can be configured to perform actions based on patterns matched in header items as well as the body of a mail message. Actions include filing, forwarding, and further processing. Many anti-spam mechanisms covered in this book utilize Procmail from either the delivery agent or the Unix mail client side. It is usually preferable to invoke Procmail at MDA time, rather than for each user individually. In this manner, Procmail setup is performed once, rather than having to go into each user's home directory to set it up.

Typically, Procmail is used when the desired anti-spam program requires it or when no other mechanisms are available. As with many Unix utilities, Procmail is lean and mean, making it difficult to understand and use. For every spam-fighting utility covered in the book that requires the use of Procmail, a canned Procmail recipe is provided. For newcomers to Procmail, the availability of preexisting recipes makes learning the tool much easier.

INSTALLATION

Procmail is included by default in most Linux distributions. However, many commercial Unix implementations do not include it, requiring you to install it if needed. We cover Procmail version 3.22 here, but you should be able to use any recent version of the tool with the recipes provided in this book.

The installation of Procmail is required only on certain versions of Unix. Most distributions of Linux contain Procmail. However, Solaris doesn't contain Procmail, so it must be built (or the binary package must be downloaded).

To install Procmail, perform the following steps. First, download the current sources by transferring them from *ftp://ftp.procmail.net* and downloading `procmail-3.22.tar.gz` into a directory such as `/usr/local/src`. Un-tar the package by executing the following commands:

```
bash% gunzip procmail-3.22.tar.gz
bash% tar xf procmail-3.22.tar
bash% cd procmail-3.22
```

After changing directories into the Procmail source directory, you will need to edit the `Makefile` variable `BASENAME` to install the package to the base location, `/usr/local`. (All of the examples assume Procmail is installed here.) A few other options can be specified in the `config.h` file; check the `INSTALL` for additional installation options if desired.

After the `Makefile` and `config.h` settings have been changed appropriately as outlined previously, compile and install Procmail as follows:

```
bash% make
bash% sudo su
# make install
```

Once installed, `procmail` must be hooked into the mail transfer agent (MTA). These steps are the subjects of the following sections.

INVOKING PROCMAIL

There are two different ways procmail can be invoked or called. The most efficient way is for the MTA to invoke it directly. This is more difficult to set up, but it uses fewer system resources. The MTA invocation topic is covered in the section titled "Delivery Agent Invocation" and requires MTA setup. The second way is to call it via .forward (or in qmail's case, .qmail) files in each user's home directory. Although easier to set up, the per-user forward method uses additional system resources.

There are two different ways Procmail recipes can be called, either system-wide in /etc/procmailrc or per-user (by default, a file called .procmailrc located in each user's home directory). The system-wide file is called first, and then the per-user recipes are called second.

.forward FILE

Both Postfix and Sendmail support .forward files, and procmail can be invoked from them. Create a file called .forward in your home directory and place the following line in it:

```
| /usr/local/bin/procmail
```

This will tell Sendmail or Postfix to process all messages through procmail for this user.

.qmail FILE

Unlike Sendmail and Postfix, it is not easy to use Procmail as a delivery agent in a qmail installation. However, Procmail can be used by the Unix user as a filtering or processing agent. procmail can be invoked by the user by placing appropriate lines in each user's .qmail file. For example, the following line in a user's .qmail-default file will cause messages for that user to be processed by procmail:

```
| /usr/local/bin/procmail
```

This line in the .qmail-default file will cause qmail to process messages through Procmail by default.

DELIVERY AGENT INVOCATION

When built from source as outlined previously, the procmail command itself is installed in /usr/local/bin. Most Linux distributions install the procmail binary in /usr/bin/procmail. In the next sections, we show how to invoke procmail under the covered MTAs, which include Sendmail, Postfix, and qmail.

Sendmail

Sendmail can be configured to use procmail as the delivery agent. Procmail is enabled by a FEATURE setting in the Sendmail configuration file, such as $SRC/cf/sendmail.mc.

```
FEATURE(`local_procmail')
```

If procmail is not in the standard place, you have two choices. Perhaps the simplest way to tell Sendmail where to find procmail is use a second argument to FEATURE to tell it where it is:

```
FEATURE(`local_procmail', `/usr/bin/procmail')
```

Alternatively, you can define the macro PROCMAIL_MAILER_PATH before the FEATURE statement:

```
define(`PROCMAIL_MAILER_PATH', `/usr/bin/procmail')
FEATURE(`local_procmail')
```

After the appropriate changes are made to the sendmail.mc file, remake the sendmail.cf file from the m4 sources and restart Sendmail like this:

```
# m4 ../m4/cf.m4 sendmail.mc > sendmail.cf
# cp sendmail.cf /etc/mail
# /etc/init.d/sendmail restart
```

After restarting Sendmail, Procmail recipes can be tested and deployed.

Postfix

Postfix can be configured to use procmail as the delivery agent. Enable it inside the main Postfix configuration file, typically /etc/postfix/main.cf, like this:

```
mailbox_command = /usr/local/bin/procmail
```

After the setting is changed, the Postfix system is restarted to enable changes:

```
# postfix reload
```

When Postfix is reloaded, you are ready to install procmail filters as necessary.

qmail

Unfortunately, qmail doesn't hand off messages to delivery in a standard way because the "envelope From:" line is stripped. It also doesn't handle standard exit codes. Instead, qmail expects a certain set of exit codes to indicate either a soft or hard failure. A soft failure indicates that delivery should be attempted again in the future. A hard failure indicates that delivery attempts should be abandoned. As a result, it is not possible to easily use Procmail as a delivery agent. In order to integrate qmail with Procmail, you are stuck doing it on a per-user basis and must invoke procmail via .qmail files, as outlined previously in the ".qmail File" section.

CONFIGURATION

The configuration of procmail is independent of the MTA used, so everything in the rest of this chapter applies to Sendmail, Postfix, and qmail (if using .qmail files for each user). By default, Procmail can use a common configuration file, /etc/procmailrc, as well as a user-supplied one, ~/.procmailrc. The file is made up of variable assignments and recipes. Recipes consist of patterns or conditions that are matched against mail header items and actions to take in the event of a match.

There are two kinds of recipes: delivering and nondelivering. Delivering recipes write the mail message to a file, pipe it to a program, or forward it in the event of a match, and further processing stops. Nondelivering recipes continue processing the email message after performing the action associated with a particular successful match.

A nondelivering recipe would be one recipe in a chain of recipes. They can be called in series and processed that way. Delivering recipes would be called at the end of a string of recipes.

Delivering recipes can be configured to act as nondelivering with the c flag. This causes a copy of the mail message to be delivered while processing continues as in a non-delivering recipe. Using this option is useful for sending a message to a second user, to log the message before processing or similar sorts of functions.

Recipes begin with :0 followed by optional flags. Zero or more conditions qualify as a match and indicate that one action is to be performed.

OPTION FLAGS

Here you will find some commonly used `procmail` options. Additional flags are documented on the `procmailrc man` page.

- c—A copy of the message is used for continued processing following this delivering recipe
- e—This recipe only executes if the previous one failed, indicated by a non-zero exit status
- f—The pipe in the action of this recipe is to be treated as a filter whose output will be used for further processing
- w—`procmail` waits for the filter or program to finish and checks its error status before proceeding

CONDITIONS

The conditions are expressed as message header items and extended regular expression similar to `egrep`. Additional special conditions include

- ^TO_—Matches destination specifications including To:, Cc:, Bcc:, and `Apparently-to:` containing a specific address
- ^TO—Matches destination specifications including `To:, Cc:, Bcc:,` and `Apparently-to:` containing a specific word

ACTIONS

An action is a path to the mailbox (or mbox) formatted folder in which the message is to be filed. If the path ends with a / character, then the folder is assumed to be a `maildir` format folder.

If the action is prefixed with a special character, it is treated differently:

- !—The action is treated as a mail address to which the message will be forwarded
- |—The action is treated as a program to which the message will be piped
- {—The action is treated as a nested block of further Procmail recipes

EXAMPLES

This assignment identifies `$HOME/Maildir` as the root directory that will be used as the starting point for paths not beginning with /:

```
MAILDIR=$HOME/Maildir
```

This identifies a file in which Procmail's actions will be recorded. It grows without bound, so be sure to rotate it appropriately:

```
LOGFILE=$MAILDIR/procmail.log
```

A recipe with no condition always matches. This example filters all messages through the program called `/usr/local/bin/bogofilter`, checking the exit status:

```
:0 fw
| /usr/local/bin/bogofilter
```

In this recipe, subjects with the word *SPAM* are placed in an mbox-formatted file called `spam`:

```
:0
*   ^Subject:.*SPAM
spam
```

Mail originally sent to `securityjobs@securityfocus.com` is filed in a maildir-style folder (individual mail files located in the user's mail folder) named `$MAILDIR/SecurityJobs`:

```
:0
* ^TO_.*securityjobs@securityfocus.com
SecurityJobs/
```

A copy of mail sent to `webmaster@example.com` is forwarded to `staff@example.com`:

```
:0 c
* ^TO_.*webmaster@example.com
! staff@example.com
```

BLACKLISTING AND FILTERING EXAMPLE

In this example, we want to filter messages with certain attributes to a folder called Spam (see Figure 2.1). We receive a lot of spam with subject lines containing ADV, along with messages that may be filtered by another anti-spam mechanism. For example, some anti-spam software places a word or phrase in the subject line such as Possible UCE. Figure 9.18 contains a list of subject line modifications made by software programs covered in this book.

In addition, we receive messages from people we never want to see, so we want to implement a blacklist based upon this list. A single Procmail recipe can be written to automatically file these messages for you, without any effort on your part.

```
MAILDIR=$HOME/Maildir
DEFAULT=$MAILDIR/
ORGMAIL=$MAILDIR/
LOGFILE=$MAILDIR/procmail.log

# file emails with subjects matching undesired regexes in the Spam folder
:0
* ? formail -xSubject: \
   | egrep -i -f spamSubjects > /dev/null 2>&1
.Spam/

# file emails with from addresses matching undesired domains in the Spam folder
:0
* ? formail -xFrom -xFrom: -xReply-To: -xReturn-Path: -xSender: -xTo: \
   | egrep -i -f spammers > /dev/null 2>&1
.Spam/
```

Figure 2.1 Blacklist/subject line filtering script.

The Procmail recipe invokes the procmail program called formail. The two lines that begin with formail are the basis for this Procmail recipe. The options used in the example echo out the contents of the header specified on the formail command line. The header contents are piped through egrep, and the return value of egrep (success or fail depending on whether a match was found) is used to conditionally trigger the recipe. That's the meaning of the ? in front of the command line. The first formail matches any subject that is listed in the spamSubject file, located in the user's home directory. If matched, the message is filed into the Spam folder. The second formail matches any header listed on the line with the addresses listed in the spammers file. Any message matched ends up in the user's Spam folder. The headers that are checked for addresses are as follows:

- From

- `From:`
- `Reply-To:`
- `Return-Path:`
- `Sender:`
- `To:`

`From` (without the trailing colon) is the envelope from, which always exists. `From:` (with the colon) is not always specified by the sending SMTP server and therefore may or may not exist. Spammers often omit the `From:` line, but they cannot omit the envelope `From`, however.

We could put the headers for the other anti-spam utilities we use into the `spamSubject` file, and all spam messages would end up in our `Spam` folder. See Figure 9.18 for a complete list of modified subject lines used by programs in this book.

CONCLUSION

Procmail is a mail delivery agent that is used by a number of applications in this book to filter messages according to various attributes. The utility comes with most distributions of Linux, and it is easy to install and configure for use with Sendmail, Postfix, and qmail. `procmail` can be called directly by the mail delivery agent for Postfix and Sendmail or indirectly by `.forward` files on a per-user basis. Under qmail, `procmail` must be invoked via `.qmail` files because qmail has no direct integration with Procmail (besides per-user `.qmail` files).

Procmail recipes are terse in nature, which also makes them somewhat cryptic and difficult to grasp. Recipes can live in `/etc/procmailrc` for all users or `.procmailrc` in each user's directory. All spam-fighting utilities in this book that utilize Procmail have cookbook recipes that can be used to filter spam messages caught by those spam-identifying programs into your spam folder. This makes learning and implementing Procmail-based solutions much easier.

SpamAssassin 3

In this chapter, we introduce SpamAssassin, which is a widely used interface to other anti-spam mechanisms as well a spam classifier in its own right. SpamAssassin has its own rules base, which is used to assign a "score" to each mail message. The methods Spam-Assassin uses to classify whether email is spam are as follows:

- **Header analysis**—SpamAssassin can analyze these headers of an email message and generate a score based on them.
- **Body analysis**—The body of a spam message often contains phrases (i.e., "Reduce your debt!") that can easily identify it as spam.
- **Bayesian analysis**—Bayes is a statistical methodology where both the headers and body of a message are compared against a known database of phrases. This book dedicates several chapters to Bayesian analysis due to its effectiveness.
- **Distributed checksums** (Vipul's Razor and DCC)—In this process, a message is check-summed and put into a distributed database along with a count. The higher the count for the checksum associated with the message, the more likely the message is spam.
- **Blackhole listing checking** (MAPS RBL, etc.)—Blackhole lists are ranges of IP addresses where spam originates. If a message comes from such a network, the message score can be adjusted accordingly.
- **Automatic whitelisting/blacklisting** (AWL)—SpamAssassin can automatically add email addresses to databases of whitelists or blacklists.
- **Manual whitelisting/blacklisting**—The software can accept/reject known good/bad email addresses.

SpamAssassin rules can be defined by the administrator and by the user if certain conditions are met. SpamAssassin's power is evident when the individual scores are summed—the final score is worth much more than the individual scores themselves. After SpamAssassin has "scored" a message, the tool can do a number of things:

- Add headers (for example, a spam score like X-SpamAssassin-Score: 40)
- Modify existing mail headers (i.e., change the subject line)
- Send a new message regarding the spam (i.e., report the spam to someone)
- Submit the spam to a database for tracking purposes
- Send a message to the sender (spamtrap-related keywords)

Arguably the most useful function in SpamAssassin is the act of scoring the message and adding an appropriate header indicating the score. Adding a score enables email clients (such as Outlook, Mozilla Messenger, etc.) to filter mail into folders as the end user wishes. However, setting up and training end users takes considerable time and effort from the administrator.

Our coverage of SpamAssassin is designed for Unix-based systems. If you are interested in running SpamAssassin on a Microsoft Windows product such as XP, you should read the writeup available at *http://www.openhandhome.com/howtosa260.html*. This web page covers the largely manual process for making SpamAssassin work on MS Windows platforms.

SpamAssassin can be set up to work at mail delivery time (when mail is being written to the users' mailbox, often called "per-user") or transfer time (when mail is coming into the system). Both are useful in the fight against spam, although normally the administrator picks one approach per system. Per-user checking is good for a small number of users and for working out bugs. Figure 3.1 shows a possible SpamAssassin integration with a mail system on a per-user basis.

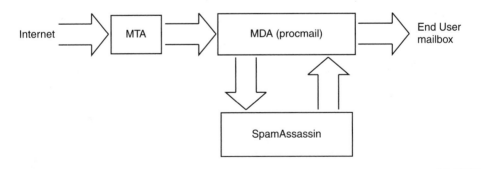

Figure 3.1 SpamAssassin deployed per user.

When you are happy with the per-user installation, you can roll the setup system-wide and implement SpamAssassin for all user accounts at mail transfer time. SpamAssassin documentation refers to this mode as "site-wide," but that is a bit of a misnomer, which is why this book will use the term interchangeably with "system-wide." Figure 3.2 illustrates SpamAssassin integration at MTA time (system-wide).

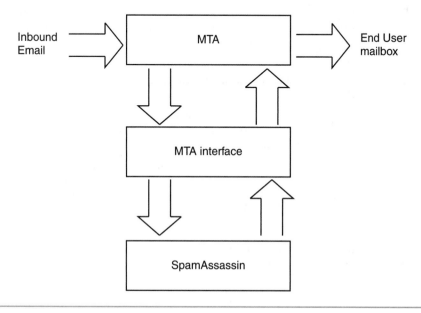

Figure 3.2 SpamAssassin deployed system-wide.

The box labeled *MTA interface* in Figure 3.2 is the mechanism that calls SpamAssassin, which is the topic of the next section.

SPAMASSASSIN AND MTA INTEGRATION

Before we get to the actual installation of SpamAssassin, it is useful to cover how to integrate it into your environment. Each MTA has its own way of adding in third-party components like SpamAssassin. In addition, each MTA itself can have several methods of integrating SpamAssassin into it.

SpamAssassin is often integrated into a large email infrastructure via an MTA filter such as milter, MIMEdefang, and Qmail-Scanner. These programs enable a number of actions on messages, including anti-virus, filtering, and, of course, anti-spam. The other way to integrate SpamAssassin into your email system is to use a facility such as Procmail, which can be enabled on a per-user basis. Using Procmail might be good for initial testing or for use on a small site. Although this approach will certainly work, the per-user procmail method requires more work on the administrator's part. Any site with more than a handful of users is probably going to want to use a site-wide method.

In the case of Sendmail, there is a standard facility called Sendmail Mail Filter (or milter), which allows administrators to call programs to perform desired functions (including filtering and spam detection), which are not part of Sendmail itself. We use milter and MIMEdefang as the method of integration between Sendmail and SpamAssassin.

With Postfix, the options are more varied. SpamAssassin integration methods could include MailScanner, MIMEdefang, or amavisd-new, among others. We chose to use amavisd-new as our Postfix integration method.

Regarding qmail, the options are fewer. We chose the Qmail-Scanner software as our integration. As with other MTAs utilizing Procmail for individual users, qmail's .qmail function could be used to call a script to invoke SpamAssassin. This would be good for a small organization, but larger sites will want to use something like Qmail-Scanner.

Table 3-1 summarizes what we use in this chapter for implementing SpamAssassin from each MTA and where to get more information.

Table 3-1

MTA	Interface(s)	More Information
Sendmail	MIMEDefang	http://www.mimedefang.org/
	milter	http://www.milter.org/
Postfix	amavisd-new	http://www.ijs.si/software/amavisd/
qmail	Qmail-Scanner	http://qmail-scanner.sourceforge.net/
	maildrop	http://www.courier-mta.org/maildrop/

INSTALLING SPAMASSASSIN

Before getting to the specifics of installing the supporting software for each MTA, we first cover the installation of SpamAssassin. If SpamAssassin is installed first, several of the packages will automatically determine that SpamAssassin has been installed and adjust their configuration.

The first step is to download the sources, which are available from the SpamAssassin site: *http://useast.spamassassin.org/released/Mail-SpamAssassin-2.63.tar.gz*. After you have downloaded them to a location such as /usr/local/src, uncompress and extract the files as follows:

```
bash$ gzip -d Mail-SpamAssassin-2.63.tar.gz
bash$ tar xf Mail-SpamAssassin-2.63.tar.gz
bash$ cd Mail-SpamAssassin-2.63
```

To install SpamAssassin, perform the following:

```
bash$ perl ./Makefile.PL
What email address or URL should be used in the suspected-spam report
text for users who want more information on your filter installation?
(In particular, ISPs should change this to a local Postmaster contact)
default text: [the administrator of that system] user@mydomain.com

Checking if your kit is complete...
Looks good
Writing Makefile for Mail::SpamAssassin
Makefile written by ExtUtils::MakeMaker 6.03

bash$ make
bash$ sudo su
# make install
```

SpamAssassin is now installed. Configuration of SpamAssassin is covered later in this chapter.

SPAMASSASSIN AND SENDMAIL

To give you an idea of how SpamAssassin is integrated into Sendmail, Figure 3.3 illustrates the flow of email through a Sendmail system filtered with SpamAssassin and MIMEDefang on a system-wide basis.

The first step is to download and install SpamAssassin. After that is accomplished, milter and MIMEDefang must be installed to complete the installation.

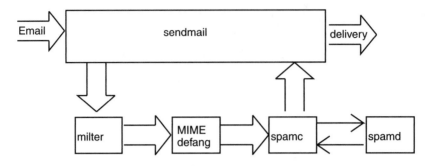

Figure 3.3 SpamAssassin and Sendmail.

Installing milter

The next task is to ensure that milter is installed. Under most Linux/Unix distributions, milter is not enabled, so Sendmail must be recompiled with milter support. To check whether your version of Sendmail was compiled with milter support, run this command: *path-to-sendmail*/sendmail -bp -d0.4 | grep MILTER. If the command returns a blank, then you need to install milter. Otherwise, you can skip this section.

We start off by installing milter. In order to enable Sendmail milter functionality, Sendmail must be recompiled. Let's assume the Sendmail sources are located in the /usr/local/src/sendmail-8.12.10 directory. Create a file in the devtools/Site directory of the Sendmail sources called site.config.m4 with the following contents:

```
dnl Milter
APPENDDEF(`conf_sendmail_ENVDEF', `-DMILTER')
APPENDDEF(`conf_libmilter_ENVDEF', `-D_FFR_MILTER_ROOT_UNSAFE')
```

These lines tell Sendmail to run milter and the environment for its execution. After making the changes to the configuration file, rebuild Sendmail by executing ./Build.sh from the root of the Sendmail source directory. Install Sendmail by executing the ./Build.sh install command, and you now have a Sendmail binary that supports milter.

Installing MIMEDefang

The final step is to install MIMEDefang. It is important to note that the MIMEDefang installation automatically detects the SpamAssassin installation and will configure itself appropriately. So, installing SpamAssassin prior to MIMEDefang is a time-saver.

There are two aspects to installing MIMEDefang. MIMEDefang depends upon a number of Perl modules. The developers of MIMEDefang have made a nice package of all the required Perl modules, which can be installed in one shot. Point your browser to *http://www.mimedefang.org/node.php?id=1* and download the `MIME-tools-5.411a-RP-Patched-02.tar.gz` sources. Then install them like this:

```
bash$ tar xzvf MIME-tools-5.411a-RP-Patched-02.tar.gz

bash$ cd MIME-tools-5.411a-RP-Patched-02

bash$ perl Makefile.PL
Checking if your kit is complete...
Looks good
Writing Makefile for MIME-tools

bash$ make
bash$ sudo su
# make install
```

The second step is to download the MIMEDefang sources from a repository. A good choice would be the MIMEDefang page at *http://www.mimedefang.org/node.php?id=1*. After downloading, the package is installed as follows:

```
bash$ tar xzf mimedefang-2.39.tar.gz
bash$ cd mimedefang-2.39
bash$ ./configure

bash$ sudo groupadd defang

bash$ sudo useradd -c 'MIMEDefang user' -d /var/empty -s /bin/false defang

bash$ make
bash$ sudo su
# make install

# mkdir /var/spool/MIMEDefang
# chmod 700 /var/spool/MIMEDefang

# cp -p examples/init-script /usr/local/bin/mimedefang.sh

# chown defang.defang /usr/local/bin/mimedefang.sh
```

The configuration file `mimedefang-filter` that the installation package includes is reasonable. However, you might need to change some of the parameters, including the following.

To change the email address and name to where notifications go:

```
$AdminAddress = 'postmaster@mydomain.com';
$AdminName = "MIMEDefang Administrator's Full Name";
```

To change the email address MIMEDefang uses to send email, change this:

```
$DaemonAddress = 'mimedefang@mydomain.com';
```

If you want warnings as part of the message instead of an attachment (default is 0), set this variable to 1:

```
$AddWarningsInline = 1;
```

The default action is to send logs via email:

```
md_graphdefang_log_enable(mail,1);
```

Activating MIMEDefang/SpamAssassin

To activate SpamAssassin, edit `sendmail.mc` from your Sendmail source directory to include the following line:

```
INPUT_MAIL_FILTER(`mimedefang', `S=unix:/var/spool/MIMEDefang/mimedefang.sock,
➥F=T, T=S:1m;R:1m')
```

This line tells Sendmail to invoke MIMEDefang, which will in turn call SpamAssassin. The Sendmail configuration file is built by running the following command while in the `$SRC/cf/cf` directory:

```
# m4 ../m4/cf.m4 sendmail.mc > sendmail.cf
```

The resulting `sendmail.cf` file can be installed in `/etc/mail` and the server restarted by issuing `/etc/init.d/sendmail restart`.

SPAMASSASSIN AND POSTFIX

The flow of mail under Postfix integrated with SpamAssassin is diagrammed in Figure 3.4 for a system-wide basis setup.

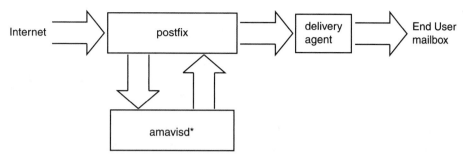

*Note: amavisd calls SpamAssassin libraries directly

Figure 3.4 SpamAssassin and Postfix.

SpamAssassin is activated under Postfix by using the amavisd-new package. More information is available online for amavisd-new at *http://www.ijs.si/software/amavisd/*. amavisd-new calls the SpamAssassin libraries directly, making the installation a bit simpler than qmail and Sendmail, which both require additional pieces of software to activate SpamAssassin. Calling the SpamAssassin libraries directly also saves some overhead because additional system resources are not required if `spamc` and/or `spamd` are not invoked.

Installing amavisd-new

amavisd-new requires a number of Perl modules to be installed on the target. The INSTALL file notes regarding prerequisites from amavisd-new are as follows:

```
Archive::Tar   (Archive-Tar-x.xx)
Archive::Zip   (Archive-Zip-x.xx) (1.09 or later is recommended!)
Compress::Zlib (Compress-Zlib-x.xx)
Convert::TNEF  (Convert-TNEF-x.xx)
Convert::UUlib (Convert-UUlib-x.xxx)
MIME::Base64   (MIME-Base64-x.xx)
MIME::Parser   (MIME-Tools-x.xxxx)
(the patched MIME-tools by David F. Skoll is recommended over 5.411,
  as it better handles broken/bad MIME syntax:
    http://www.mimedefang.org/ -> Download section.
  The new 6.2xx from http://search.cpan.org/dist/MIME-tools/
  also includes these patches, and more.
Mail::Internet (MailTools-1.58 or later have workarounds for Perl 5.8.0 bugs)
Net::Server    (Net-Server-x.xx)
Net::SMTP      (libnet-x.xx)    (use libnet-1.16 or later for performance)
Digest::MD5    (Digest-MD5-x.xx)
```

```
IO::Stringy    (IO-stringy-x.xxx)
Time::HiRes    (Time-HiRes-x.xx) (use 1.49 or later; some older cause problems)
Unix::Syslog   (Unix-Syslog-x.xxx)
```

Make sure all of these Perl modules are installed on the target system. If any are missing, download and install them from *http://www.cpan.org*.

Unfortunately, there is no install script, so the software must be installed and configured manually. To begin, download the amavisd-new sources from *http://www.ijs.si/software/amavisd/amavisd-new-20030616-p6.tar.gz* in a directory, such as /usr/local/src. Extract it and change directory into the directory by running:

```
# gzip -d amavisd-new-20030615-p6.tar.gz
# tar xvf amavisd-new-20030615-p6.tar.gz
# cd amavisd-new-20030616
```

Then create a directory under /var called amavis as the amavisd home directory:

```
# mkdir /var/amavis
```

Create the group amavis and user amavis:

```
# groupadd amavis
# useradd -c 'Amavis Daemon' -d /var/amavis -g amavis -s /bin/false amavis
```

Make the permissions and ownership correct on the directory /var/amavis:

```
# chown amavis:amavis /var/amavis
# chmod 750 /var/amavis
```

Copy the amavisd executable to /usr/local/sbin and change the permissions appropriately:

```
# cp amavisd /usr/local/sbin/
# chown root /usr/local/sbin/amavisd
# chmod 755  /usr/local/sbin/amavisd
```

Copy the amavisd.conf configuration file to its default location, /etc, and make the permissions correct:

```
# cp amavisd.conf /etc/
# chown root /etc/amavisd.conf
# chmod 644  /etc/amavisd.conf
```

(If you change the location, you must start up amavisd with the -c option to tell it where to read its configuration from.)

Next, you must create the quarantine directory (where amavisd stores viruses that are caught) and set the permissions and ownership:

```
# mkdir /var/quarantine
# chown amavis:amavis /var/quarantine
# chmod 750 /var/quarantine
```

Finally, you need to adjust the amavisd.conf configuration file to reflect the appropriate settings. If you followed the preceding recommendations, then set the following values as follows:

```
$mydomain = 'example.com';
$daemon_user   = 'amavis';
$daemon_group = 'amavis';
$TEMPBASE = "$MYHOME/tmp";
$forward_method = 'smtp:127.0.0.1:10025'; # for postfix
$notify_method = $forward_method;         # for postfix
$inet_socket_bind = '127.0.0.1';          # improves security
$QUARANTINEDIR = '/var/quarantine';
```

You will want to change example.com to the name of the domain you are receiving email for. $daemon_user and $daemon_group are set to the name of the amavisd-new user—in our case, amavis. $TEMPBASE is set to the amavisd-new variable $MYHOME appended with /tmp. You may want to set this to /var/tmp or /tmp, depending upon your setup. The $forward_method setting tells amavisd-new what to do with the message after processing it. In our case, Postfix expects to receive the message on port 10025 of the local machine. $notify_method tells amavisd what to do with notify messages—in our case, treat them the same as the $forward_method. $inet_socket_bind is set to loopback in order to restrict the IP addresses that are allowed to connect to amavisd. Finally, the $QUARANTINEDIR keyword tells amavisd-new what to do with messages if they are identified as a problem and need to be set aside.

If you are not running virus checks, you will want to enable this line:

```
@bypass_virus_checks_acl = qw( . );
```

This will disable virus checking, if necessary. The log level can be set anywhere from 0 (no logging) to 5 (everything is logged). For debugging purposes, start with 5 and then reduce it down to 2 after everything is running smoothly.

```
$log_level = 2;
```

After all of the settings have been changed, start amavisd with the debug option to check for any missing Perl libraries or other misconfigurations:

```
bash$ sudo su
# /usr/local/sbin/amavisd debug
```

After it starts cleanly, enable amavisd-new to start on bootup by executing the following, assuming you are running a recent version of Linux:

```
# cp amavisd_init.sh /etc/init.d/
# ln -s /etc/rc.d/init.d/amavisd_init.sh /etc/rc.d/init.d/rc2.d/amavisd
```

Configuring Postfix

The Postfix configuration required to activate SpamAssassin and amavisd-new is relatively straightforward. Only a few lines need to be added to your `main.cf` and `master.cf` located by default in `/etc/postfix`.

In `main.cf`, add the following line:

```
content_filter = smtp-amavis:[127.0.0.1]:10024
```

The above line tells Postfix to invoke the amavisd-new content filter by connecting to the loopback interface on port 10024. In `master.cf`, add the following lines:

```
#
# The amavis interface
#
smtp-amavis unix - - y - 2 smtp
        -o smtp_data_done_timeout=1200
        -o disable_dns_lookups=yes

127.0.0.1:10025 inet n - y - - smtpd
        -o content_filter=
        -o local_recipient_maps=
        -o relay_recipient_maps=
        -o smtpd_restriction_classes=
        -o smtpd_client_restrictions=
        -o smtpd_helo_restrictions=
        -o smtpd_sender_restrictions=
        -o smtpd_recipient_restrictions=permit_mynetworks,reject
        -o mynetworks=127.0.0.0/8
```

The first configuration entry beginning with `smtp-amavis` here tells `smtp` (Postfix's delivery agent) to run in a chroot'ed environment with a maximum of two instances. It invokes `smtpd`, sets the `smtp` done timeout to 1200 seconds, and disables DNS lookups to improve performance. The second configuration entry starting with `127.0.0.1` tells amavisd-new to reinject the filtered results into a `chroot`'ed instance of Postfix's `smtpd` on port 10025 configured with the listed restrictions.

The next step is to tell Postfix to re-read its configuration files:

```
bash$ sudo postfix reload
```

You should now be up and running with SpamAssassin/amavisd-new support in Postfix. You may skip ahead to the "Verifying SpamAssassin Operation" section now.

SPAMASSASSIN AND QMAIL

The flow of mail when utilizing SpamAssassin and qmail on a system-wide basis is shown in Figure 3.5. For the purposes of this book, it is assumed that qmail (and required associated programs) have been previously installed by the administrator.

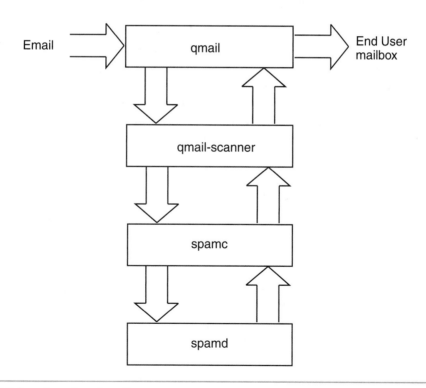

Figure 3.5 SpamAssassin and qmail.

In order to integrate SpamAssassin into qmail, a number of additional packages are required. These include

- Qmail-Scanner (*http://qmail-scanner.sourceforge.net/*)
- qmail-queue patch (*http://www.qmail.org/qmailqueue-patch*)
- maildrop 1.3.8 or higher (*http://www.courier-mta.org/maildrop/*)
- Perl module Time::HiRes (*http://search.cpan.org/dist/Time-HiRes/*)
- Perl module DB_File (may be included in your Perl distribution; if not, it's available at *http://search.cpan.org/dist/DB_File/*)
- Perl module Sys::Syslog (most distributions come with it preinstalled; if not, it's available at *http://search.cpan.org/~nwclark/perl-5.8.2/ext/Sys/Syslog/Syslog.pm*)

Qmail-Scanner allows anti-virus and anti-spam tools such as SpamAssassin to be invoked by qmail. More information on Qmail-Scanner is available at *http://qmail-scanner.sourceforge.net/*. The qmail sources need to have the qmail-queue patch, which is available at *http://www.qmail.org/qmailqueue-patch*, installed. The qmail-queue patch allows filtering, header rewriting, and other functionality required for programs like SpamAssassin. If you are running Linux, a qmail-queue patched version of qmail-1.03 pre-built RPM prepackaged binary is available at *http://untroubled.org/qmail+patches/*. The instructions here assume that you are building qmail from scratch and not using the RPM.

To enable qmail to invoke SpamAssassin, you must apply a simple patch to qmail-1.03. From the *http://www.qmail.org/qmailqueue-patch* site, copy the lines beginning with `diff` to the last line from the qmail-queue patch page to a file called `patchfile` in your `qmail-1.03` directory. Apply the patch from the directory containing the root of `qmail-1.03` like this:

```
bash$ patch -p0 < patchfile
```

Become root and reconfigure, recompile, and reinstall qmail:

```
bash$ sudo su
# ./config
```

Next, install maildrop. Please note that you need to have GNU `make` installed in order to build maildrop. GNU `make` is installed on most free operating systems such as Linux and BSD variants. To install maildrop, download the sources from *http://www.courier-mta.org/maildrop/* to `/usr/local/src` and unpack them:

```
bash$ bzip2 -d maildrop-1.6.3.tar.bz2
bash$ tar xf maildrop-1.6.3.tar
bash$ cd maildrop-1.6.3
```

Then, compile and install the package as follows:

```
bash$ ./configure
bash$ make
bash$ sudo su
# make install
```

Next, we must prepare to install Qmail-Scanner. The Qmail-Scanner package has a number of prerequisites, namely:

- Perl module Time::HiRes
- Perl module DB_File
- Perl module Sys::Syslog

Be sure they are downloaded and installed prior to continuing the installation. After the environment is set, download qmail-scanner 1.20 from *http://prdownloads.sourceforge.net/qmail-scanner/qmail-scanner-1.20.tgz?download* to a location on your system, such as /usr/local/src. Unpack the archive:

```
bash$ gzip -d qmail-scanner-1.20.tgz
bash$ tar xf qmail-scanner-1.20.tar
bash$ cd qmail-scanner-1.20
```

After that is accomplished, compile and install Qmail-Scanner:

```
bash$ ./configure
bash$ sudo su
# ./configure --install
```

After Qmail-Scanner has been installed, you need to update the tcprules to have qmail run the qmail-scanner-queue.pl executable instead of the default qmail-queue binary. This is accomplished by copying the following lines into a file in your local directory called tcprules.tmp:

```
127.:allow,RELAYCLIENT="",RBLSMTPD="",QMAILQUEUE="/var/qmail/bin/qmail-queue"
10.:allow,RELAYCLIENT="",RBLSMTPD="",QMAILQUEUE="/var/qmail/bin/qmail-scanner-queue.pl"
:allow,QMAILQUEUE="/var/qmail/bin/qmail-scanner-queue.pl"
```

When loaded into the local tcprules.tmp file, update your tcprules by executing the following command as root:

```
# tcprules /etc/tcp.smtp.cdb ./tcprules.tmp < /etc/tcp.smtp
```

This command builds a new `tcp.smtp.cdb` file with the new configuration from your `./tcprules.tmp` file. After the `tcprules` have been updated and qmail restarted, qmail will process incoming messages through SpamAssassin.

SPAMASSASSIN SCORING

SpamAssassin's main strength is its ability to score messages for their likelihood to be spam. The set of rules distributed with SpamAssassin is located by default in `/usr/local/share/spamassassin`. The rules are covered here to give you a taste of how the scoring engine works. SpamAssassin rules should be changed only after fully understanding the ramifications of modifying them.

RULES

A rule is a test that determines the spam score of a message. Rules can act on various parts of the message, including the full message and headers, headers only, body only, etc. Rules can be positive (definitely spam) or negative (definitely legitimate email) and can be fractional. An example rule is given in the "Privileged Parameters" section later. An explanation of the default ruleset as shipped with SpamAssassin 2.63 is contained in Appendix C, "Default SpamAssassin Ruleset."

There are a number of rules that incorporate features of SpamAssassin or that make administration easer. One test is called GTUBE. This test forces a message to be considered spam by assigning a high score, in the case of GTUBE, 1000. GTUBE is useful for the administrator when testing a setup. There are also a number of tests associated whitelisting/blacklisting, which implement the whitelisting/blacklisting features of SpamAssassin.

SPAMASSASSIN CONFIGURATION

In the last part of this chapter, we look at the SpamAssassin application: how to use it and how to integrate it into your mail infrastructure.

SpamAssassin is broken down into the following major user-accessible components:

- `spamassassin` —The Perl program meant to be used as a per-user command line interface. It is not designed to be used in high-volume environments; instead, use `spamc/spamd` or call the libraries directly.

- `spamc`—A very efficient interface to the SpamAssassin processor, written in C. It is meant to be called from scripts and designed to communicate with `spamd`, the daemonized version of `spamassassin`.
- `spamd`—The daemonized version of the `spamassassin` program. It is meant to be used with `spamc`, but it doesn't have to be. `spamd` is designed for high-volume environments, where speed is of the essence. It is optimized for running as a standalone program, where clients would connect to it on port 783. There are options for connecting to a MySQL database or LDAP server for large installations.
- `sa-learn`—The program that populates or retrains SpamAssassin's Bayesian classifier database of spam.

Along with these four programs, which can be run by the end-user/administrator, the SpamAssassin libraries themselves are also available. These are the Perl libraries that actually perform the analysis and scoring of email messages. An example of a user program that calls the libraries directly is amavisd-new, one of the SpamAssassin MTA interfaces we cover. The end user can write programs in Perl that execute SpamAssassin library calls, enabling custom programs to be written for processing email. The complete set of command options for `spamassassin`, `spamc`, `spamd` and `sa-learn` commands are contained in Appendix D, "SpamAssassin Command Line Interface Reference."

THE SPAMASSASSIN COMMAND LINE INTERFACE

The `spamassassin` command line interface (CLI) is meant for users who have command line access to the machine that houses their email box. Alternatively, the CLI could be used to process messages for testing purposes or in a setup with a small number of users. The Procmail, forwarding, or `.qmail` functions in MTAs invoke the `spamassassin` command to process messages when SpamAssassin is not set up to be run at MTA time for the entire organization. For example, you would use the CLI if you were not integrating SpamAssassin into your MTA via milter, amavisd-new, or Qmail-Scanner.

The `spamassassin` command line interface can be used for the following purposes:

- To identify a message as spam to collaborative filtering services
- To retrain the internal Bayesian filters
- To send a warning message to spam senders
- To add addresses to whitelists/blacklists

Running SpamAssassin via Procmail

We will use the example of a per-user installation, where we had a small number of users or we wanted to test SpamAssassin prior to rolling it into full production. If you were running Sendmail or Postfix and were set up to call `procmail` as your MDA, this could easily be done by using the following Procmail recipe:

```
:0fw
| /usr/local/bin/spamassassin
```

`/usr/local/bin/spamassassin` could be replaced with `/usr/local/bin/spamc`, the fast interface to spamassassin, if desired. This recipe could alternatively be placed in `/etc/procmailrc`, which would cause `spamassassin` to be invoked for all users. qmail installations would use the `.qmail` functionality outlined next.

Running SpamAssassin in qmail

In a qmail installation, if you wanted to have SpamAssassin process your messages as a regular user, you would place something like this in the `.qmail` file:

```
|/usr/local/bin/spamassassin -P | maildir ./Maildir/
```

This example would route all messages through `spamassassin`, outputting messages in the maildir formatted mailbox located in the user's home directory in folder called `Maildir`.

sa-learn

`sa-learn` is used by a command line user to retrain the Bayesian filters. It accepts a file name as an argument, or messages can be piped to it if desired. It accepts a number of options, the most useful of which are `--ham` for messages that need to be reclassified as non-spam and `--spam` for messages that were mistakenly classified as spam. For example, if you wanted to submit a mail message contained in the file called `spam.txt` in your home directory, you would execute the following command:

```
/usr/local/bin/sa-learn --spam spam.txt
```

This would be used for reclassifying a message that SpamAssassin misidentified as spam.

VERIFYING SPAMASSASSIN OPERATION

In order to be sure that your SpamAssassin installation is working, there are a couple of tests that can be performed. These tests will determine if the SpamAssassin engine is able to identify spam messages with the default installation. The first test is to see if a spam message is identified by the filters correctly, and the second test determines whether a non-spam message is allowed through the program.

TESTING A SPAM MESSAGE

Fortunately, SpamAssassin ships with a message that you can use to easily verify that the filters identify a spam message correctly. The message SpamAssassin ships with is shown in Figure 3.6.

```
Subject: Test spam mail (GTUBE)
Message-ID: <GTUBE1.1010101@example.net>
Date: Wed, 23 Jul 2003 23:30:00 +0200
From: Sender <sender@example.net>
To: Recipient <recipient@example.net>
Precedence: junk
MIME-Version: 1.0
Content-Type: text/plain; charset=us-ascii
Content-Transfer-Encoding: 7bit

This is the GTUBE, the
    Generic
    Test for
    Unsolicited
    Bulk
    Email

If your spam filter supports it, the GTUBE provides a test by which you
can verify that the filter is installed correctly and is detecting incoming
spam. You can send yourself a test mail containing the following string
of characters (in upper case and with no white spaces and line breaks):

XJS*C4JDBQADN1.NSBN3*2IDNEN*GTUBE-STANDARD-ANTI-UBE-TEST-EMAIL*C.34X

You should send this test mail from an account outside of your network.
```

Figure 3.6 SpamAssassin test spam message.

The test is run by emailing yourself the sample spam message like this:

```
bash$ mail user@mydomain.com < sample-spam.txt
```

This command assumes that the `sample-spam.txt` file containing the test Spam Assassin message is in the current directory. Replace `user@mydomain.com` with your email address on the machine running SpamAssassin. If this message is caught by the filter, by default you will receive a message (see Figure 3.16) from SpamAssassin telling you about the spam message.

TESTING A NON-SPAM MESSAGE

In order to test a non-spam message, take a message from your inbox and mail it to your-self. For example, from the command line, issue the following command:

```
bash$ mail user@mydomain.com < sample-not-spam.txt
```

We assume that the `sample-not-spam.txt` file, a regular email message with a header and body, is in the current directory. Replace `user@mydomain.com` with your email address as in the previous example. This message should not be caught by the filters but rather should be allowed through SpamAssassin to your inbox.

SPAMASSASSIN CONFIGURATION FILES

SpamAssassin can be run with the as-shipped configuration files, requiring little or no change. Due to the large number of configuration parameters available, only highlights of the configuration files are presented here. A complete description of all configuration parameters is contained in Appendix E, "SpamAssassin Configuration File." Figures 3.7–3.15 and 3.17 are based on information from *http://spamassassin.apache.org*.

CONFIGURATION FILE LOCATIONS

The SpamAssassin configuration files live by default in `/usr/share/spamassassin` and `/etc/mail/spamassassin`. Note that all files with a `.cf` extension are read in alphabetically at `spamassassin` startup time. The site-wide configuration is by convention called `local.cf` and should be placed in `/etc/mail/spamassassin`. You should not place config-uration files in `/usr/share/spamassassin`, as those files may get deleted during future SpamAssassin upgrades.

The individual user configuration file is called `user_prefs` and is normally located in the user's home directory in the `.spamassassin` subdirectory. The ability for individual users to have their own `user_prefs` is a tunable parameter. Also, with the virtual support available within `spamd`, user preferences can be located in a variable location, depending upon the mail account's domain and/or username. This makes integration with large mail systems easier.

CONFIGURATION FILE PRECEDENCE

You need to be aware that the SpamAssassin rule processing is "last touched wins." In other words, the last setting is the one that is used. So, it is important to know that the files are processed in this order:

1. SpamAssassin default rules directory, in alphabetic order (defaults to `/usr/share/spamassassin`)
2. Local rules directory, in alphabetic order (by default `/etc/mail/spamassassin`)
3. Local `user_prefs` file (user's home directory, in a directory called `.spamassassin`)

Configuration settings come in different classes. The three classifications of keywords are as follows:

- Those that can be changed globally, by the user and/or system-wide (in other words, both `user_prefs` and `local.cf`)
- Options that are changeable with permission of the SpamAssassin administrator (if `allow_user_rules` is enabled)
- Settings that can only be changed by the SpamAssassin administrator in `local.cf`

The following classes of users are allowed to manipulate the privileged commands:

- The administrator via the system-wide `/etc/mail/spamassassin` file
- Users running `spamassassin` from their `procmailrc` or forward files

`spamd` users are not allowed to change the privileged files unless the administrator has set `allow_user_rules` to 1.

Please consult Appendix E for a complete list and description of available configuration options for all three classes of keywords (global, administrator permitted, and administrator only).

UNPRIVILEGED OR GLOBAL KEYWORDS

Under the unprivileged class of configuration keywords available to anyone, the available options can be broken down as follows:

Scoring

The scoring keywords define what is to be considered spam and the scores assigned by rules (see Figure 3.7).

```
required_score n.nn (default: 5)
score SYMBOLIC_TEST_NAME n.nn [ n.nn n.nn n.nn ]
```

Figure 3.7 Scoring options.

The `required_score` defines what SpamAssassin considers to be spam. This value can be adjusted higher or lower, depending upon the point at which you want SpamAssassin to consider a message to be spam. If you feel SpamAssassin is being too aggressive and creating lots of false positives, adjust the score threshold upward. If it is too conservative, letting a lot of spam get through, adjust it downward.

Whitelist and Blacklist

The settings in Figure 3.8 control how SpamAssassin processes and manages whitelists and blacklists as well as the auto-whitelisting feature.

```
whitelist_from add@ress.com
unwhitelist_from add@ress.com
whitelist_from_rcvd addr@lists.sourceforge.net sourceforge.net
def_whitelist_from_rcvd addr@lists.sourceforge.net sourceforge.net
whitelist_allows_relays add@ress.com
unwhitelist_from_rcvd add@ress.com
blacklist_from add@ress.com
unblacklist_from add@ress.com
whitelist_to add@ress.com
more_spam_to add@ress.com
all_spam_to add@ress.com
blacklist_to add@ress.com
```

Figure 3.8 Whitelist and blacklist options.

These settings are a matter of personal preference and should be set as the user and administrator see fit.

Tagging

The options in Figure 3.9 control how headers are added to spam messages and header processing.

```
rewrite_header { subject | from | to } STRING
add_header { spam | ham | all } header_name string

Defaults to:
add_header spam Flag _YESNOCAPS_
add_header all Status _YESNO_, score=_SCORE__ required=_REQD_ tests=_TESTS_
   autolearn=_AUTOLEARN_ version=_VERSION_
add_header all Level _STARS(*)_
add_header all Checker-Version SpamAssassin _VERSION_ (_SUBVERSION_) on _
   HOSTNAME_

remove_header { spam | ham | all } header_name
clear_headers
report_safe { 0 | 1 | 2 } (default: 1)
```

Figure 3.9 Message tagging and header processing options.

The defaults here are reasonable. If you want to adjust the headers, use the `add_header` keyword. If you want to tell SpamAssassin not to send a separate email message for every message it has identified as spam, set `report_safe` to 0, and then only `X-Spam-` headers will be added to the message.

Language

The keywords in Figure 3.10 define geographic locations and language.

```
ok_languages xx [ yy zz ... ] (default: all)
ok_locales xx [ yy zz ... ] (default: all)
```

Figure 3.10 Location and language options.

The default is set to allow all locations and languages, which should be acceptable for most situations.

Network Test

These settings include Razor, Pyzor, DCC, RBL, trusted networks, and other related areas (see Figure 3.11).

```
use_dcc ( 0 | 1 ) (default: 1)
dcc_timeout n (default: 10)
dcc_body_max NUMBER (default 999999)
dcc_fuz1_max NUMBER (default: 999999)
dcc_fuz2_max NUMBER (default: 999999)
use_pyzor ( 0 | 1 ) (default: 1)
pyzor_timeout n (default: 10)
pyzor_max NUMBER (default: 5)
pyzor_options [option ...] (default: none)
trusted_networks ip.add.re.ss[/mask] ... (default: none)
clear_trusted_networks
internal_networks ip.add.re.ss[/mask] ... (default: none)
clear_internal_networks
use_razor2 ( 0 | 1 ) (default: 1)
razor_timeout n (default: 10)
skip_rbl_checks { 0 | 1 } (default: 0)
rbl_timeout n (default: 15)
check_mx_attempts n (default: 2)
check_mx_delay n (default: 5)
dns_available { yes | test[: name1 name2...] | no } (default: test)
```

Figure 3.11 Network test options.

These options control the parameters for various network checking and whether checks happen or not. Trusted networks are networks that you know never emit spam and are exempt from certain tests. This series of parameters also allows you to control timeouts and DNS checks. The defaults are reasonable for most installations.

Learning

The options in Figure 3.12 control the operation of the Bayesian analyzer and whitelisting integration with the Bayesian engine.

Most of the Bayesian learning options are acceptable as shipped and don't need to be adjusted. If there are issues with Bayesian scores, the thresholds can be adjusted via the bayes_auto_learn_threshold parameters. In case you want to turn off the Bayesian processing totally, set use_bayes to 0.

```
use_bayes ( 0 | 1 ) (default: 1)
use_bayes_rules ( 0 | 1 ) (default: 1)
auto_whitelist_factor n (default: 0.5, range [0..1])
auto_whitelist_db_modules Module ... (default: DB_File GDBM_File NDBM_File SDBM_File)
bayes_auto_learn ( 0 | 1 ) (default: 1)
bayes_auto_learn_threshold_nonspam n.nn (default: 0.1)
bayes_auto_learn_threshold_spam n.nn (default: 12.0)
bayes_ignore_header header_name
bayes_ignore_from add@ress.com
bayes_ignore_to add@ress.com
bayes_min_ham_num (Default: 200)
bayes_min_spam_num (Default: 200)
bayes_learn_during_report (Default: 1)
bayes_sql_override_username
bayes_use_hapaxes (default: 1)
bayes_use_chi2_combining (default: 1)
bayes_journal_max_size (default: 102400)
bayes_expiry_max_db_size (default: 150000)
bayes_auto_expire (default: 1)
bayes_learn_to_journal (default: 0)
```

Figure 3.12 Bayesian analysis engine options.

Miscellaneous

These keywords (Figure 3.13) define the templates for functions and other areas not defined previously.

```
lock_method {nfssafe |  flock | win32 } (default: no default)
fold_headers { 0 | 1 } (default: 1)
report_safe_copy_headers header_name ...
envelope_sender_header Name-Of-Header.
describe SYMBOLIC_TEST_NAME description ...
report_charset CHARSET (default: unset)
report ...some text for a report...
clear_report_template
report_contact ...text of contact address...
report_hostname ...hostname to use...
unsafe_report ...some text for a report...
clear_unsafe_report_template
```

Figure 3.13 Miscellaneous options.

In the miscellaneous category, `fold_headers` controls whether the headers that Spam-Assassin adds are broken up (the default) or kept as one single long line. If a mail client has issues with divided headers, this parameter can be adjusted.

Privileged Parameters

The end user is allowed to create his or her own spam checking rules if certain conditions apply.

```
allow_user_rules { 0 | 1 } (default: 0)
header SYMBOLIC_TEST_NAME header op /pattern/modifiers [if-unset: STRING]
header SYMBOLIC_TEST_NAME exists:name_of_header
header SYMBOLIC_TEST_NAME eval:name_of_eval_method([arguments])
header SYMBOLIC_TEST_NAME eval:check_rbl('set', 'zone' [, 'sub-test'])
header SYMBOLIC_TEST_NAME eval:check_rbl_txt('set', 'zone')
header SYMBOLIC_TEST_NAME eval:check_rbl_sub('set', 'sub-test')
body SYMBOLIC_TEST_NAME /pattern/modifiers
body SYMBOLIC_TEST_NAME eval:name_of_eval_method([args])
uri SYMBOLIC_TEST_NAME /pattern/modifiers
rawbody SYMBOLIC_TEST_NAME /pattern/modifiers
rawbody SYMBOLIC_TEST_NAME eval:name_of_eval_method([args])
full SYMBOLIC_TEST_NAME /pattern/modifiers
full SYMBOLIC_TEST_NAME eval:name_of_eval_method([args])
meta SYMBOLIC_TEST_NAME boolean expression
meta SYMBOLIC_TEST_NAME boolean arithmetic expression
tflags SYMBOLIC_TEST_NAME [ {net|nice|learn|userconf|noautolearn} ]
priority SYMBOLIC_TEST_NAME n
```

Figure 3.14 Administrator enabled or privileged settings.

A simple rule is shown in Figure 3.14 for illustrative purposes. More complex rules may require changes to configuration files and are beyond the scope of this book.

Example Rule

We want to create a simple rule that scans the message body and adds 10 points to the spam score if the phrase this is a test of spamassassin is present. Rules can be placed in the user's configuration file if allowed by the administrator. More commonly, they are placed in /etc/mail/spamassassin/local.cf by the administrator, which is the method we use here.

If you want to look at the default rules that are distributed with SpamAssassin, they are located by default in /usr/local/share/spamassassin. Although you can add or update the rules located here, this can cause problems when upgrading to future versions of SpamAssassin. The rules files that are distributed with SpamAssassin 2.63 are shown in Figure 3.15.

```
0_misc.cf
20_anti_ratware.cf
20_body_tests.cf
20_compensate.cf
20_dnsbl_tests.cf
20_fake_helo_tests.cf
20_head_tests.cf
20_html_tests.cf
20_meta_tests.cf
20_phrases.cf
20_porn.cf
20_ratware.cf
20_uri_tests.cf
23_bayes.cf
25_body_tests_es.cf
25_body_tests_pl.cf
25_head_tests_es.cf
25_head_tests_pl.cf
30_text_de.cf
30_text_es.cf
30_text_fr.cf
30_text_it.cf
30_text_pl.cf
30_text_sk.cf
40_myrule.cf
50_scores.cf
60_whitelist.cf
```

Figure 3.15 SpamAssassin distributed rules.

We update the `local.cf` file in `/etc/mail/spamassassin` with our new rule. The rule we want to add in `local.cf` consists of the following three lines:

```
body MY_SPAMASSASSIN_RULE          /this is a test of spamassassin/is
describe MY_SPAMASSASSIN_RULE      Test of my spamassassin rule
score MY_SPAMASSASSIN_RULE         10
```

The name of the rule is `MY_SPAMASSASSIN_RULE`. The line starting with body defines the test to run. In our case, the test is to match the pattern `this is a test of spamassassin`, ignoring the case of the string (indicated by `i`) and matching with embedded newlines (indicated by `s`). The pattern modifiers (our rule has one, `is`) are Perl regular expressions.

The second line gives a human-readable description to our rule—in our case `Test of my spamassassin rule`. Finally, the number of points to be added to the score is indicated by `score`—in our case 10. Note that the score can be any positive, negative, whole, or fractional value.

If SpamAssassin is configured to run this test, and a message is processed by the server that contains the string `this is a test of spamassassin`, a message similar to that in

Figure 3.16 should be sent to the recipient. Sending a message like this is the default method of spam notification under SpamAssassin. The original message is included at the bottom of the message from SpamAssassin.

```
Subject: Spamassassin rule test
From: somebody@example.com
Date: Tue, 20 Jul 2004 11:07:27 -0400
To: dale@woody.cushman.avacoda.com

Spam detection software, running on the system "woody.cushman.avacoda.com",
has identified this incoming email as possible spam.  The original message
has been attached to this so you can view it (if it isn't spam) or block
similar future email.  If you have any questions, see
the administrator of that system for details.

Content preview:  This is a test of spamassassin. This message should be
  marked as spam. [...]

Content analysis details:   (15.0 points, 5.0 required)

 pts  rule name               description
 ----  --------------------    --------------------------------------------------
 0.3  NO_REAL_NAME            From: does not include a real name
  10  MY_SPAMASSASSIN_RULE    BODY: Test of my spamassassin rule
 3.3  MSGID_FROM_MTA_SHORT    Message-Id was added by a relay
 1.4  DNS_FROM_RFCI_DSN       RBL: From: sender listed in dsn.rfc-ignorant.org




Subject: Spamassassin rule test
From: somebody@example.com
Date: Tue, 20 Jul 2004 11:07:27 -0400
To: dale@woody.cushman.avacoda.com

This is a test of spamassassin.  This message should be marked as spam.
```

Figure 3.16 Example of SpamAssassin notification message.

SpamAssassin assigned this message a score of 15.0 points, activating the following rules and associated scores:

Test	Score
NO_REAL_NAME	0.3
MY_SPAMASSASSIN_RULE	10
MSGID_FROM_MTA_SHORT	3.3
DNS_FROM_RFCI_DSN	1.4

The tests were activated due to the lack of a name in the From: header, the test rule we built containing the test phrase, the fact that a header was generated by a mail relay, and the fact that the From: sender is listed in a BLS blacklist.

ADMINISTRATOR-ONLY SETTINGS

The settings that can be modified only by the administrator include paths, directory locations, library modules, username/password, and similar parameters.

```
test SYMBOLIC_TEST_NAME (ok|fail) Some string to test against
razor_config filename
pyzor_path STRING
dcc_home STRING
dcc_dccifd_path STRING
dcc_path STRING
dcc_options options (default: -R)
use_auto_whitelist ( 0 | 1 ) (default: 1)
auto_whitelist_factory module (default: Mail::SpamAssassin::DBBasedAddrList)
auto_whitelist_path /path/to/file (default: ~/.spamassassin/auto-whitelist)
bayes_path /path/to/file (default: ~/.spamassassin/bayes)
auto_whitelist_file_mode (default: 0700)
bayes_file_mode (default: 0700)
bayes_store_module Name::Of::BayesStore::Module
bayes_sql_dsn DBI::databasetype:databasename:hostname:port
bayes_sql_username
bayes_sql_password
user_scores_dsn DBI:databasetype:databasename:hostname:port
user_scores_sql_username username
user_scores_sql_password password
user_scores_sql_custom_query query
```

Figure 3.17 Administrator-only configuration settings.

Most of these settings are acceptable as distributed and only need to be changed if you use non-standard software installation locations or are using LDAP, MySQL, or other optional features.

CONCLUSION

SpamAssassin is a Perl program that scores email messages on the basis of several different criteria, including heuristics, Bayesian, distributed checksums, blackhole listing service checks, and blacklists/whitelists. It allows administrators and certain users to generate their own rules for helping to determine whether or not a message should be considered spam.

For our coverage, SpamAssassin is run on a per-user basis by Procmail (Sendmail/ Postfix) or .qmail files (qmail). It is configured to run on a system-wide basis by milter/ MIMEDefang (Sendmail), amavisd-new (Postfix), or Qmail-Scanner (qmail). Spam-Assassin has many configuration parameters in three separate classes. The as-distributed settings can produce a reasonable and working implementation for most organizations. Rules can be defined by administrators and certain users, allowing customized scoring rules to be enabled.

Native MTA
Anti-Spam Features

In this chapter, we look at native anti-spam features in the covered MTAs, as well as black-listing/whitelisting support. Blacklisting/whitelisting can be accomplished by both static lists located on the server and dynamic lists updated by domain name system (DNS) style protocols. Although not all of the techniques shown in this chapter should be implemented by every organization, they are certainly worthy of consideration. Your organization's email or anti-spam policy may address these issues.

MTA native anti-spam features generally fall into the following broad categories:

- Whitelisting/blacklisting
- Strictness of adhering to RFC2822, the mail transfer standard
- Removing SMTP commands that are used primarily for spamming
- Reverse DNS checks for connecting mail servers and From: domains

Messages can be accepted or rejected based upon the information received during the initial connection to the SMTP server. The connecting client's IP address can be checked against a locally maintained database as well as various DNS-based blackhole listing services (BLS). The sender's username and domain name received in the SMTP MAIL FROM portion of the SMTP Client Server dialog can be checked in the same way.

Many MTAs enable the administrator to select how strict of a policy the email server should enforce on connections and what commands to allow. For example, requiring the use of the HELO/EHLO command when remote servers connect will discourage spammers, as will disabling the pipelining capability. However, these may cause interoperability issues with other email servers and should be deployed with care.

A third way to reduce the amount of spam is the use of reverse DNS checks at SMTP connection time. For example, many MTAs allow the administrator to require remote systems trying to connect to their server to resolve via reverse DNS. Also, forging envelope From: (the SMTP MAIL FROM command) addresses is a common way for spammers to hide their tracks. Many MTAs allow the administrator to configure these settings.

STATIC FILTERS

One of the first methods available to block spammers was to parse the inbound SMTP connection MAIL FROM field and compare a static list of known spammers against that field. If the username and/or domain attempting a connection was contained on that list, then the message was rejected. If the username/domain in MAIL FROM line was not on that list, then the message was allowed to continue through subsequent checks. Rejecting mail in this manner is often called "blacklisting." This mechanism can also be used to allow certain addresses through, otherwise known as a "whitelist." The list of MAIL FROM addresses allowed or denied is usually a static file generated by the mail system administrator and placed into files for comparison as inbound mail is processed by the MTA.

Implementing static white/blacklists was very effective until the spammers began forging their mail headers. The next step was to block known spam servers (open relays, or mail servers that allowed spammers to spam) via the IP address on the inbound SMTP connection. If your message was not destined for a local user (a user the mail server knew about), and the server's IP address wasn't on the list, your message was rejected.

This functionality is often called "mail relaying" and is still in use today for providers or enterprises that want to offer mail relay services to a limited number of users, such as a provider who sells Internet access to customers in a business park and needs to allow its customers to send mail. An enterprise might use mail relaying for an employee who needs to send mail through the company's email servers. However, in new deployments today, one is likely to use STARTTLS and/or SMTP Authentication to restrict who can send email through a mail relay. See Chapter 5, "SMTP AUTH and STARTTLS," for more information on this topic.

BLACKHOLE LISTING

Soon there became too many "open relay" mail servers to block statically, and other mechanisms needed to be implemented. MAPS RBL was one of the first blackhole listing services that became available and is now a pay for service. The blackhole listing service is similar in nature to the static IP listing, except that the lookups happen in real time. Usually, blackhole listing is implemented through pseudo name records via DNS. Clients perform lookups when processing inbound messages to see if the IP address of the connecting SMTP client is listed in the service. If the IP address is on the list, the message is not accepted, and an error is generated, without the message being delivered to the recipient.

Many worthwhile blackhole listing services are available. MAPS (*http://mail-abuse.org/*) was the first and is the most widely known. However, MAPS is no longer a free service, so it may not be right for those on low budgets. Some of the more widely used free services include:

- **SORBS**—*http://www.dnsbl.au.sorbs.net/*
- **Spamcop**—*http://www.spamcop.net/bl.shtml*
- **Spamhaus**—*http://www.spamhaus.org/SBL/*

In order to allow systems to look up only portions of their data, some blackhole listing providers split out the information in their databases. For example, the SORBS service breaks down blackhole lists as follows:

Name	DNS Name	Lookup by IP addr
SORBS-BLOCK	dnsbl.sorbs.net	127.0.0.8
SORBS-DUL	dnsbl.sorbs.net	127.0.0.10
SORBS-HTTP	dnsbl.sorbs.net	127.0.0.2
SORBS-MISC	dnsbl.sorbs.net	127.0.0.4
SORBS-SMTP	dnsbl.sorbs.net	127.0.0.5
SORBS-SOCKS	dnsbl.sorbs.net	127.0.0.3
SORBS-SPAM	dnsbl.sorbs.net	127.0.0.6
SORBS-WEB	dnsbl.sorbs.net	127.0.0.7
SORBS-ZOMBIE	dnsbl.sorbs.net	127.0.0.9

In this list, SORBS-DUL indicates the list of IP addresses SORBS has identified as dial up. This list contains the IP addresses that SORBS believes are dial-up pools that shouldn't be originating messages. Another example is SORBS-ZOMBIE. The zombie list contains the IP addresses that SORBS believes are compromised hosts and that are likely being used by spammers to send their messages.

Choosing the wrong blocklist can cause headaches by wasting computing and network resources. If your blocklist service is too strict and includes many legitimate mail servers, genuine messages will be blocked, your false positive rate will go up, and users will complain. On the other hand, if the service is too lenient, there isn't much point in using a blackhole listing service at all because many spam messages will leak through.

Many of the blocklist services break out their lists into sublists, allowing administrators to pick the type of lists they want to use. For example, if your organization has road warriors who connect to your mail server in order to relay outbound messages, enabling a blocklist that blocks dial-up IP address space will likely cause a problem for roaming users.

Here are a few URLs that list many additional blacklist services:

- **Declude's listing**—*http://www.declude.com/JunkMail/Support/ip4r.htm*
- **Spamlink's listing**—*http://spamlinks.net/filter-dnsbl.htm*
- **Jeff Makey's comparison**—*http://www.sdsc.edu/~jeff/spam/Blacklists_Compared.html*

Choosing a Blackhole Listing Service

It is very difficult to choose a DNS-based blocklist to use. Adding to this complexity, the MTA's covered here allow the administrator to specify multiple blocklists if desired. The best method is to have personal knowledge or talk to other administrators and find out what blocklists they use. One option would be to run a pilot project with a certain set of your users and see the results of using various blocklists. Also, it can be helpful to find answers to the following questions regarding the lists you want to use:

- What are the criteria for being placed on the list?
- What actions must be performed to get off the list?
- How long does it take a host listed to get off the list?
- Are there organizations on that list with which you or your users need to communicate?
- How responsive is the blocklist operator in queries from people on the list and from users like you?

If your organization can spend money on a blocklist, you should consider utilizing a commercial list such as MAPS RBL. A commercial blocklist operator will likely be more responsive and may have higher quality data on its blocklists.

OTHER METHODS

Some administrators implement other methods besides blacklisting on MTAs in order to reduce the amount of spam coming into their email systems. These methods generally fall under three categories, including

- Strictly adhering to SMTP-related protocols
- Eliminating access to certain SMTP commands that are commonly abused by spammers
- Reverse DNS checks

Before discussing these approaches, it is important to point out that most, if not all, of these approaches will cause some legitimate messages to be rejected. If this behavior is acceptable to you, your users, and your organization, then you can implement any or all of these restrictions.

However, if you are concerned about not receiving messages (and not receiving clear indication of missing these messages, unless you spend a lot of time looking at log files), then you should tread carefully here. These methods violate the "be generous in what email you accept and strict in what email you send" philosophy.

Strict Protocol Adherence

There is nothing wrong with enforcing protocols exactly as they are designed, except that not everyone does. Whether on purpose or by design, the systems that don't precisely adhere to the protocol can cause you to lose messages. For example, some MTAs don't do much checking of the MAIL FROM: and RCPT TO: arguments passed to them from remote systems. As a result, you will stop a lot of legitimate email, as well as spam, from ending up on your systems if you enforce strict protocol adherence.

Eliminating Certain SMTP Commands

Some commands are often used by spammers to speed up the delivery of their junk to unsuspecting people. For example, consider the case of pipelining, which is a way to *optionally* speed up transfers of large amounts of messages via SMTP. This command is primarily used by spammers to distribute their messages. Because it is an extension, it is not required to be implemented by mail servers; it is only to enhance the performance of the protocol. As a result, some administrators choose to turn this command off.

Reverse DNS checks

The third method often used by some administrators to reduce the amount of spam is to require reverse DNS checks of mail systems at the connection level, as well as the From:

address. Although many spammers use mail systems that don't have reverse DNS set for them, many legitimate sites don't either. What can be more useful is requiring From: address domains to be legitimate. Again, implementing a From: address domain check is more worthwhile than a connecting system reverse DNS check, which can and will block legitimate messages from reaching your users.

SENDMAIL

Sendmail is one of the most widely used MTAs available. Although Sendmail can be somewhat difficult to set up and maintain, it has several m4 macros already written that can perform many functions in the fight against spam. Information on Sendmail can be found on the web at *http://www.sendmail.org/*.

UPDATING THE CONFIGURATION

Before we get into specific methods for controlling spam with Sendmail, some background coverage for manipulating the configuration files under Sendmail is required. Please note that these steps will need to be performed in order to enable each of the methods outlined for Sendmail. These instructions should be good for any recent version of Sendmail (anything above version 8.10).

The Sendmail configuration file is usually located in `/etc/mail/sendmail.cf`. This file is normally created from source files using the m4 macro processor. (It can be built by hand, although this is not recommended.) The m4 configuration source files are in `$SRC/cf`, where `$SRC` is the root of the Sendmail source distribution directory tree. Normally, if Sendmail is installed from a binary package, `$SRC` would be `/usr/share/sendmail`.

Where noted, certain steps require the Sendmail configuration file to be rebuilt. The Sendmail configuration file is built by running the following command while in the `$SRC/cf/cf` directory:

```
# m4 ../m4/cf.m4 sendmail.mc > sendmail.cf
```

The resulting `sendmail.cf` file can be installed in `/etc/mail` and the server restarted by issuing `/etc/init.d/sendmail restart`.

Further m4 documentation is available at *http://www.sendmail.org/m4/intro_m4.html*.

Static Filter Setup

In Sendmail, blocking/allowing messages by IP or sending domain is handled by an access database file. Sendmail's configuration must include the access database feature for the database to be consulted and messages blocked or allowed accordingly. There are several types of back-end database formats available depending upon your hardware and flavor of Unix. The examples here use the "hash" format unless otherwise noted.

Sendmail Access Database

The top-level Sendmail configuration source file, `$SRC/cf/cf/sendmail.mc`, must include the `access_db` feature, specified as follows:

```
FEATURE(`access_db')
```

Note the use of backquote (`` ` ``) and quote (`'`); these are specific m4 syntax required for proper operation! After the `sendmail.mc` file has been updated, it needs to be compiled and installed per the preceding instructions.

The access database, `/etc/mail/access.db`, is a binary file created from a plain text file called `/etc/mail/access`. This file is translated to database (in this case, a simple hash) format using the `makemap` command that comes with Sendmail:

```
# makemap hash /etc/mail/access < /etc/mail/access
```

The format of the `access` file consists of two fields. The left hand side (LHS) is the entity for which you want to block, which might be an IP address, email address, or domain. The LHS can contain prefixes that specify classes like `Connect:`, `From:`, and `To:` but are of limited use. The right hand side contains the keyword `RELAY`, `OK`, `ERROR`, or `REJECT`. The `RELAY` keyword can be used for allowing relaying to other domains, but it is not useful in most situations, unless you have users who originate email messages from static IP addresses. For example, if you provide Internet access in a building and need to allow customers to send messages to nonlocal users, you would use `RELAY` to allow this functionality.

The IP address or domain to block or allow is specified as follows:

- **Email address**—`user@example.com`
- **Domain name**—`example.com`
- **Single IP address**—`192.168.64.78`
- **/24 or Class C IP address block**—`10.5.3`

The action field is as follows:

- REJECT—Bounce the message back with a generic error message.
- ERROR "### custom message"—Bounce the message back with the specified message and error code specified by ###.
- OK—Accept the message that would otherwise be rejected by a more general rule.

Here is an example of a Sendmail access database:

```
#
# sendmail access database
#
# reject specific from address
spammer@spamalot.com REJECT
# reject entire from domain with custom error message
spammer.net       ERROR:"550 We don't accept mail from spammers"
# accept exception to rejected
domainokay.spammer.net OK
# a spammer.net user that we want to get mail from
cooldude@spammer.net OK
# reject specific ip address
192.168.16.8     REJECT
# reject ip address block
192.168.16       REJECT
# allow specific ip address from rejected block
192.168.16.11    OK
```

Using this access database, mail from spammer@spamalot.com would be rejected with the following message:

```
550 5.7.1 spammer@spamalot.com... Access denied
```

Mail from anyone at spammer.net would be rejected with this message:

```
550 5.0.0 xxx@spammer.net... We don't accept mail from spammers
```

If the SMTP client attempting to send mail has the IP address 192.168.16.8, it will be rejected with this message:

```
550 5.7.1 Access denied
```

A message beginning with 5xx means the failure was permanent, and no retry will be made. 4xx indicates a temporary failure, and the server will retry sending the message at a later time.

BLOCKING BY BLACKHOLE LISTING SERVICES

Blocking by blackhole listing is handled in the m4 sources with the `dnsbl` feature using the name of the blackhole-listed domain as an argument as follows:

```
FEATURE( `dnsbl', `rbl.example.com' )dnl
```

This specifies that the IP address of the connecting server will be looked up in the `rbl.example.com` domain. For example, if the host with the IP address `10.1.2.3` connects, Sendmail will try to resolve the name `3.2.1.10.rbl.example.com`. If the lookup is successful, then the message is rejected; otherwise, it passes on to whatever other checks are in place.

Information available to Sendmail can be given to a sender via an error message. For example, use this command to return the IP address when rejecting a message via the `dnsbl` method:

```
FEATURE(`dnsbl', `bl.spamcop.net', `"Spam blocked see:
➥http://spamcop.net/w3m?action=checkblock&ip="$&{client_addr}')dnl
```

This results in the sender receiving this error message:

```
Spam blocked see: http://spamcop.net/w3m?action=checkblock&ip=1.2.3.4
```

This messsage is useful because the sender receiving this message can simply copy and paste the URL into a web browser and can see exactly why the message is being rejected.

Ordinarily, if the blackhole lookup results in a temporary failure, the message will be allowed through. A third argument to the `dnsbl` keyword can be specified to return an error and temporarily reject the message instead. An argument of `t` returns a generic message; otherwise, the text of the message is specified:

```
FEATURE(`dnsbl', `rbl.example.com', `', `t')dnl
```

and this is the resulting error message:

```
451 4.7.1 Temporary lookup failure of 10.1.2.3 at rbl.example.com
```

This message indicates that the server was unable to perform a lookup of the IP address on the blocklist server. This message tells the sending system that it should retry sending the message again later when the blocklist is available.

There is an enhanced version of the `dnsbl` feature available called `enhdnsbl`, which causes messages to be rejected only if the return value of the blackhole list "name" lookup matches particular values. The value to match is specified as a fourth argument to the feature. The other arguments have the same meaning as for `dnsbl`.

```
FEATURE(`enhdnsbl', `rbl.example.com', `', `t', `127.0.0.2.')dnl
```

This line causes Sendmail to block a message only if the sender resolves to 127.0.0.2. This is useful for some blackhole listing services that want to separate their master list into a number of sublists.

Overriding Entries on BLS

Occasionally, you need to allow access from a particular IP address that may be listed on a blackhole listing service that you really want to keep. In order to do this in Sendmail, list the IP addresses or names with an OK in the access database as outlined previously in the section "Sendmail Access Database."

POSTFIX

Postfix is another widely used MTA written by Wietse Venema. More information on Postfix is available online at *http://www.postfix.org/*. Unless otherwise noted, all configuration information in this section pertains to Postfix version 2.x.

UPDATING THE CONFIGURATION

In a "standard" Postfix installation, the /etc/postfix directory is the home of all Postfix configuration files. main.cf contains the parameters that control the operation of Postfix. These settings include the SMTP clients and sender domains from which Postfix will accept mail. The clients and domains can be listed directly in the main.cf configuration file.

Whenever you modify any Postfix configuration file, including main.cf, you must reload the Postfix server by issuing the postfix reload command, typically located in /usr/sbin or /usr/local/sbin. postfix reload will force Postfix to re-read all of its configuration files and make active any changes you have made.

STATIC FILTER SETUP

Similar to Sendmail, Postfix implements blocking/allowing messages by IP addresses or sending domain by using an access database. You can specify the database to use for enforcing sender IP address restrictions in the Postfix configuration file, /etc/postfix/main.cf.

The main.cf parameter smtpd_client_restrictions lists the IP address restrictions of SMTP clients. By default, this parameter is empty, which causes Postfix to accept mail from any mail server. Restrictions are specified in a comma- or space-separated list. For example, consider the following entry:

```
smtpd_client_restrictions = check_client_access hash:/etc/postfix/client_access
```

This line specifies that connecting SMTP clients will be checked against the access database stored in the hash file /etc/postfix/client_access.

The parameter smtpd_sender_restrictions lists the restrictions for sender addresses and domains. By default, this parameter is empty, and Postfix will accept mail from any sender. Restrictions are specified in a comma- or space-separated list.

For example, look at this configuration file entry:

```
smtpd_sender_restrictions = check_sender_access hash:/etc/postfix/sender_access
```

This entry specifies that the sender addresses and domains will be checked against the access database stored in the hash file /etc/postfix/access. Note that the same file can contain both sender and recipient restrictions. See the example at the end of the next section for more information.

The Postfix Access Database

The Postfix access database, /etc/postfix/access.db, is a BerkeleyDB format file created from a plain-text file, /etc/postfix/access, using the postmap command that comes with Postfix:

```
# postmap hash /etc/postfix/access
```

This command converts the /etc/postfix/access text file into a hash database file that Postfix can read efficiently. The format of the access file consists of two fields similar to Sendmail. The left hand side (LHS) specifies the address to block or allow and is specified as:

- **Email address**—user@example.com
- **Domain name**—example.com
- **Single IP address**—192.168.64.78
- **/24 or Class C IP address block**—10.5.3

The right hand side (RHS) indicates the action to take for the specified address:

- REJECT—Bounce the message back with a generic error message.
- 4## custom message—Temporarily defer delivery of the message with the specified custom message.

- `5## custom message`—Bounce the message back with the custom specified message.
- `OK`—Accept the message that would otherwise be rejected by a more general rule.

Consider the following example Postfix access file:

```
#
# postfix access database#
# reject specific from address
spammer@spamalot.com  REJECT
# reject entire from domain with custom error message
spammer.net       550 We don't accept mail from spammers
# accept exception to rejected domain
okay.spammer.net OK
# a spammer.net user that we want to get mail from
cooldude@spammer.net OK
# reject specific ip address
192.0.34.166      REJECT
# reject ip address block
192.168.16      REJECT
# allow specfic ip address from rejected block
192.168.16.11     OK
```

Using this access database, mail from `spammer@spamalot.com` would be rejected with the following message:

```
554 <spammer@spamalot.com>: Sender address rejected: Access denied
```

Mail from any user at spammer.net would be rejected with this message:

```
550 <anyuser@spammer.net>: Sender address rejected: We don't accept mail from spammers
```

If the SMTP client attempting to send mail has the IP address `192.0.34.166`, it will be rejected with this message:

```
554 <www.example.com[192.0.34.166]>: Client host rejected: Access denied
```

It is important to note the different treatment an access database entry receives, depending on whether the check is being made on the client or sender. For example, using the previously described access database, a message would be rejected using the client restrictions if the connecting client's IP address mapped to the `spammer.net` domain unless it originated from the address associated with `okay.spammer.net`.

Using the sender restrictions, Postfix would reject the message if it were from spammer@spamalot.com or any user from `spammer.net` (except domainokay.spammer.net and cooldude@spammer.net), regardless of the address of the connecting client. In a similar fashion, in this example, the entire block of 192.168.16 addresses are not allowed, except for 192.168.16.11, which is specifically allowed.

In the preceding example, the access databases for client and sender restrictions are combined for convenience. They can also be kept separate. For example, the following parameter settings in main.cf would use separate access databases for each:

```
smtpd_client_restrictions = check_client_access hash:/etc/postfix/access_sender
smtpd_sender_restrictions = check_sender_access hash:/etc/postfix/access_client
```

Complete documentation for the access file is at *http://www.postfix.org/access.5.html*.

BLOCKING VIA BLACKHOLE LISTING

Postfix uses the reject_rbl_client restriction in the smtpd_client_restictions list. This restriction takes an argument specifying the blackhole-listed domain to use:

```
smtpd_client_restrictions = reject_rbl_client rbl.example.com
```

These restrictions can be combined with others on the same main.cf parameter line:

```
smtpd_client_restrictions = check_client_access
hash:/etc/postfix/access_sender,
reject_rbl_client rbl.example.com
```

The message returned for rejected messages can be customized using the default_rbl_reply parameter, which is set in main.cf. There are many built-in macros that can be used, such as

- $rbl_class—The class of the blacklisted entity, such as client host, sender address.
- $rbl_domain—The domain serving the blacklist that the entity was on.
- $rbl_code–The numerical reply code. The default is 554, but it can be changed by setting $maps_rbl_reject_code.
- $rbl_what—The blacklisted entity, such as IP address, domain, sender address.
- $rbl_reason—The reason the domain is blacklisted.

Complete documentation is at *http://www.postfix.org/uce.html#additional*.
Consider the following entry:

```
default_rbl_reply = $rbl_code Service unavailable; $rbl_class [$rbl_what] blocked
➥see http://$rbl_domain
```

A message sent by a client listed in `rbl.example.com`'s map would then be rejected with this message:

```
554 Service unavailable; Client host [192.168.16.7] blocked see http://rbl.example.com
```

Overriding Entries on BLS

In order to allow servers that might be listed on blackhole listing services such as MAPS to send you email, simply list the name or IP address of the server in the Postfix access database as OK. This will allow you to override any BLS list entries with which you or your email users need to communicate.

QMAIL TCPSERVER AND RBLSMTPD

True to its minimalist design, qmail has no built-in mechanism for blocking connecting SMTP clients by address. As a result, tcpserver must be used in combination with rblsmtpd for this purpose. tcpserver is part of Dan Bernstein's ucspi-tcp package. It allows programs to easily control access to arbitrary TCP/IP connections. It is similar to inetd/xinetd in nature.

Qmail's SMTP server doesn't run as a daemon listening on the SMTP port waiting for incoming connections as Sendmail and Postfix do. Another daemon, tcpserver, is used to listen for incoming connections. When an SMTP connection is received, tcpserver invokes qmail, connecting stdin and stdout to the socket, much as inetd does for the services it manages. tcpserver is started with qmail as an argument. Here is a simple example for starting qmail under tcpserver control:

```
tcpserver -v -u <qmail-uid> -g <qmail-gid> 0 smtp /var/qmail/bin/qmail-smtpd 2>&1 &
```

ucspi-tcp (a package required by qmail, which includes tcpserver) is distributed with a program called rblsmtpd. rblsmtpd blocks or allows messages depending upon the value of an environment variable $RBLSMTPD. If the variable $RBLSMTPD is set and non-empty, the email message is rejected with the text value of $RBLSMTPD used as the bounce message. If the variable is set and empty, the message is accepted. If the variable is not set, then the blackhole-listed databases are consulted to determine whether the message should be accepted or rejected. $RBLSMTPD is set by /usr/local/bin/rblsmtpd.

rblsmtpd is invoked by a call from tcpserver. tcpserver takes an -x argument, which specifies the name of a file containing rules to be used for blocking or allowing connecting clients by IP address. Furthermore, environment variables can be set depending upon the IP address of the connecting client. For example, the following command configures qmail to use rblsmtpd and the IP address connection rules located in /etc/tcp.smtp.cdb:

```
tcpserver -v -x /etc/tcp.smtp.cdb -u <qmail-uid> -g <qmail-gid> 0 smtp \
/usr/local/bin/rblsmtpd /var/qmail/bin/qmail-smtpd 2>&1 &
```

TCPSERVER RULES

The tcpserver rules file is actually a database created from a plain-text file using the tcprules program. For example, if the rules database was /etc/tcp.smtp.cdb and the text file source for it was /etc/tcp.smtp, the following command would update it after a change was made:

```
# tcprules /etc/tcp.smtp.cdb /etc/tcp.smtp.cdb.tmp < /etc/tcp.smtp
```

(Note: tcprules's second argument is the name of a temporary file to hold the new database before it is renamed to that of the old.)

BLOCKING AND ALLOWING MESSAGES BY IP ADDRESS

CDB is a database format used by tcpserver to manage the IP addresses that are allowed to connect to the qmail server. A CDB rule consists of two fields separated by the colon (:) character. The LHS of the colon is an address, and the RHS is an instruction beginning with allow or deny. The instruction can also have environment variable assignments. The first rule that matches is applied.

For the purposes of using rblsmtpd to reject specific addresses, the addresses to be blocked are listed with the allow instruction followed by the RBLSMTPD environment variable assignment that will cause rblsmtpd to reject the incoming mail with the specified message. Simply setting the instruction to deny drops the connection before rblsmtpd can return an error message, causing the sender to re-queue and retry the mail as if a network failure had occurred.

The message is sent back as error 451, which indicates a temporary failure, and the sender re-queues the message. If the message text is prepended with a hyphen (-), the message is sent back as a permanent failure, 553.

For example:

```
# defer messages from a specific IP address
192.0.34.166:allow,RBLSMTPD="We don't accept mail from spammers"
# allow specfic IP address from rejected block
192.168.16.11:allow,RBLSMTPD=""
# reject messages from an IP address block
192.168.16.:allow,RBLSMTPD="-We don't accept mail from spammers"
```

Using this `tcp.smtp.cdb` database, a message relayed from `192.0.34.166` would be rejected with the message

```
451 We don't accept mail from spammers
```

A message relayed from `192.168.16.11` would be accepted, though a message from all other addresses in `192.168.16.xx` would be rejected with the message

```
553 We don't accept mail from spammers
```

Further `tcprules` documentation can be found at *http://cr.yp.to/ucspi-tcp/tcprules.html.*

BLOCKING AND ALLOWING MESSAGES BY EMAIL ADDRESS

In order to block non-IP addresses via qmail, we must move our focus back to qmail. Messages may be blocked based on the envelope From: address by listing the addresses in the file `badmailfrom` typically located in the `/var/qmail/control` directory. Addresses are listed in `badmailfrom` as `user@domain.com` or `@domain.com`. For example, consider the following entries:

```
spammer@spamalot.com
spammer.net
```

Using this `badmailfrom` entry, `spammer@spamalot.com` or any user from `spammer.net` would be rejected with the following message:

```
553 sorry, your envelope sender is in my badmailfrom list (#5.7.1)
```

BLOCKING VIA BLACKHOLE LISTING

As mentioned previously, the `rblsmtpd` program will look up connecting clients IP addresses in blackhole lists to determine whether to block or allow the connection. Unlike Sendmail and Postfix, qmail looks up a DNS TXT record associated with the address rather than a DNS A record. A DNS TXT record is essentially a text comment string, and an A record is an address record, indicating the IP address associated with a name.

For this reason, some commonly used blackhole listing services won't work with `rblsmtpd`. Blackhole listing sources to use for the lookup are specified with the `-r` option to `rblsmtpd`. Additionally "anti-rbl" sources may also be specified using the `-a` option. An anti-blackhole listing queries for an A record. Each specified source is used in order until a lookup is successful. If the successful lookup is from a blackhole listing source, the mail is blocked, and the text returned by the lookup is used as the error message. If the successful lookup is from an anti-blackhole listing source, the message is accepted.

A 451 error code deferring delivery temporarily is returned by default for mail rejected as a result of a blackhole listing lookup. The -b flag causes a 533 error code, indicating permanent failure to be returned. You probably should use the -b flag so that messages aren't continually queued by the sender, causing resources to be consumed on your email system for no benefit to you.

By default, if the lookup fails temporarily, the mail is accepted. The -c flag causes delivery to be deferred with a 451 error message.

For example, to use rbl.example.com as an rbl source, add -r rbl.example.com to the tcpserver command line. The -b causes a 553 error code to be returned:

```
tcpserver -v -x /etc/tcp.smtp.cdb -u <qmail-uid> -g <qmail-gid> 0 smtp \
/usr/local/bin/rblsmtpd -b -r rbl.example.com /var/qmail/bin/qmail-smtpd 2>&1 &
```

If the TXT record for 7.16.168.192.rbl.example.com is

```
7.16.168.192.rbl.example.com. IN TXT    "listed in rbl, see http://rbl.example.com"
```

then messages relayed from a host listed on rbl.example.com will be rejected with the following message:

```
553 listed in rbl, see http://rbl.example.com
```

Overriding Entries on BLS

In order to override BLS entries that block messages from mail servers you need to receive messages from, set the RBLSMTPD variable in the tcp.smtp line to be blank. So, if you wanted to allow mail from the server 1.2.3.4, which was listed in a BLS you were using, you would enter the following line:

```
1.2.3.4:allow,RBLSMTPD=""
```

This would allow 1.2.3.4 to send email to your qmail server, even though it was listed in a BLS you were using.

OPTIONAL MTA CONFIGURATION CHANGES

The following section shows how to implement certain MTA checks that may reduce both the amount of spam and legitimate messages received. These parameters should be used with caution! The following types of controls are covered here:

- Strict Protocol Adherence
- Eliminating Certain SMTP commands
- Reverse DNS checks

These methods are discussed for each covered MTA in the following sections.

SENDMAIL

As of Sendmail 8.12, many of the old default settings that were helpful to spammers have been turned off. As a result, the administrator doesn't need to make as many changes, unless an older version of Sendmail is running or the defaults need to be changed to something more permissive.

Sendmail doesn't have as many options for restricting or eliminating SMTP commands as Postfix does. Although you can write your own m4 macros to customize Sendmail to do just about anything, this section covers the available prebuilt macros that are distributed with Sendmail.

All of these configuration parameters go in the Sendmail configuration directory and are updated per our instructions in this chapter.

FEATURE(`delay_checks')

This keyword delays the `check_mail` and `check_relay` calls when a connecting client issues the `MAIL` command. Instead, they are called by the `check_rcpt` ruleset later in the processing of the message.

FEATURE(`accept_unresolvable_domains')

By default, Sendmail rejects servers that don't have reverse DNS entries when connections (i.e., at the `MAIL FROM:` command) are made to your Sendmail server. Enabling this feature allows your server to connect to remote systems that are not properly in reverse DNS.

FEATURE(`accept_unqualified_senders')

In its default setup, Sendmail rejects `MAIL FROM:` arguments that don't have fully qualified addresses (i.e., `sender@domain.com`). Enabling this feature allows `MAIL FROM:` arguments without a domain.

POSTFIX

Postfix gives the mail administrator more control over how it deals with the SMTP protocol and DNS checks. The changes outlined here go into `main.cf`, which requires a `postfix reload` after editing to become active.

strict_rfc821_envelopes

By default, Postfix isn't strict about header checking. This can be set to `yes` or `no` (default). Setting this option to `yes` may eliminate some spam but also some legitimate messages.

smtpd_helo_required

Postfix doesn't require a connecting SMTP session initiate a `HELO` command. Setting this option to `yes` forces a server to issue `HELO` prior to sending a message.

smtpd_helo_restrictions

This keyword lists the various controls that can be put on connecting clients' use of the SMTP `HELO` command. In order to be stricter about controlling access to Postfix, the following controls can be specified:

- `permit_mynetworks`
  The connection is permitted if the client address matches `$mynetworks`.
- `reject_invalid_hostname`
  The connection is rejected because the client issued a `HELO` *host* with bad syntax.
- `reject_unknown_hostname`
  The client connection is rejected because the *host* specified in the `HELO` *host* command didn't contain DNS A or MX record.
- `reject_non_fqdn_hostname`
  The requested client connected is rejected due to the fully qualified domain name not being specified in the `HELO` *host* command.
- `check_helo_access maptype:mapname`
  This causes Postfix to look up `HELO` hostname or parent domains in the specified map.

restrict_unauth_pipelining

This causes Postfix to not allow pipelining unless the connecting server follows the proper protocol.

disable_vrfy_command

Not an anti-spam parameter per se, but this command will disable the connecting server's ability to validate the existence of accounts on your system to stop so-called account fishing attacks.

QMAIL

In qmail's minimalist approach, not many anti-spam functions are available in the default qmail-1.03 distribution, short of the anti-relaying functionality. Third-party patches are available to perform the following checks:

- Rejecting SMTP connections from hosts with bad DNS
- Not accepting messages with invalid domain names on the envelope From:
- Analyzing headers for common spammer traits and rejecting the message
- Verifying that MAIL FROM: domain part of addresses exist

Pointers to these patches are included in Appendix G, "References."

CONCLUSION

The native anti-spam controls in Sendmail and Postfix are quite similar. Patches can be installed against the regular qmail distribution, which implements many of the anti-spam functionality in Sendmail and Postfix. Each MTA has the ability to block messages based on local lists of IP addresses (and email addresses) as well as querying dynamic lists of IP addresses such as SORBS. Local, static lists of IP addresses and email addresses will only go so far in the fight against spam. The static lists can be used to exempt particular IP addresses from the dynamic lists. This enables the administrator to use the blackhole listing service but preserve access to required email servers that might be listed on the BLS.

There are many dynamic DNS-based block lists to choose from, making selecting a list or lists an issue. If you block inbound connections at MTA time, selecting the wrong list can lead to loss of messages. Also, you will receive no indication of lost messages unless you dig through email server logs or hear complaints from your users. Postfix and Sendmail have a few optional settings that can be adjusted to control connections to your server. qmail has patches that contain similar functionality. However, these changes should be made carefully because loss of messages may be experienced if these techniques are implemented without appropriate consideration.

SMTP AUTH and STARTTLS

To prevent a system from being a source of spam while still enabling legitimate users to send outbound messages, a secure mechanism must be provided to relay messages that are destined for email recipients located on remote hosts. In the past, relay restrictions were usually based upon IP addresses, which work fine for certain classes of users such as enterprise networks located on high-speed networks. However, the advent of roaming users created a need for dial-in users to send email from remote networks. As a result, a method of authenticating these mobile users had to be developed.

There several ways users can be authenticated prior to allowing them to send email to arbitrary email boxes:

- POP/IMAP-before-SMTP
- Secure SMTP
- SMTP AUTH and STARTTLS

Each method has its strengths and weaknesses and is covered briefly here. Perhaps the oldest method is the "POP before SMTP" method. This is where an email client who wants to send email must authenticate via POP (or IMAP) prior to the email relay allowing an SMTP connection from that client. In this case, the POP server usually logs the IP address in a database of some sort. Then, when the email client initiates an SMTP session, the SMTP server checks the database for allowed IP addresses prior to allowing the connection to be started for that IP address.

The benefits of the POP (or IMAP)-before-SMTP method are as follows:

- No email client setup/changes are necessary.
- Existing protocols are used.
- Little additional server overhead for implementation.

Issues with this approach are

- It's only as secure as the underlying POP/IMAP protocols.
- MTAs lack built-in support due to architecture.

The POP-before-SMTP method is useful for certain clients that lack support for the more advanced methods described next. It is a good method for handling outbound email for small devices such as cellular phones and personal digital assistants.

Secure SMTP (sometimes known as SMTPS,) is a method whereby an alternate TLS-encrypted port is used to accept inbound mail. The benefit of this approach is that it is a simple protocol with no history of security issues (as opposed to SMTP AUTH and STARTTLS). However, this approach has a number of drawbacks:

- Email client requires additional setup or external software
- Additional overhead (i.e., Stunnel required at the server level)
- Requires use of a certificate to work

Stunnel is a universal wrapper that allows you to encrypt any TCP-based protocol via SSL. If a protocol has no higher level of encryption, Stunnel can be used to encrypt it. The method we have chosen to cover here is SMTP AUTH/STARTTLS. These methods are defined by RFCs 2554 and 3207, respectively, which are extensions to the SMTP protocol itself.

The benefits of using SMTP AUTH/STARTTLS are as follows:

- Wide client support, straightforward to enable
- Good native MTA support (except for qmail)
- Flexibility in the use of encryption

The biggest limitation in using SMTP AUTH/STARTTLS is the potential for security issues. Unfortunately, due to the lack of better alternatives available until the underlying SMTP protocol is changed, this is what we are forced to use today.

The Simple Authentication and Security Layer (SASL) is a protocol defined by RFC2222. The Cyrus SASL library is an implementation of the RFC, and it supports a number of front-end authentication methods; that is, methods that email clients connecting to your server would use to perform SMTP authentication. The methods that are implemented via the SASL library include the following:

- PLAIN
- LOGIN
- ANONYMOUS
- DIGEST-MD5
- CRAM-MD5
- OTP
- KERBEROS_V4
- GSSAPI

In theory, all of the methods could be used, though in practice this is usually not the case. You would implement only the methods you need. The authentication types allowed can be reduced at Cyrus SASL compile time by using appropriate configuration switches. Authentication methods available at Cyrus SASL compile time will define the available authentication methods to the MTA. If the method is not available via Cyrus SASL, it won't be available for use at the MTA.

You may select all available methods or only a subset of the available methods via MTA configuration parameters, which results in a lot of flexibility for the administrator. We compile all available methods and then only allow LOGIN and PLAIN via MTA configuration for our examples. Although LOGIN and PLAIN are not as secure as other authentication methods that could be used, these two methods work with almost every major email client. Utilizing STARTTLS encrypts the SMTP AUTH session data, providing a secure mechanism for sending sensitive email data across untrusted networks. If STARTTLS is not used, then email authentication data is sent unencrypted, which could cause a security breach.

The choice of which front-end methods to use is largely dependent upon the email clients connecting to your server. Be aware that Microsoft Outlook and other email clients only support the LOGIN method.

STARTTLS AND MTAS

Under most distributions of Linux, Sendmail and Postfix RPMs are not enabled for SASL authentication. As a result, our instructions show how to build Sendmail and Postfix manually with support for SMTP AUTH/STARTTLS.

qmail supports only basic SMTP functions with the base distribution, so you must use a third-party patch in order to get the SMTP AUTH/STARTTLS functionality. We use netqmail-1.05, which has a number of patches for features that don't exist in the base qmail version, including SMTP AUTH/STARTTLS.

CYRUS SASL

Our approach is to use the Cyrus SASL 2.1.8 SMTP AUTH/STARTTLS package for most of the underlying work. The appropriate hooks in the covered MTAs will be activated to support the Cyrus SASL implementation.

Back-end authentication methods for Cyrus SASL include

- /etc/passwd—The traditional Unix password file is enabled by default. Set pwcheck_method to getpwent in order to activate this method.
- **kerberos**—Kerberos version 4 is enabled if the configuration script finds the appropriate libraries. Set pwcheck_method to kerberos_v4 to activate this method.
- **Pluggable authentication method (PAM)**—If PAM libraries are found during configuration time, support for PAM will be included, and it will be the default method. PAM can authenticate via a number of back ends, including RADIUS, NIS, and /etc/passwd. To explicitly set PAM as the authentication method, set pwcheck_method to pam.
- sasldb—Cyrus SASL has its own internal authentication mechanism, distinct from the other methods outline here. This mechanism uses its own username/password database, which must be updated by the Cyrus SASL saslpasswd command. To activate this method, set pwcheck_method to sasldb.

Also, Cyrus SASL includes support for writing your own back-end authentication method. Please refer to the documentation if you are interested in writing your own. We use PAM with /etc/passwd as the back end in our examples.

The order of installation is important here. Cyrus SASL must be installed first so that the subsequent Sendmail/Postfix compilations find the correct SASL libraries and are subsequently linked in successfully.

Installing

The installation of Cyrus SASL is the same for all three covered MTAs and is covered here. Requirements for building Cyrus SASL include

- BerkeleyDB 4.2 or later
- OpenSSL 0.9.7d or later

For the purposes of installation here, we assume BerkeleyDB (version 4.2) was preinstalled and is located in /usr/local/BerkeleyDB.4.2. Also, we assume SSL is located in the regular system locations (/usr/lib, /usr/include, etc.)

The sources for Cyrus SASL are available for download here: *ftp://ftp.andrew.cmu.edu/pub/cyrus-mail/cyrus-sasl-2.1.18.tar.gz.* Place the file in /usr/local/src and extract and install it as follows:

```
bash$ tar xzvf cyrus-sasl-2.1.18.tar.gz
bash$ cd cyrus-sasl-2.1.8
bash$ ./configure --sysconfdir=/etc/sasl2 \
--with-bdb-incdir=/usr/local/Berkeley DB.4.2/include \
--with-bdb-libdir=/usr/local/BerkeleyDB.4.2/lib --enable-login
bash$ make
bash$ sudo make install
bash$ sudo ln -s /usr/local/lib/sasl2 /usr/lib
```

Configuring

In order to use PAM, the mechanism needs to be set up to tell PAM what to use when Cyrus SASL wants to authenticate someone. This is performed by creating/modifying the file /etc/pam.d/smtp and adding the following line:

```
auth        required      pam_unix.so nullok try_first_pass
```

If you wanted to use some other back end other than PAM, this line would be modified to include that library instead of pam_unix.so. You will probably want Cyrus SASL to be started whenever the system starts. This can be done by adding the startup script listed in Figure 5.1 to your system startup directory as /etc/init.d/saslauthd.

```
#! /bin/sh

case $1 in
  start)
    /usr/local/sbin/saslauthd -a pam
    echo -n "Starting up saslauthd"
    ;;

  stop)
      # Stop daemons.
      echo -n "Shutting down saslauthd: "
      killproc /usr/local/sbin/saslauthd
      ;;
  restart)
      $0 stop
      $0 start
      ;;
  *)
      echo "Usage: $0 {start|stop|restart}"
      exit 1
esac

exit 0
```

Figure 5.1 saslauthd startup script.

Then link this script into your system startup by placing links from the appropriate startup directories at the appropriate run levels to this file. Installation of Cyrus SASL is complete. Next, we show how to set up Sendmail and Postfix to work with Cyrus SASL and complete our SMTP AUTH/STARTTLS setup.

SENDMAIL

Unfortunately, most binary distributions of Sendmail don't include support for SMTP AUTH/STARTTLS, so the programs must be built manually. We use Sendmail version 8.12.11 in our installation instructions, available for download from *ftp://ftp.sendmail.org/pub/sendmail/sendmail.8.12.11.tar.gz*. It is always good practice to use the latest version of Sendmail. Other versions can be used, although the installation procedure might vary from how it is covered here.

Installation and Configuration

The Sendmail build script is quite good at self configuring, so as long as all of the components are in their correct places, the build script should find them without a problem.

We start off by untar'ing and running the build script and building/installing Sendmail:

```
bash$ cd /usr/local/src/sendmail-8.12.11
bash$ ./Build
bash$ sudo ./Build install
```

Now, changes must be made to two of the m4 configuration file macros. In /usr/local/src/sendmail-8.12.11/cf/cf/site.config.m4, add the following lines:

```
APPENDDEF(`conf_sendmail_ENVDEF', `-DSASL=2')
APPENDDEF(`conf_sendmail_LIBS', `-lsasl2')
APPENDDEF(`confLIBDIRS', `-L/usr/local/lib')
APPENDDEF(`confINCDIRS', `-I/usr/local/include/sasl')
APPENDDEF(`conf_sendmail_ENVDEF', `-DSTARTTLS')
APPENDDEF(`conf_sendmail_LIBS', `-lssl -lcrypto')
```

These lines tell Sendmail where to find the SASL libraries and other related parameters when building the Sendmail configuration file. In the sendmail.mc file located in the same directory, add the following lines:

```
define(`confAUTH_OPTIONS', `A')dnl
define(`confAUTH_MECHANISMS', `LOGIN PLAIN')dnl
```

```
TRUST_AUTH_MECH(`LOGIN PLAIN')dnl
define(`confCACERT_PATH', `/etc/mail/certs')dnl
define(`confCACERT', `/etc/mail/certs/MYcert.pem')dnl
define(`confSERVER_CERT', `/etc/mail/certs/MYcert.pem')dnl
define(`confSERVER_KEY', `/etc/mail/certs/MYkey.pem')dnl
define(`confCLIENT_CERT', `/etc/mail/certs/MYcert.pem')dnl
define(`confCLIENT_KEY', `/etc/mail/certs/MYkey.pem')dnl
```

These changes tell Sendmail to enable the SMTP AUTH/STARTTLS functionality, the methods we wish to support (LOGIN and PLAIN), and where to find the certificates for SSL (encryption) support. The second and third lines where the mechanisms are listed can be modified to include whatever back-end authentication types you desire. We include only the LOGIN and PLAIN methods. Change the name of the certificate (MYcert.pem) and key (MYkey.pem) as appropriate. Also, if you don't care about TLS (SSL) encryption support, simply remove the last six lines, which define certificates and keys, and you will have SMTP AUTH support only.

After these changes have been made, run make sendmail.cf from the /usr/local/src/sendmail-8.12.11/cf/cf/ directory to generate the production sendmail.cf file. This is copied into /etc/mail/sendmail.cf after making a backup of any existing sendmail.cf file that may be present.

Certificates

If you want to support STARTTLS, you must generate and install certificates. We cover using a self-signed certificate here. If you have a certificate already, you may skip this step. To create a self-signed certificate/key pair, run the following command:

```
bash$ sudo openssl req -new -x509 -days 3650 -nodes -out \
MYcert.pem -keyout MYkey.pem
```

This will generate a key that is good for 3,650 days or 10 years to the filenames listed. These files are copied to the /etc/mail directory by executing the following steps:

```
bash$ sudo cp -p *.pem /etc/mail/certs
bash$ sudo chmod 400 /etc/mail/certs/*.pem
```

Starting and Testing

One file must be adjusted in order to support Sendmail with Cyrus SASL. The link between Sendmail and Cyrus SASL is provided by placing the following line in /usr/local/lib/sasl2/Sendmail.conf:

```
pwcheck_method: saslauthd
```

This tells the Cyrus SASL libraries to use `saslauthd` when Sendmail asks to authenticate a user. If you are running PAM, set this to `pam`. After Sendmail has been installed and configured, start Sendmail by running the startup command `/etc/init.d/sendmail start`. When it is running, you can check the methods allowed by executing the SMTP `EHLO` command to see what authentication types are available, like this:

```
220 pegasus.isp.com ESMTP Sendmail 8.12.11/8.12.11; Mon,
5 Jul 2004 16:48:23 -0400 (EDT)
ehlo smtp.example.com
250-pegasus.isp.com Hello localhost [127.0.0.1], pleased to meet you
250-ENHANCEDSTATUSCODES
250-PIPELINING
250-EXPN
250-VERB
250-8BITMIME
250-SIZE
250-DSN
250-ETRN
250-AUTH PLAIN LOGIN
250-DELIVERBY
250 HELP
```

The `250-AUTH PLAIN LOGIN` line indicates that SMTP AUTH is active and is accepting PLAIN and LOGIN as authentication mechanisms.

Postfix

Our implementation for SMTP AUTH/STARTTLS for Postfix requires Cyrus SASL, similar in fashion to Sendmail. Thus, you should first follow the steps listed previously for installing Cyrus SASL and then proceed here. Postfix requires a patch to its sources in order to facilitate STARTTLS. If you are looking for only SMTP AUTH capability, you can safely skip the patch instructions outlined next. Our example assumes that you want to use PAM as the back end, with LOGIN and PLAIN as the authentication types available for SMTP clients. Although they are not as secure as the encrypted types, they work with more email clients.

Installation and Configuration

First download the Postfix sources from *ftp://ftp.porcupine.org/mirrors/postfix-release/ official/postfix-2.1.3.tar.gz* and patches from *ftp://ftp.aet.tu-cottbus.de/pub/postfix_tls/ pfixtls-0.8.18-2.1.3-0.9.7d.tar.gz*. Note that the Postfix TLS patches are dependent upon the version of OpenSSL libraries in use on your system. We are using version 0.9.7d.

After the Postfix sources are downloaded to /usr/local/src/postfix-2.1.4 and the TLS patches to the subdirectory pfixtls-0.8.18-2.1.3-0.9.7d within the Postfix directory, perform the following steps to create the necessary Postfix user, and to group, configure and install like this:

```
bash$ cd /usr/local/src/postfix-2.1.3
bash$ patch -p0 < pfixtls-0.8.18-2.1.3-0.9.7d/pfixtls.diff
bash$ sudo groupadd postdrop
bash$ sudo useradd -c 'Postfix Daemon' -d /nonexistent -s /sbin/nologin postfix
bash$ make makefiles CCARGS="-DUSE_SASL_AUTH \
-I/usr/local/include/sasl -DHAS_S SL -I/usr/include/openssl" \
AUXLIBS="-L/usr/local/lib -R/usr/local/lib -lsasl2 -l ssl -lcrypto"
```

At the make install stage, the installer will ask you a number of questions regarding locations of files, among other things. Be sure you have good backups if you have a prior version of Sendmail or Postfix so that you can recover any files that may be inadvertently deleted during this process. When you are happy with the state of your backups, install the software and make a required directory for the program's socket to listen on:

```
bash$ sudo make install
bash$ mkdir /var/spool/postfix/var/sasl2
```

You must now make Postfix configuration file changes to enable activation of the SMTP AUTH and STARTTLS services. Start by modifying the /etc/postfix/main.cf file and adding the following lines:

```
# SASL
smtpd_sasl_auth_enable = yes
smtpd_sasl_security_options = noanonymous
smtpd_sasl_tls_security_options = $smtpd_sasl_security_options
smtpd_sasl_local_domain =
broken_sasl_auth_clients = yes

# TLS
smtpd_tls_cert_file = /etc/postfix/server.pem
smtpd_tls_key_file = $smtpd_tls_cert_file
smtpd_tls_CAfile = /etc/postfix/server.pem

#change next parameter to be no to allow people to connect via
#SMTPAUTH without STARTTLS
smtpd_tls_auth_only = yes
smtpd_tls_received_header = yes
smtpd_use_tls = yes
```

```
smtpd_tls_session_cache_timeout = 3600s
tls_random_source = dev:/dev/urandom
```

If you don't want to force people to use STARTTLS, set `smtpd_tls_auth_only` to no. This will enable those clients who only want to use SMTP AUTH to authenticate. Next, tell `smtpd` what type of authentications to allow from inbound SMTP connections. This is done by adding the following line to `/etc/postfix/smtpd.conf`:

```
mech_list:      plain login
```

Of course, you would add whatever other authentication mechanisms you wanted to allow through your Postfix server to the end of the line.

Certificates

In order to support encrypted (TLS) connections, a certificate must be made available to the server. Generating a certificate is not required for using SMTP AUTH without STARTTLS. A certificate signed by a certificate authority can be used, but in our example, we use a self-signed certificate. A self-signed certificate for Postfix is generated by issuing the following command:

```
bash$ openssl req -new -x509 -days 3650 -nodes -out server.pem -keyout server.pem
bash$ sudo cp server.pem /etc/postfix/server.pem
```

This command generates an X509-formatted certificate valid for 10 years in a single file called `server.pem`. It is installed into the default Postfix directory, `/etc/postfix`.

Starting and Testing

To finish up, you must perform a couple of additional tasks. First, add a file called `smtpd.conf` to the `/usr/local/lib/sasl2` directory with the following contents:

```
pwcheck_method: saslauthd
mech_list:      plain login
```

These lines enable the PAM authentication method for users in the back end. If another back-end mechanism is desired, use the appropriate keyword here. The second line tells SASL to allow PLAIN and LOGIN front-end authentication mechanisms. Other authentication methods can be listed here if desired.

Finally, start the authentication mechanism by running this command:

```
saslauthd -m /var/spool/postfix/var/sasl2 -a pam
```

If you were using a different back-end authentication mechanism (for example, sasldb), you would change pam to sasldb. Figure 5.2 contains a sample /etc/init.d startup script that can be used if desired. Be sure to modify the authentication method if you are using something other than PAM.

```
#! /bin/sh

case $1 in
  start)
    /usr/local/sbin/saslauthd -m /var/spool/postfix/var/sasl2 -a pam
    echo -n "Starting up saslauthd"
    ;;

  stop)
        # Stop daemons.
        echo -n "Shutting down saslauthd: "
        killproc /usr/local/sbin/saslauthd
        ;;
  restart)
        $0 stop
        $0 start
        ;;
  *)
        echo "Usage: $0 {start|stop|restart}"
        exit 1
esac

exit 0
```

Figure 5.2 /etc/init.d/saslauthd startup script.

To start the Postfix system, enter sudo postfix start, and it should start up. To check for correct operation, telnet to port 25 on the machine running Postfix, enter EHLO *machine name* at the prompt, and verify that the authentication mechanisms you have put into the configuration appear. For our example, you should see a line like this:

```
250-AUTH PLAIN LOGIN
```

This output indicates that the server has been enabled for SMTP AUTH using the PLAIN and LOGIN methods. Entering QUIT will exit from the SMTP session.

QMAIL

qmail doesn't contain native support for STARTTLS or SMTP AUTH, so patches and additional software must be used to allow this functionality. We use the netqmail-1.05 distribution, which contains most of the patches needed to enable STARTTLS and SMTP AUTH.

It is assumed that this software will be installed on a server already running a version of qmail, so setup has already taken place. For example, we assume ucspi-tcp and daemontools are installed. In addition, the checkpassword-0.90 needs to be installed to support qmail and STARTTLS/SMTP AUTH authenticating against the /etc/passwd file. Unfortunately, there is no support for alternative authentication back ends like PAM with qmail.

The front-end authentication methods are hard-coded and consist of the following:

- LOGIN
- PLAIN
- CRAM-MD5

These methods cannot be altered, except by changing the sources.

Installation

For the purposes of the discussion here, we assume that you have already installed qmail and just want to update the binaries to support SMTP AUTH/STARTTLS. If you want to build qmail from scratch, an excellent site is Dave Sills' Life With qmail, *http://www.lifewithqmail.org*.

In order to support SMTP AUTH, we use the netqmail-1.05 distribution, which is a collection of patches for qmail-1.03. We also need the checkpassword package from the qmail author's web site and the SMTP AUTH patch itself. Download the netqmail-1.05 sources and the two other files from the appropriate sites into /usr/local/src:

- netqmail—*http://www.qmail.org/netqmail-1.05.tar.gz*
- checkpassword—*http://cr.yp.to/checkpwd/checkpassword-0.90.tar.gz*
- qmail smtpauth patch—*http://shupp.org/patches/netqmail-1.05-tls-smtpauth-20040705.patch*

First, we will install netqmail-1.05 using the following steps:

```
bash$ cd /usr/local/src
bash$ sudo su
# tar xzvf netqmail-1.05.tar.gz
```

```
# cd netqmail-1.05
# ./collate.sh
# patch -p0 < /usr/local/src/netqmail-1.05-tls-smtpauth-20040705.patch
bash$ sudo su
# make setup check
```

A version of qmail that incorporates the SMTP AUTH functionality is now installed. Next, we install checkpassword, which enables qmail to check passwords against the /etc/passwd file to support SMTP AUTH. checkpassword is installed as follows:

```
bash$ cd /usr/local/src
bash$ sudo su
# tar xzvf checkpassword-0.90.tar.gz
# cd checkpassword-0.90
# patch < /usr/local/src/netqmail-1.05/other-patches/checkpassword-0.90.errno.patch
# make
# chmod 4711 /bin/checkpassword
```

The qmail run script must be adjusted to check for a password when relaying a message. This is accomplished by adjusting the /var/qmail/supervise/qmail-smtpd/run script as follows. Change the last line in the file, which usually reads

```
-u "$QMAILDUID" -g "$NOFILESGID" 0 smtp /var/qmail/bin/qmail-smtpd 2>&1
```

to this:

```
-u "$QMAILDUID" -g "$NOFILESGID" 0 smtp /var/qmail/bin/qmail-smtpd
/bin/checkpassword /bin/true 2>&1
```

Changing the run script as shown here invokes checkpassword so that email relay requests can be authenticated by the SMTP AUTH protocol. The installation of checkpassword and netqmail-1.05 is now complete.

Certificates

To build a self-signed certificate in order to support STARTTLS, simply run a make cert in the /usr/local/src/netqmail-1.05 build directory. The build script copies the certificates over to /var/qmail/control automatically for you. Of course, a "real" certificate signed by a certificate authority can be substituted. Note that this is not required in order to perform simple unencrypted SMTP AUTH authentication.

Testing

To restart qmail after upgrading or changing configuration files, restart using your qmail control script. If you have installed qmail using the Life With qmail site, this will be `qmailctl restart`. To test, simply telnet to port 25 on your server, execute an `EHLO`, and see what authentication types are available, similar to this:

```
250-AUTH PLAIN LOGIN CRAM-MD5
```

This line indicates that all of the default qmail authentication types are installed and available, including PLAIN, LOGIN, and CRAM-MD5. Entering `QUIT` exits from the SMTP session.

CONCLUSION

Email systems that provide email-relaying services to end users can be secured in a number of ways. Among the methods are POP before SMTP, tunneling SMTP via a TLS channel, and SMTP AUTH/STARTTLS. We chose to cover SMTP AUTH/STARTTLS because it has wide support among email clients and servers and is relatively easy to implement on the covered MTAs.

The basis for implementing SMTP AUTH/STARTTLS for Sendmail and Postfix is the Cyrus SASL library. Although there are a number of front-end mechanisms, we decided to cover only the LOGIN and PLAIN front-end mechanisms because they are supported in the most modern email clients. In order to get full end-to-end encryption, TLS must be used. qmail support for SMTP AUTH/STARTTLS is provided by the netqmail-1.05 package, which is qmail-1.03 with a set of patches including SMTP AUTH and START-TLS functionality. The patches only provide for limited front- and back-end authentication methods.

Distributed Checksum Filtering

In this chapter, we look at a classification of filtering called Distributed Checksum Filtering (DCF). This method of fighting spam involves a network of mail transfer agents (MTAs), which exchange mail message signatures with each other. A signature is a small unique numeric value that represents the message, similar to a checksum used in verifying data transfers.

Two approaches use the DCF method:

- Exchange checksums for spam messages (Vipul's Razor and Pyzor)
- Exchange checksums and counts from all messages (Distributed Checksum Clearinghouse, or DCC)

The method of exchanging only spam message checksums theoretically reduces the amount of traffic between checksum servers because after a message is identified and reported as spam, it doesn't need to be reported again. The second method (reporting all message checksums) relies on large counts of messages to help indicate whether or not a given message is spam. Obviously, opt-in list sending addresses need to be whitelisted in order for this to work, as legitimate mailing lists would be misidentified as spam. Figure 6.1 illustrates how the DCF approach works.

Because spammers broadcast their messages to a wide audience, and given a relatively large network of MTAs exchanging signatures and counts, you can safely say that spam messages (and other messages, like opt-in lists) will have very high message checksum counts. As a result, many of these messages can be identified as spam and the non-spam messages allowed through by means of a whitelist.

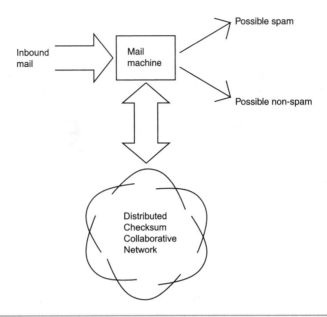

Figure 6.1 Distributed checksum filtering.

The DCF methods can be implemented natively with certain MTAs or in conjunction with a tool like SpamAssassin. We cover the following DCF methods:

- Vipul's Razor (Razor)
- Distributed Checksum Clearinghouse (DCC)

We illustrate how to hook DCC and Razor into Sendmail, Postfix, and qmail. We also show how to set up DCC for sharing checksums with their respective DCF networks so that others can benefit from your users' "knowledge" of spam messages.

Spammers have attempted to circumvent the DCF checksums by placing random words in order to change the resultant signatures. By adjusting the algorithms used to generate the checksums, the DCF software authors play a game of "cat and mouse," where each successful tweak of the algorithm by software authors causes the spammers to adjust their methods, resulting in additional changes, and so forth. However, perhaps the best way to implement a DCF solution is by using a "scoring" system such as SpamAssassin. By using a scoring method, false positives can be reduced (although not eliminated).

VIPUL'S RAZOR

Vipul's Razor is a system for identifying and filtering spam emails in a distributed fashion. (We will refer to Vipul's Razor throughout this book as both Razor and VR.) It consists of a set of Razor servers that hold a database of known spam emails. Razor was initially designed to be run from the command line, but it has been extended to work with SpamAssassin.

In standalone mode, the user's email client is configured to submit incoming emails to a Razor client that queries a Razor server to determine if it is a known spam email and delivers it accordingly. Additionally, users can register with the server so that they can add spam emails to the database or so that they can flag emails misidentified as spam by the system. The weight assigned to a given user's classification of emails is determined by a trust level associated with the submitter. This trust level is maintained by the server, which considers the "correctness" of previous classifications by that submitter in generating a trust level for that submitter.

The client side of Vipul's Razor is implemented as a set of Perl scripts, which are installed in /usr/local/bin; associated libraries are installed in /usr/local/lib/perl5.

INSTALLING VIPUL'S RAZOR

There are two pieces to Vipul's Razor. The first piece is the required Perl modules, provided by Vipul's Razor as part of the software development kit. Download the latest v2 razor-agents tarball from *http://razor.sourceforge.net/download/*. Also, download the latest v2 razor-agents-sdk tarball from *http://razor.sourceforge.net/download/*.

The Razor SDK contains the following Perl modules, which are required for Razor operation:

Net::Ping
Net::DNS
Time::HiRes
Digest::SHA1
Getopt::Long
File::Copy
Digest::Nilsimsa
URI::Escape

After downloading it to /usr/local/src, untar the Razor Agents SDK package and install as follows:

```
bash$ perl Makefile.PL
bash$ make
bash$ sudo su
# make test
# make install
```

Next, the Razor package itself must be installed. Untar the razor-agents tar file and execute the following commands:

```
bash$ perl Makefile.PL
bash$ make
bash$ sudo su
# make test
# make install
```

The Vipul's Razor package and required Perl modules are now installed. To finish up the installation, razor-client must be run as root in order to install appropriate symbolic links:

```
# razor-client
```

This completes the installation of Vipul's Razor.

COMMANDS

The following sections show you how to manipulate Razor using command line access to the Linux shell. The Razor distribution includes a configuration file called razor-agent.conf and the following commands:

- razor-admin—Perform administrative Razor functions.
- razor-check—Check a message against the Razor database.
- razor-report—Report spam to the Razor network.
- razor-revoke—Change a spam report back to non-spam in the Razor network.

Each of the individual components is covered in the following sections.

razor-agent.conf

The operation of the client is controlled by the `razor-agent.conf` configuration file. The following configuration keyword/value pairs are available:

`razorhome = directory` (Default is razor-agent.log)

This specifies the directory where Razor should look by default for Razor-agent files. Files specified without a full path are relative to this path. If the directory doesn't exist, Razor creates it. Defaults are

- `/etc/razor/` for root
- `~/.razor/` for other users

`logfile = filename` (Default is razor-agent.log)

This is the log file for the Razor Agents.

`debuglevel = integer from 0-20` (Default is 5)

This specifies the amount of debug information Razor should produce.

- Low values (0–4) log startup and error messages.
- Mid values (5–10) show all events going through server.
- High values (11+) show events in great detail and should only be used with care, as files can grow large very quickly.

`identity = filename` (Default `razorhome/identity-user`)

Running `razor-admin` specifies an identity file for storing a newly registered identity. Razor uses this identity while authenticating with Razor servers when using the `razor-report` and `razor-revoke` commands.

`razorzone = DNS zone` (Default is razor.cloudmark.com)

This keyword identifies the DNS zone where Razor agents expect to find Razor discovery servers. Razor agents that use this include

- `razor-admin`
- `razor-check`
- `razor-report`
- `razor-revoke`

`listfile_nomination = ` *`filename`* ` (Default is servers.nomination.1st)`

This specifies the file where Razor nomination servers are listed, in order of closest ping time. The file is created automatically. This list is used by

- `razor-report`
- `razor-revoke`

`listfile_catalogue = ` *`filename`* ` (Default is servers.catalogue.1st)`

This specifies the file where Razor catalogue servers are listed, in order of closest ping time. The file is created automatically and is used by `razor-check`.

`listfile_discovery = ` *`filename`* ` (Default is servers.discovery.1st)`

This specifies the file where Razor discovery servers are listed, in random order. The contents of this file are created automatically using DNS.

`rediscovery_wait_dns = ` *`seconds`* ` (Default is 604800)`

This indicates the maximum time in seconds Razor agents will wait before computing a new `listfile_discovery` using DNS.

`rediscovery_wait ` *`seconds`* ` (Default is 172800)`

This sets the maximum time in seconds Razor Agents will wait before computing a new `listfile_nomination` and a new `listfile_catalogue`.

`turn_off_discovery (0 | 1) (Default 0, or off)`

This sets the closest host discovery function. When set to 1, the following files are not updated:

- `listfile_catalogue`
- `listfile_nomination`
- `listfile_discovery` (not read or updated)

`ignorelist (0 | 1) (Default is 0, or off)`

When this value is set to 1, it will cause Razor to automatically ignore mailing list posts. If set to 0, mailing list posts will be handled like all other mail. Mailing list posts are identified by this regular expression: `$headers =~ /\n((X-)?List-Id[^\n]+)/i`. This expression will match headers such as `List-Id` or `X-List-Id`.

```
whitelist filename (Default is razor-whitelist)
```

This sets the Razor whitelist file. Razor agents can consult a whitelist of addresses and SHA1 hashes before checking email with Razor servers. No check will be made against the Razor server if an address is on the list.

Lines in the whitelist consist of header name and value pairs, separated by white space. Headers can be any valid header line, such as `to`, `from`, `cc`, and the special keyword, `sha1`. `sha1` indicates a Razor whitelisting signature. It's important to note that if any part of the string matches, it will return a match. Examples of entries in this file include

```
to someone@special.com
from me@somewhere.com
cc @friends.com
sha1 75f8bcc2357366bbfa9c6ab0b6e5648ed0cf7083
```

```
min_cf
```

This is the minimum confidence score that a message must be to be considered spam. When checking spam, the server can optionally return a spam confidence value ranging from 0 (not confident) to 100 (absolutely or 100% confident). To be considered spam, the server's spam confidence value must be greater than or equal to `min_cf`. `min_cf` can be a number or an expression containing `ac`, the average confidence published by a Razor server. Examples: 0, 60, 100, ac, ac + 10, and ac - 20. If an expression evaluates to less than 0, it becomes 0; likewise, those greater than 100 become 100. The default is `ac`.

```
report_headers (0 | 1) (Default is 1, or on)
```

If set to 1, when reporting spam, the entire email message (including header and body) is sent to a Razor nomination server. When set to 0, all the headers are removed except for headers beginning with `Content-`. A special header beginning with `X-Razor2` is added to note this action.

```
use_engines (1,2,3,4) (Default is 1,3,4)
```

This keyword specifies which signatures to use when checking an email against Razor. Each integer (comma-separated, whitespace ignored) represents an engine that is to be used to compute a signature from. The integer's meanings are as follows:

1. SHA1 of entire email (compatible with Razor version 1)
2. SHA1
3. Nilsimsa
4. Ephemeral Hash

Notes:

- Engines 2 and higher are Razor v2-compatible; that is, they compute signatures of individual body parts (MIME attachments).
- In order to send signatures to the server, the server must support the engines, and they must be available locally.

razor-admin

`razor-admin` is used to administer Razor. It is most commonly used to set up the system for use with a user. The first argument is the action you want performed, and it is required.

The three actions can be `register`, `discover`, or `create`, which mean the following:

`-register`

This option registers a new Razor identity, used for authenticating with Razor nomination servers. Identities are a user and password pair stored in *razorhome*/`identity-`*user*. Both `razor-report` and `razor-revoke` require the user reporting the message to be registered in order to determine the trust of each user reporting spam.

`-discover`

This forces discovery of Razor catalog servers. This will create `server.*.lst` files in *razorhome*.

`-create`

This explicitly creates a `razor-agent.conf` file in *razorhome*, and creates *razorhome* if it does not exist. By default, this option loads `/etc/razor/razor-agent.conf` if it exists, using defaults for anything not found.

Some of the more useful optional flags are as follows:

`-d | --verbose`

This prints extra debugging information.

`-user=user@domain.com`

This option asks Razor to register the specified username spam reports to the Razor server for this identity, if available. Razor will assign a username if none is specified. Normally, this should be the email address of the user submitting the message.

`-pass=password`

This sets the password assigned with this Razor identity. If not specified, it will be assigned.

`-1`

This option tells Razor that this is the default identity.

razor-check

`razor-check` compares an email message against the Razor distributed database. It is normally invoked at the command line pipe via Procmail or a similar mechanism, or less often directly with spam messages as arguments. Some of the more useful command line arguments are as follows:

`-d | --verbose`

This prints debugging information.

`-s`

This simulates a Razor lookup but doesn't perform a server check.

`-rs=razor server`

This tells the program to use the specified Razor catalogue server instead of the default list (usually `servers.catalogue.lst`).

`-H`

This tells Razor to just compute and print the signature of the email message without doing anything else.

`-S=string`

This tells Razor to accept a list of precomputed (with `-H`) signatures on the command line, instead of computing one from mail content. Signatures can be submitted in hex or base64 (preferred); this requires `-e` to specify which engine to use.
Example:

`razor-report -e 1 -S d3b07384d113edec49eaa6238ad5ff00`

`-e=integer`

This specifies the engine used to create signatures, currently 1, 2, 3, or 4. Engine 1, or -e=1, is used for Razor 1.x signatures. Used only with -S=*string* or -H.

razor-report

razor-report is used to report spam to the distributed Razor server network. Normally, it is called via Procmail or a mail user agent. You need to be authenticated prior to reporting your results to the Razor network. Be careful when reporting messages to the network because the more "correct" your results are, the more trust your reporting results will receive by the Razor network. "Correct" means how well your scores agree with others in the Razor network.

The options accepted by razor-report are very similar to razor-check, so see that section for details. One interesting flag is different, though:

-f

This indicates to stay in the foreground; do not detach and run in the background.

razor-revoke

razor-revoke is used to reclassify emails marked incorrectly as spam. This command is meant to be run as a filter, meaning that messages should be piped to it. However, it can be used on the command line. As with razor-report, all submissions are tagged with the ID of the reporter, so a level of trust can be developed for each submitter.

Switches are very similar to razor-report, except for -f (discussed previously) and an option to process an entire mailbox:

-M | --mbox *mailbox*

This tells the system to accept a mailbox name on the command line and revoke every mail in the mailbox against the database. If in foreground with the -f option, razor-revoke will print out the mail number of every mail that was accepted by the Razor catalogue server.

Configuration

The default configuration file is kept in /etc/razor/razor-agent.conf and is initially created by the razor-admin command invoked with the necessary options:

```
# razor-admin -d -create -home=/etc/razor
```

Individual users need to run the razor-admin command in order to set up their own .razor directory, which holds user-specific configuration information.

```
bash$ razor-admin -create
```

This command sets up the Unix account that invokes the command for Razor operation.

Whitelisting

A whitelist may be created that holds a list of addresses or message signatures that will not be processed by the spam checking or reporting commands. This file is `~/.razor/white-list` by default, but that may be changed in the `razor-agent.conf` file. Each line consists of two fields. The first indicates the type of address, and the second is the address itself. For example, consider the following whitelist:

```
from someguy@example.com
cc spamme@example.net
sha1 d3b07384d113edec49eaa6238ad5ff00
```

This prevents messages from `someguy@example.com` from being processed as well as messages cc'd to `spamme@example.net`. The third example prevents a message with the listed `sha1` signature from being processed.

USAGE

Although you must be a registered Razor user to report spam, querying the Razor network for spam scores does not require authorization. Checking individual messages against the database is handled by the `razor-check` command. It checks individual messages or a mailbox in mbox format. With no arguments, it reads the message or mailbox from `stdin`. With filename arguments, it reads from the named files.

If the message is found in the database, `razor-check` exits with status 0; otherwise, it returns 1. If more than one message is processed at once, the index of spam messages is returned. Only one of the named files may be a mailbox in mbox format. If the message matches the whitelist, 1 is returned.

```
bash$ razor-check /path/to/message
```

This reads the message located in the specified location and returns a 0 if the message is listed in the Razor network or a 1 if it is not.

```
bash$ razor-check mailbox
```

The `razor-check` command returns a spam score for all messages in the named mbox-formatted mailbox.

Registering

You must register an identity with the system in order to report spam. Your identity is used to track your reports and revokes to build up your reputation, which determines what weight your reports carry. You register with the `razor-admin` command with the `-register` flag. You are assigned an identity that is recorded in your `.razor` directory. Optionally, you may use the `-user` flag to select an identity. Your registration fails and an error message is displayed if the identity is unavailable.

```
bash$ razor-admin -register
```

Running the `register` command without a `-user` argument causes the Razor network to assign you an ID and password, which is saved in your `.razor` directory.

```
bash$ razor-admin -register -user me@example.com
```

This command causes the Razor ID `me@example.com` to be registered with the Razor network. An error is returned and registration fails if the specified identity is not available.

Reporting and Revoking Spam

After registering, you may use the command `razor-report` to report spam. It either reads from `stdin` or from named files. Only one of the named files may be a mailbox in mbox format. There appears to be an undocumented restriction that the named files must have absolute paths. The message isn't processed if it matches the whitelist.

```
bash$ razor-report /path/to/message1 /path/to/message2
```

This command reports the named messages to the Razor network as spam.

If you find that non-spam messages have been misclassified as spam, you may report that as well with the `razor-revoke` command. It, too, reads messages or a mailbox in mbox format from `stdin` or named files supplied as arguments.

```
bash$ razor-revoke /path/to/message1 /path/to/message2
```

This command tells the Razor network that the messages previously submitted were in fact not spam.

DISTRIBUTED CHECKSUM CLEARINGHOUSE

The following section describes the Distributed Checksum Clearinghouse (DCC). More information is available at *http://www.rhyolite.com/anti-spam/dcc/*.

INTRODUCTION

DCC is a system for identifying bulk email messages. It is made up of a distributed collection of servers, where counts of email messages received by clients are maintained. Each participating client computes checksums for each email it receives and sends them to a DCC server, which in turn floods this information to other participating servers. It should be emphasized that messages are never forwarded to the DCC servers, only the checksums.

The server can be set up to tag messages with a header indicating the DCC scores or to reject messages on the basis of the DCC results. Usually, tagging messages is safer than outright rejection of suspected email because not accepting messages can mean lost legitimate email.

DCC utilizes the concept of "greylists." These are messages that you might not want to accept because there isn't enough data on them yet. Greylisting is optional, and it requires some additional configuration to use.

The server returns the count for the referenced message back to the client. The client can then decide whether or not to accept the message based upon that count. Counts are returned for the following items:

- IP—The IP address of the sending client
- env_From—The envelope From: address
- From—The From: address from the message header
- Message-Id—The message ID field from the header
- Received—The last received line from the header
- Body—The body of the message (ignoring white space)
- Fuz1, Fuz2—Two filtered (or "fuzzy") checksums, arrived at with different algorithms

Whitelists prevent the client from submitting emails that match a configurable set of header information or checksums. DCC specifically makes no judgment as to the "spamminess" of emails, only their "bulkiness." Whitelists must be used to prevent legitimate bulk email (for example, mailing lists) from being considered spam.

There are two modes of attaching to the DCC network:

- anonymous
- named

The default method is "anonymous," where you are not identified to the DCC network. The alternative, "named," is where you are identified to the server. If you choose to submit scores to the DCC network, your scores as an anonymous submitter will have less impact than those submitted as a named user.

There are two ways to invoke DCC processing of messages: per-user via Procmail or site-wide utilizing milter. Both are covered here.

INSTALLING DCC

The DCC system is composed of the following components:

- dccproc—For use with MTAs other than Sendmail, such as Procmail
- dccifd—Generic Perl and MTA interface
- dccm—Sendmail milter interface
- dccd—The dcc daemon, for sharing checksums with others
- cdcc—Administrative information such as server names, addresses, passwords, and similar data

DCC sources are available in three flavors, listed in increasing order of functionality:

- dcc-dccproc.tar.Z—Contains dccproc, dccifd, cdcc, and all of the manual pages and documentation.
- dcc-dccm.tar.Z—Everything in the dcc-dccproc.tar.Z, plus dccm
- dcc-dccd.tar.Z—Everything in dcc-dccm.tar.Z plus dccd

Although you don't need the entire package if you aren't sharing checksums with other servers, we will use that tar file in our installation because we cover how to set up your own dccd server.

First, cd to your local source area, download the DCC sources from Rhyolite, and extract them:

```
bash$ cd /usr/local/src
bash$ lynx http://www.rhyolite.com/anti-spam/dcc/source/dcc-dccd.tar.Z
bash$ uncompress dcc-dccd.tar.Z
bash$ tar xf dcc-dccd.tar
```

Make sure Sendmail has been built with milter support (see Chapter 3, "SpamAssassin"). By default, DCC uses the following file locations:

- DCC "home directory"   `/var/dcc`
- libexec directory   `/var/dcc/libexec`
- binaries directory   `/usr/local/bin`

The `configure` defaults are reasonable and should work for most installations. Following are a few notes on configure options you might need to use:

- If you are running a large installation, you may want to increase the hash table size by enabling the `--enable-big-db` configure flag.
- To specify the location of Sendmail milter files, use the `--with-sendmail=DIR` keyword.

If you are an end user and just want to run DCC yourself, configure it like this:

```
bash$ ./configure --disable-sys-inst  --disable-server \
--disable-dccm --disable-dccifd \
--homedir=path-to-home-directory \
--bindir=path-to-home-directory/bin
bash$ make
bash$ make install
```

To activate DCC system-wide, use the usual configure `make` routine:

```
bash$ ./configure
bash$ make
bash$ sudo make install
```

DCC provides a daemon, `dccm`, that implements Sendmail's milter interface to allow Sendmail to process incoming messages through DCC prior to delivery, optionally bouncing them. To activate the Sendmail milter interface to `dccm`, perform the following steps. From the DCC source directory, copy the `misc/dccdnsbl.m4` files to your `/usr/local/src/sendmail-8.12.11/cf/feature` directory like this:

```
$bash cp misc/dcc.m4 /usr/local/src/sendmail-8.12.11/cf/cf/feature
$bash cp misc/dccdnsbl.m4 /usr/local/src/sendmail-8.12.11/cf/cf/feature
```

Add the line FEATURE(dcc) to your sendmail.mc configuration file. Then rebuild and reinstall your sendmail.cf and restart Sendmail:

```
bash$ cd /usr/local/src/sendmail-8.12.11/cf/cf
bash$ sudo su
# make sendmail.cf
# cp /etc/mail/sendmail.cf /etc/mail/sendmail.cf.old
# /etc/init.d/sendmail stop
# /etc/init.d/sendmail start
```

CONFIGURING DCC

DCC has a number of configuration files that specify how the server works. These are outlined in the sections here.

Files

By default, DCC support files are installed in /var/dcc. The following files are used to configure DCC, noting whether they are associated with the server, client, both, or neither:

- Makefile—(n/a) The file used to build the rest of the configuration files in this directory.
- Makefile.in—(n/a) The Makefile as distributed, before customization by configure.
- dcc_conf—(Server) The primary DCC configuration file.
- dcc_conf.in—(n/a) The dcc_conf as distributed, before customization by configure.
- flod—(Server) The file used to tell DCC what servers to send checksums to. Only used if distributing your checksums to other servers.
- grey_flod—(Server) Used to tell DCC what servers to send greylisted checksums to. Only used if distributing checksums that originate on your server to other servers in the DCC network.
- grey_whitelist—(Server) Identifies greylisted machines.
- ids—(Server) Contains usernames and passwords for various parts of DCC.
- make-dcc_conf—(n/a) Generates a new dcc_conf from an existing file.
- map.txt—(clients) Specifies what DCC servers to connect to.
- whiteclnt—(clients) Client-side whitelist file.
- whitecommon—(both) Whitelisted addresses common on both client and server side.
- whitelist—(Server) Server-side whitelist file.

Basic DCC Setup

The following sections cover how to set up DCC in a basic mode. This is enough information to get the DCC system up and running under Sendmail and evaluating incoming email. The setup has the following attributes:

- Anonymous binds to the DCC server
- Only remote servers are used
- No flooding
- No greylisting
- Tagging messages with a DCC score

Setting up your own servers, flooding, and greylisting are covered in the sections following the basic setup.

dcc_conf

The main DCC configuration file is dcc_conf in the DCC home directory (usually /var/dcc). For the most part, the configuration file as delivered after the software is built is acceptable. There is one flag you might change, and that has to do with rejecting messages instead of the default behavior of simply adding a header. The distributed version of dcc_conf is not set to reject messages. Instead, it adds a header item indicating the results of DCC processing. Consider the following header:

```
X-DCC-dcc.uncw.edu-Metrics: sluggo.cushman.avacoda.com 1201; Body=42 Fuz1=42 Fuz2=many
```

The scores are at the end of the line. There are three tests run—Body, Fuz1, and Fuz2—with scores of 42, 42, and many, respectively. These three scores are the results from running the message through three algorithms that DCC uses to identify messages as spam or not. The Fuz2=many score indicates that the message exceeded a large number, so it is likely spam (or a bulk emailing).

Rather than simply rejecting email outright, adding X-DCC headers gives users the opportunity to whitelist the mailing lists they're on. When you're satisfied that things are working correctly, the DCCM_REJECT_AT parameter may be set to the count threshold for rejecting emails. For example, the following line will cause DCC to reject any message that has a count of many, which normally indicates spam:

```
DCCM_REJECT_AT=many
```

However, any message rejection based only upon DCC scores should be used with caution. Otherwise, legitimate messages may be blocked, and the end user (or administrator) won't know that messages are being rejected unless further action is taken.

ids

The ids file contains the authentication information for attaching to the DCC network. It is not used in the anonymous mode. The file contains username password pairs separated by white space, such as

```
1405      secret
8203      asecret
```

map.txt

The map.txt file contains the names or IP addresses of DCC servers that should be used. The package ships with the following list:

```
dcc1.dcc-servers.net
dcc2.dcc-servers.net
dcc3.dcc-servers.net
dcc4.dcc-servers.net
dcc5.dcc-servers.net


# local DCC server
127.0.0.1    RTT-1000 ms     32768 secret1

# local greylist server
127.0.0.1    GREYLIST        32768 secret1
```

Check the DCC home page for other servers that might be better for you. Although the servers listed on the home page all allow anonymous access, it doesn't hurt to drop the listed administrator an email and let her know that you are using her server.

Whitelist Files (whiteclnt, whitecommon, and whitelist)

Update the whitelisting-related files with any email addresses that you do not want DCC to reject. Note that changes to whitelist are not effective until dbclean is run. (See "DCC File Maintenance" later; note that dbclean can also be run by hand.) Unless your setup is very complex, you can probably make changes in one file (whitecommon) and simply include it in the whiteclnt and whitelist files.

Enabling DCC at System Startup

A startup script, /var/dcc/libexec/rcDCC, should be run to start dccm and other DCC-related daemons. It reads /var/dcc/dcc_conf to determine which daemons should be started.

To activate, simply copy the file misc/rcDCC under the DCC distribution to the location of all the system startup scripts, usually /etc/init.d, and activate it like this:

```
# cp misc/rcDCC /etc/init.d
# ln -s /etc/init.d/rcDCC /etc/rc2.d/S65rcDCC
```

Please note that DCC must be started *before* Sendmail in order to ensure proper operation. Be sure that the number of the DCC file (in our case, 65) is *lower* than the Sendmail startup number.

DCC File Maintenance

In order to maintain DCC database consistency, you need to run a daily cron job. Copy the file misc/cron-dccd to a location on your system such as /usr/local/sbin like this:

```
# cp misc/cron-dccd /usr/local/sbin
```

Add the following line to your crontab to run the DCC cleanup every day at 3:15 am:

```
15 3 * * * /usr/local/sbin/cron-dccd > /dev/null 2>&1
```

DCC AND PROCMAIL

This section covers using DCC with Procmail to filter incoming email. The DCC command that is designed to do this is called dccproc. Invoking DCC by Procmail is less efficient than using milter; using Procmail to call DCC is useful. For example, Procmail could be used to prototype DCC or to implement it for a certain subset of users.

dccproc

dccproc is a program that reads messages on stdin and writes them to stdout with a header item added indicating the results of DCC processing. It is intended to be used by delivery agents such as Procmail.

dccproc supports many options, including

```
-w whiteclnt_file
```

This specifies a user-supplied whitelist to augment the server's whitelist.

```
-c type,[log_threshold,]reject_threshold
```

This specifies the thresholds for determining whether a given message is bulk or not. The type refers to the checksum type. CMN is shorthand for indicating that if any of the common types—Body, Fuz1, and Fuz2—have exceeded the specified thresholds, then the message should be considered bulk. The log_threshold and reject_threshold refer to the cutoff point for logging (saving in a separate directory) or rejecting (returning exit code EX_NOUSER, typically 63) the message being processed. The threshold may be a number or the keyword MANY, indicating that the DCC server network has seen millions of messages with this checksum.

The following Procmail recipe can be included in an individual user's .procmailrc file or in the system-wide /etc/procmailrc file to cause messages to be processed through DCC as they are delivered.

```
MAILDIR=${HOME}/Maildir
LOGFILE=${MAILDIR}/procmail.log

:0fW
| /usr/local/bin/dccproc -w ${HOME}/.dcc/whiteclnt -c cmn,many

:0e
{
  EXITCODE=67
  :0
  spam
}
```

This Procmail recipe runs the message through the dccproc and routes the message to the spam folder when the EXITCODE from dccproc is 67.

Please note:

- The user's mail folders are stored in ${HOME}/Maildir.
- procmail keeps a log of messages processed in ${MAILDIR}/procmail.log.
- dccproc uses a whitelist located in ${HOME}/.dcc/whiteclnt.

ADVANCED DCC SETUP

The following sections illustrate how to perform some of the more advanced functions within DCC:

- Create your own local DCC server
- Activate flooding
- Activate greylisting

You want to activate your own DCC server if you

- Have a large number of email users
- Want to share checksums with others

Activate greylisting if you wanted extra spam filtering. Note that it isn't worthwhile to set up a server unless you are going to activate flooding or greylisting! Also, before activating the more advanced features of DCC, be sure your existing DCC infrastructure is running smoothly and the way you want it to.

Local DCC Server

The first step in setting up flooding or greylisting is to set up your own local DCC server. In order to run a server, you must have a unique ID that identifies your system to the DCC network you join. Right now, the maintainer of the DCC server network is the DCC developer, Vernon Schryver. Contact him and obtain the server ID.

In dccd_conf, set the following values appropriately:

```
DCCD_ENABLE=on
SRVR_ID=Server ID
BRAND=string
```

These lines enable dccd for operation, identify the DCC server to the rest of the DCC network, and specify the identification string the server uses when reporting the message checksums to the DCC network.

Next, choose a password and place it in your ids file as follows:

```
Server_ID password
```

The left column is the server ID assigned to you by the DCC administrator, and the right-hand argument is the password string used for authenticating DCC sessions. You now are set up to authenticate servers. To enable clients for authentication, add them to the ids file in a similar fashion to the server.

Flooding

Flooding is sending checksums to peers in the DCC network. To set up flooding, you need to

- Obtain the passwd-ID and its password of each peer and add them to your /var/dcc/ids file
- Add a line for each flooding peer to the /var/dcc/flod file

The format of the flod file is as follows:

```
server port password [out options] [in options]
```

server	remote DCC server
port	DCC port
password	password for server and port
out options	optional parameters for running dccd
in options	optional parameters for running dccd

To check that flooding is happening, use the following commands to check the status of the server:

```
# cdcc stats
# cdcc "id X; flood list"
# /var/dcc/libexec/dblist -Hv
```

Greylisting

Greylisting uses a modified DCC server to maintain a database of checksums of the following classes of entities:

- Frequent email senders
- Recurrent senders' email addressees
- IP addresses of frequent senders' SMTP clients

The setup of greylisting is similar to flooding. You must arrange with a member of the DCC network to gain access to the greylist checksums. When you receive the client IDs and passwords, place them in the /var/dcc/map.txt file. It is convenient to share server IDs between regular blacklists and greylists. If you want to grant access to your servers to others, simply generate the client IDs and passwords and place them in the ids file.

Within the `dcc_conf` file, set the following parameters:

- `GREY_ENABLE=on`
- If a DCC server is not being run, set `GREY_SRVR_ID`. Otherwise use the default line to use the DCC server-ID.
- Override the following values in `GREY_DCCD_ARGS` if necessary:
  - embargo
  - wait
  - white
- add `-G` to `DCCM_ARGS`

Local greylist flooding can be enabled by placing appropriate lines in the `grey_flod` files, in the same manner as `flod` files.

Ports and Firewalls

DCC servers use TCP and UDP ports 6276 and 6277. The exact mapping is as follows:

Protocol	Port	Use
TCP	6277	DCC flooding between servers
UDP	6277	DCC communictions to clients
UDP	6276	DCC greylisting between servers

Firewalls on your DCC machine and on your network may need to be adjusted appropriately to allow these protocols through.

CONCLUSION

DCF is a useful method for determining whether or not a message is spam. There are two variations of this method. One method (Vipul Razor) exchanges checksums of messages its users has identified as spam. The second method (DCC) exchanges checksums of all messages processed by servers in the network, counting the number of times each checksum has been identified. The DCC method requires a whitelist, as legitimate bulk email will be identified as spam unless the sender is identified in a whitelist.

Both Vipul Razor and DCC are implemented as part of the SpamAssassin package, which is an excellent way to utilize DCF. Using a scoring method rather than rejecting messages based upon DCF eliminates the worry of legitimate messages getting rejected as spam based upon a single method.

Introduction to Bayesian Filtering

One particularly powerful scheme for fending off spam takes a statistical approach. Instead of looking for individual elements of a message, this approach examines the message's entire contents and tries to infer mathematically whether the message is spam or not.

In August of 2002, famous anti-spam crusader Paul Graham wrote "A Plan for Spam" [1], which relates his experiences and frustrations trying to write individual spam detection rules and his epiphany that a statistical approach might be better.

In hindsight, this approach makes good sense. For instance, Graham identified a word used only in his own field ("Lisp") that, for him, was a powerful discriminator in detecting spam (and legitimate email). Identifying the indicative keywords, of course, requires more of a statistical approach than simply trying to recall all of the special words one might expect to receive in email.

Graham examined his body of human-identified spam and non-spam email and calculated probabilities that various single words appear. He made two tables of word counts: one for spam messages and one for non-spam messages. He learned that words like "perl," "python," "tcl," "scripting," and "morris" each appeared in only 1% of his spam. On the other hand, words like "guarantee," "cgi," and "prices" appeared in over 90% of his spam.

To gain insight into a new mail's spam status, Graham broke the new message down into a set of words and examined the spam probabilities for all the words that appeared in his calculated lists. He then looked at the 15 words that had the highest spam probability and the 15 words that had the lowest spam probability. He applied a formula to these 30 numbers to decide whether the message was spam or not.

This probabilistic formula enables one to answer the interesting statistical question, "What is the probability that a certain event (or property) will occur, given that other events (or properties) are true (or present)?"

THE MATH

(Readers who don't require the nuts-and-bolts math for every concept of an algorithmic technique can skip this section.)

The type of statistical property that addresses questions of the probability that events or properties happen—given the context of other events' or properties' existence—is known as "conditional probability."

Probabilities of the form "The probability that the word 'foo' appears in a spam message" are more precisely stated as "The probability that a message is spam given the word 'foo' in its text" and are written like this in statistical mathematics:

$$P \text{ (message is spam | 'foo' in text)}$$

or, more concisely,

$$P \text{ (spam | 'foo')}$$

A simple pair of tables of word counters (i.e., the number of times a given word appears in spam and non-spam) enables easy calculation of these probabilities, including the "probability that the word 'foo' appears in a non-spam message":

$$P \text{ (non-spam | 'foo')}$$

Now the question is how to calculate the probability that a message is spam. Presumably, such mail would be rejected or filed into a spam folder.

The probability that a message containing a set of words is spam can be written as

$$P \text{ (spam | words)}$$

The formula that calculates this probability is given by Bayes Rule.

This rule embodies an approach pioneered by Thomas Bayes. Born in 1702, Bayes was the son of a London minister who followed his father's footsteps through ordination and assignment to Turnbridge Wells, just 35 miles away from London. After his death in 1761, a friend discovered his probability theory work, which was subsequently published in 1764.

Simply stated, Bayes Rule says

$$P(A \mid B) \ = \ \frac{P(B \mid A) \times P(A)}{P(B)}$$

which is to say that knowing certain probability estimates about properties A and B enables calculation of other estimates.

Bayes Rule sometimes yields initially surprising results. Consider an example with a population of adults in which 1% have cancer (mathematically: *P (cancer) = 0.01*). Let's postulate a somewhat imperfect test for cancer. If a person has cancer, this test will yield a positive result 80% of the time. This means the test errs and yields a negative result 20% of the time a person has cancer (which, of course, is a mistake). Bayes Rule enables calculation of the probability that a person has cancer when the test is positive. Mathematically restated, this is

$$P (positive \mid cancer) = 0.8$$

$$P (positive \mid no\ cancer) = 0.2$$

Intuitively, one would imagine that a positive test for cancer would suggest a very high probability that the subject has cancer. Bayes Rule reduces speculation to a precise probability with this calculation:

$$P (cancer \mid positive) \ = \ \frac{P (positive \mid cancer) \times P (cancer)}{P (positive)}$$

Two of the values here are already known (both *P (positive | cancer)* and *P (cancer)*), but the value of P (positive) has not yet been stated. We know that only 1% of the population has cancer, so 99% of the population does not. For the 1% who do, we know that *P (positive | cancer)* is 0.8. For the 99% who don't, we know that *P (positive | no cancer) = 0.2*. This covers all the cases, so:

$$P (positive) = P (cancer) \times P (positive \mid cancer) + P (no\ cancer) \times P (positive \mid no\ cancer)$$

The numbers work out like this:

$$P (positive) = 0.01 \times 0.8 + 0.99 \times 0.2 = 0.206$$

which says that just over 20% of the subjects will yield a positive test result in a population with a 1% cancer incidence.

Thus, with substitution, the Bayes Rule formula becomes:

$$P_1 = P \ (positive \mid cancer) \times P \ (cancer)$$

$$P_2 = P \ (cancer) \times P \ (positive \mid cancer) + P \ (no \ cancer) \times P \ (positive \mid no \ cancer)$$

$$P \ (cancer \mid positive) \quad = \quad \frac{P_1}{P_2}$$

into which we can then substitute all the actual numerical probabilities already known:

$$P \ (cancer \mid positive) \quad = \quad \frac{0.8 \times 0.01}{0.01 \times 0.8 + 0.99 \times 0.2} \quad \cong 0.0388$$

That 0.0388 means that less than 4% of the people who test positive for cancer actually have cancer! This is comforting if counterintuitive news to those who test positive.

This result can be visualized by imagining a population of 100 people, one of whom has cancer. A typical result of the cancer test yields the positive result for the single actual cancer victim and about 21% positive results ($P \ (positive)$) for all the rest of the people who don't have cancer. The following diagram depicts the population of 100, where C means 'cancer,' c means 'tested positive, no cancer,' and $*$ means 'tested negative, no cancer.'

```
C c c c c c c c c c c c c c c c c c c c c * * * * * * * *
* * * * * * * * * * * * * * * * * * * * * * * * * * * * *
* * * * * * * * * * * * * * * * * * * * * * * * * * * * *
* * * * * * * * * * * * * *
```

It is easy to see that only one person in the population had cancer, even though 21 tested positive. Of those who tested positive, only 1 of 21 (1/21 = 4.76%) actually had cancer. The observed 4.76% is close enough to the theoretical 3.8%.

Applying this process to a spam message is now straightforward:

$$P \ (spam \mid word) \quad = \quad \frac{P \ (word \mid spam) \times P \ (spam)}{P \ (spam) \times P \ (word \mid spam) + P \ (not \ spam) \times P \ (word \mid not \ spam)}$$

A sample set of classified email messages yields each of these probabilities, or at least a probability for each given word. Assuming that words in spam messages are independent (i.e., $P \ (A,B) = P \ (A) \times P \ (B)$), another rule enables calculation of the probability that a spam message contains two given two words:

$$P \ (spam \mid word_1, \ word_2) = P \ (spam \mid word_1) \times P \ (spam \mid word_2)$$

or even a set of words:

$$P \ (spam \mid word_1, \ word_2, \ ..., \ word_n) = \prod_{i=1}^{n} P \ (spam \mid word_i) \times P \ (word_i)$$

One then sets a threshold value for *P (spam | words)* and rejects those messages that are above that threshold and thus likely to be spam.

Mathematically, this is a challenge because multiplying together, say, 500 probabilities (all less than 1) is liable to lead to an extremely small number that is difficult to express in a computer's floating point representation. (That number, of course, is combined mathematically with other small numbers to get the final probability.) To solve this problem, Paul Graham [1, 2] chooses two sets of 15 words. One Bayesian filter author [3] solves this problem by summing the logarithms of probabilities instead of multiplying the probabilities themselves. Another author [4] uses program logic to reset products that get "too small."

WORD ANALYSIS

Bayes Rule enables calculation of the probability that a message is spam, given an observed probability that various words indicated spam (or non-spam) in the past. One of the drawbacks of non-Bayesian filtering is the lack of a "big picture" about the message (for example, looking only for certain keywords, addresses, or other patterns). Initial Bayesian spam filters chose only 30 words to examine [1, 2]. Newer filters [4] look much more deeply.

One author [5] carefully determined word stems (such as reducing "mails" and "mailing" to "mail"). Graham [1, 2] was careful to generalize his analyses to include headers (which is intuitive because certain sources of email issue only spam).

Bill Yerazunis, author of the spam-filtering tool CRM114, seems to have hit on an extraordinarily fruitful approach. CRM114 considers not only every word (i.e., the string of letters and numbers separated from other words by punctuation and white space) in the message and headers, but also combinations of words.

When combinations of words are considered, the combinatoric potential grows rapidly. One might consider single words, sequences of 2, 3, . . ., *n* words, or more. Note that the phrase "The cow jumped over the moon" has several two-word sequences: "The cow," "cow jumped," "jumped over," and so on. The CRM114 program goes even further: It considers sequences with missing words. Each word is considered with the 16 different ways the next four words can be included. The first word of the phrase yields these 16 phrases as compound keywords:

The cow jumped over the
The cow jumped over
The cow jumped the
The cow jumped
The cow over the
The cow over
The cow the
The cow
The jumped over the
The jumped over
The jumped the
The jumped
The over the
The over
The the
The

Then the next word is considered ("cow"), along with its 16 potential successors. This generates a huge number of keyword phrases to characterize a message. Many of them are fairly useless (e.g., "The" and "The the"), but some intuitively feel worthwhile (e.g., "The cow jumped," or even just "cow"). In practice, the filter works extraordinarily well.

WORD CHOICE

Earlier Bayesian filter authors made interesting choices about the actual sets of words of a message they chose to analyze. Some, as mentioned earlier, derived word stems. Others processed only the text of the message.

Yerazunis's CRM114 tool looks at every string of numbers/text (i.e., all punctuation and white space is considered to be a "word" delimiter) of the message. A slight modification to his program decodes attachments. This means that every piece of the header is examined, including timestamps, message identification numbers, and other administrivia in addition to more intuitively pleasing items like the sender's email address. The training methodologies (see the next section) work to balance items that are found in both spam and non-spam messages (e.g., "Message-ID") so that they can be ignored.

TRAINING

Bayesian email filters require training—a set of identified spam and non-spam from which to derive initial probabilities for words and phrases that appear in those email messages. The community seems to disagree about how much training is necessary. One author's mailbox receives 400 spam emails per day, thus easing the availability of spam material. A pruned inbox with anything more than 100 non-spam messages is a source for non-spam material. Training with a megabyte each of spam and non-spam seems quite sufficient. (Note that this is text training, not Word or other attachments.)

Bayesian filters suffer from the general observation that they seem to be much stronger when trained for each individual mail user rather than for a larger group (hence the popular phrase "One man's spam is another man's ham"). Some people prefer to receive various emails while others don't (e.g., certain mailing lists). Pure Bayesian filtering (in the absence of whitelists) probably requires individual word probabilities databases for each user. A Bayesian filter can be combined with other techniques (source checking, blacklists, and whitelists) to provide input to decision tools like SpamAssassin.

EFFICACY AND ATTACKS

One author's appreciation of CRM114 has been unbounded. It catches more than 99% of spam, thus freeing the mailbox for its intended purpose. However, it has not quite been perfect. CRM114 (and presumably any well-implemented Bayesian filter) will either pass a little spam through or block the occasional legitimate email as "apparent spam." In the 21st century, however, the idea that "The spam filter ate your message" has gained much more respect than "My dog ate my homework" ever did!

When a spam message sneaks through, the filter needs additional training. A small program can easily add a single message to the spam mail database.

False positives are another problem. In order to keep statistics, one author skims all 400 daily spam emails to check for erroneous categorizations as spam and to perform general statistics. So far, almost every email erroneously categorized has either been found or re-sent by its sender with the obvious query. Whenever a new "kind" of email comes through (e.g., acknowledgments from United Parcel Service or any e-commerce system, replies to a general query sent to a mailing list), the filter seems to have a small probability of deciding the entire new category is spam. One email sent through the retraining filter is generally enough to reclassify all future email from that category.

Spammers now routinely include (sometimes huge) amounts of standard (English) text (i.e., a wire-service news article or a list of random words) in their messages in order to confuse Bayesian filters. Luckily, including such tiny phrases as "<font color=red>" continues to tag almost all of this as spam.

Graham [6] continues to investigate techniques for increasing Bayesian efficacy. He notes that words like "FREE" in the subject of a message are stronger markers than in the body. However, he also notes that the filters are so powerful that any improvement will be incremental at best.

OTHER BAYESIAN FILTERING PACKAGES

CRM114 is not the final word in Bayesian spam filtering. Many packages exist as of July, 2004:

AGMSBayesianSpam	JoeEmail	SpamAssassin
Annoyance Filter	Junk-Out	SpamBayes
Apple Mail	JunkChief	Spambayes
ASSP	K9	Spambayes for Outlook
BayesIt! (Russian)	KSpam	Spamcan
Bayespam	LegMail	SpamCorp
BMF	Lockspam	SpamHammer
Bogofilter	Mail-SpamTest-Bayesian	Spamhandle
BopSpam	Mail::Classifier	Spamihilator
BSFilter (Japanese)	MailPermit	Spammunition
BSpam	MailWasher Pro	Spamnix
C Bayesian Filter	Mozilla	SpamOracle
Cerebrus	MSN 8	SpamPal
CRM114	Oddpost	SpamProbe
Death2Spam	Outclass	SpamSieve
Delord's POPF	PASP	SpamStat
Disruptor OL	Pitonyak's Filter	SpamTiger
DSPAM	Plan.Scm	SpamWeed
Eudora 6.0	Pop3Proxy	SquirrelBayes
Eureka Email	POPFile	Statistical Spam Filter
Exapia	PrismEmail	Tcl Spam Filter
Funkplanet Filter	SaProxyPro	TOLD
Gauche (Japanese)	Scribe	trimMail
GFI MailEssentials	Spam Bully	VBayesSpam
Ifile	Spam Filter for VPOP	XWall for MS Exchange
ImapAssassin	Spam Inspector	yMail
InboxShield	Spam Marshall	

In addition, new packages are appearing with ever-higher frequency. These packages distinguish themselves with various features:

- Ease of installation
- Ease of training
- Ease of use beyond a single user
- Availability for platforms like Windows
- Better preprocessing (unpacking enclosures, processing HTML)
- More advanced algorithms (see the next sections)

Most packages build on Paul Graham's initial paper and expand the scope or power of the tool with various innovations.

ADVANCED TECHNIQUES: TOKENIZATION

CRM114 sported the interesting combine-successive-tokens scheme. Other schemes include

- Dealing with separators (e.g., dots or "at" signs in an address) in special ways
- Recognizing host names, IP addresses, and/or other header information
- Ignoring certain header information such as dates and message-IDs
- Choosing only the first n bytes of a message
- Handling headers specially (e.g., combining the name of the header keyword successively with each alphabetic token on that header's line)

ADVANCED TECHNIQUES: CLEVERER STATISTICS

Several spam researchers recognized a problem with the raw Bayesian approach: a word that appears only once in, say, a spam message has a probability of 100% associated with that word's "spamminess." Intuitively, this does not feel right because random words might appear in any email.

Gary Robinson [7] made several extremely useful suggestions in his Linux Journal article on spam. First of all, he defined $p(w)$ as the probability that an email with the word "w" is spam:

$$p(w) \quad = \quad \frac{b(w)}{(b(w) + g(w))}$$

where

$$b(w) \quad = \quad \frac{count\ of\ spam\ emails\ containing\ word\ w}{count\ of\ spam\ emails}$$

and similarly,

$$g(w) \quad = \quad \frac{count\ of\ non\text{-}spam\ emails\ containing\ word\ w}{count\ of\ non\text{-}spam\ emails}$$

When a training corpus has differing amounts of spam and non-spam, though, their ratio impacts the actual probabilities—but the formulae given here ignore that effect. This problem manifests itself most severely on rare words (e.g., a word that appears just once—as spam—has $p(w) = 1.0$).

Robinson proposes a new formula that mitigates this problem:

$$f(w) \quad = \quad \frac{(s \times x) + (n \times p(w))}{s + n}$$

where

- $p(w)$ is defined as stated previously
- n is the absolute number of emails that contain the word w

and two new user-defined parameters are used that tell how much *a priori* confidence exists about a new word appearing in spam.

- x is the assumed probability that any new word will first be seen in spam (versus in non-spam)
- s is a parameter that defines the "strength" of the belief that x is correct.

This statistic seems to provide a better number to use as a word's spam probability than the simpler $p(w)$ direct calculation. Some developers start with $s=1.0$ and $x=0.5$ and tune their implementations based on actual data.

Pure Bayesian filtering (à la Graham [1] and [2]) yields a score for spam and a score for non-spam. These scores are easily compared to deduce whether a message is spam or not. The results are initially counterintuitive—many email messages end up having large spam scores even when they are not spam (because their non-spam scores are even higher).

Gary Robinson proposed using "Fisher's method" for calculating the probability that a message is spam (and also the probability that it isn't). Fisher's method evaluates

$$F = -2 \, ln \prod_w p(w)$$

and then treats F as a chi-square distribution with *2n* degrees of freedom. Look up the result in a chi-square table and determine the probability of getting a result as large (or larger) than F. This is the new probability that a message is spam (or, when calculated using *1-p(w)*, the probability that a message is non-spam, a quantity defined to be F'). These statistics yield dramatically better results when tabulated against a large email corpus. Large numbers of spam and non-spam yield statistics in the range one would expect.

Tim Peters of the SpamBayes Project observed that defining

$$I \quad = \quad \frac{(1 + F - F')}{2}$$

yields a continuum in the range 0..1, where 0.5 is a good indicator of "unsureness." In one case, this happens when the mail's words are "new" to the evaluation function and also when the mail's words truly do indicate both spam and non-spam.

To accommodate these unsure states, some spam processing systems now have three states: definitely spam, definitely non-spam, and a hazy state of "not sure." Bogofilter author Eric Raymond reports that users are "quite sympathetic" with the "not sure" rating, generally agreeing that the message had elements of both spam and non-spam.

Filters that have Fisher calculations include (but are not limited to) SpamBayes, Bogofilter, SpamAssassin, SpamSieve, Mozilla, and Thunderbird.

Note that all the methods listed here are improving on very good results. The refinements reduce false positives and generally add '9's to the success probability. It is difficult to believe that the final methods have already been deduced.

CONCLUSION

Bayesian spam filtering is an incredibly powerful statistical technique—with acceptable computational complexity—for identifying spam messages. Bayesian techniques address many weaknesses of other methodologies:

- The entire message can be examined, not just special parts.
- All words are significant, not just special keywords or addresses.

- Updating is, in practice, infrequent (never more than one or two email messages per week through the training program; often none).
- So far, spam attacks on Bayesian filters have been relatively unsuccessful.
- When combined with other techniques, Bayesian filters can be a very strong component of an institution's global spam system.

The CRM114 system is just one of many available Bayesian spam filters; commercial implementations are now appearing with high frequency.

REFERENCES

[1] Graham, Paul, *http://www.paulgraham.com/spam.html.*

[2] Graham, Paul, *http://www.paulgraham.com/better.html.*

[3] *http://www.the-wabe.com/log/?entry=76.*

[4] Yerazunis, Bill, "Sparse Binary Polynomial Hash Message Filtering and the Crm114 Discriminator," *Proceedings of the 2003 Spam Conference*; download software and other info from *http://crm114.sourceforge.net/.*

[5] Pantel, Patrick and Lin, Dekang, "SpamCop—A Spam Classification & Organization Program," *Proceedings of AAAI-98 Workshop on Learning for Text Categorization.*

[6] Graham, Paul, *http://www.paulgraham.com/sofar.html.*

[7] Robinson, Gary, "A Statistical Approach to the Spam Problem," *http://www.linuxjournal.com/article.php?sid=6467.*

[8] *http://www.bgl.nu/bogofilter/fisher.html.*

Bayesian Filtering

In Chapter 7, "Introduction to Bayesian Filtering," we gave you the mathematics background of Bayesian theory. We also covered how the Bayesian theory is implemented in several of the Bayesian analyzers in this book, including SpamAssassin and the Bayesian analyzers covered in this chapter. Now, we examine a number of the available Bayesian implementations to help in the fight against spam.

HOW TO CHOOSE A BAYESIAN ANALYZER

Choosing the right Bayesian-style analyzer to run on your network is difficult because there are many Bayesian implementations to choose from. Some of the questions to ask when choosing a Bayesian implementation include

- What level of sophistication are my users?
- How many users am I supporting?
- Is message scoring (for example, SpamAssassin) "good enough?"
- Is retraining the Bayesian analyzer important to my configuration? If so, can I handle the support load? Can my users learn how to manage filter retraining?
- How accurate do I want the analyzer to be?

As with most things, choosing which Bayesian-style classifier to use is about managing trade-offs. The more features a solution has, the harder it is to manage. The fewer features a program has, the easier it is to manage.

In the end, you must look at the features of each Bayesian solution and decide which one best fits your needs, given your environment and users. Often, a pilot program where you can test solutions with a small subset of users can make the choice easier. That way, you get to see how the product performs in a controlled environment without committing to a solution that you aren't sure is going to work.

How We Chose the Bayesian Analyzers

For the purposes of illustration, we wanted to show differently architected solutions that were widely used and that had good accuracy rates. The packages we cover in this chapter include

- CRM114
- bogofilter
- Anti-Spam SMTP Proxy (ASSP)

We chose CRM114 due to its widespread use and accuracy. CRM114 (the Controllable Regex Mutilator) is a regular expression filter that actually predates most of the other more recent Bayesian methods and packages. However, Bayesian support has been extended with a Markovian system and is similar enough to the rest of the packages here that decided to include it in our discussion. CRM114 is written in ANSI C and is actually a language designed specifically for filters and offers significant ability to configure filters. Camram (covered in Chapter 12, "Sender Verification") contains a very nice front end to the CRM114 interface. More information is available for CRM114 from *http://crm114.sourceforge.net/*.

bogofilter was chosen because it is one of the most accurate Bayesian filters available, and it is written in C, making it fast and efficient. It uses procmail to process messages. bogofilter is one of the most accurate (and fastest) Bayesian classifiers available. The bogofilter home page is *http://bogofilter.sourceforge.net*.

The Anti-Spam SMTP Proxy, or ASSP, is a Perl-based program that works transparently between the Internet and your SMTP server. It was chosen primarily for its ease of use and configuration. It has a web-based setup GUI, so it is very easy to configure. ASSP also acts as an SMTP proxy, making integration into your email infrastructure transparent. More information on ASSP is available at *http://assp.sourceforge.net*.

CRM114

Unlike many of the other Bayesian filters, CRM114 is actually a language specifically designed for writing filters. The actual mail filtering in CRM114 is completely programmable. By default, most users use the package-supplied CRM program named `mailfilter.crm`, which offers a lot of configurability without a lot of work. If `mailfilter.crm` doesn't meet your needs, it's not difficult to create an entirely new filter in the CRM114 language.

For example, people have created web content filters for French elementary schools in CRM114, as well as Usenet analysis and content extraction tools. You probably don't need this at the very start, but the power is available.

INSTALLATION

In this section, we cover installation of the CRM114 package. Although we cover the BlameYokohama version here, the software is updated quite often, so you should check the web site for the latest version. The package is offered in two different forms:

- `crm114-version.i386.tar.gz` (statically linked binaries)
- `crm114-version.src.tar.gz` (complete source code and tests)

Each package will install the following four executables:

- crm—base software, the CRM114 compute engine
- cssutil—.css file checker/verifier/editor
- cssdiff—.css file comparator
- cssmerge—.css file merger

You can also choose to download a preexisting set of css (CRM114 sparse spectra) files, which are prelearned "spam body" files. If you use these, you will have better results initially. However, over time, the css files you generate from your own spam will gradually get better and eventually will be more accurate than the preexisting body of spam.

This chapter shows how to download and install the preexisting css files, but it is not necessary for operating the system. Please note that the preexisting css files are not recommended for use by the developers of CRM114 and that they are for i386 (Intel Pentium and compatible) architectures only, due to endian (byte ordering) addressing issues.

COMPILING

For the purposes of this section, we will be covering the source code installation. To begin, download the sources from the web site *http://crm114.sourceforge.net/crm114-20040221-BlameYokohama.src.tar.gz.*

The versions change quite often, so be sure to select the version you feel most comfortable with. If desired, the css files can be downloaded from *http://crm114.sourceforge.net/crm114-20040221-BlameYokohama.css.tar.gz.*

CRM114 requires TRE, an open source regular expression program. Unless you have already done so, the first task is to build and install TRE. After you've downloaded it, place the sources in /usr/local/src and build like this:

```
bash$ gunzip crm114-20040221-BlameYokohama.src.tar.gz
bash$ tar xvf crm114-20040221-BlameYokohama.src.tar
bash$ cd crm114-20040221-BlameYokohamea
bash$ cd tre-0.6.4
bash$ ./configure
bash$ make
bash$ sudo su
# make install
# cd ..
```

CRM114 by default installs its core utilities into /usr/bin. Unfortunately, CRM114 hard-codes the path /usr/bin/crm in many utilities, so it is difficult to change the location without modifying scripts.

Now, continuing from the previous CRM114 session:

```
# make clean
# make install
# crm -v
```

The final command displays the version of crm. If you want to run post-install tests, you can run make megatest from the installation directory. It is not a complete test, but it does an acceptable level of testing.

CONFIGURING MAILFILTER

The next task is to tell CRM114 what to do with your spam and non-spam. For the purposes of this section, we will assume use of Procmail as the MTA hook-in and Courier Maildir format for the mailbox.

The configuration file is called `mailfilter.cf`, which defaults to your home directory. CRM114 processes MIME-encoded messages with one of two possible programs: `mimencode` or `mewdecode`. Redhat/Fedora ships with `mewdecode`, so that program must be used. Other Unix distributions need to be checked to see what MIME decoder is available, and the correct executable should be enabled. To check which MIME decoder is distributed under your version of Linux, execute

```
bash$ locate mimencode
bash$ locate mewdecode
```

The path to the command included on the `locate` command line will be returned by `locate` in the event of a match. In `mailfilter.cf`, enable the appropriate MIME decoder by setting the variable `:mime_decoder:` to the appropriate MIME decoder. For example, if you are running RedHat/Fedora Core, you enable `mewdecode` like this:

```
:mime_decoder: /mewdecode/
```

By default, `mailfilter.cf` has a lot of logging turned on. Most of this is unnecessary and only serves to consume disk space at a rapid rate. It's probably best to disable the following logging statements:

```
:log_to_allmail.txt: /no/
:log_rejections: /no/
```

Logging can be turned on if you have issues that need to be addressed. Additionally, if you have the `normalizemime` package installed, you should turn off the internal mime/html expansion with

```
:rewrites_enabled: /no/
```

The only other line that needs to be changed here is the default password shipped with CRM114. Change the line that reads

```
alter (:spw:) /SecretPasswordGoesHere_No_Blanks!!!jkal984884hj87fryfjd9ie8ru9/
```

to

```
alter (:spw:) /your_password/
```

Next, the `rewrites.mfp` must be modified. This file contains four lines that need to be changed appropriately:

MyEmailAddress is replaced with *your email address*
MyEmailName is replaced with *your name*
MyLocalMailRouter is replaced with *your mailserver name*
MyLocalMailRouterIP is replaced with *your mail router IP*

Now we can add a recipe to procmail. Note that CRM114 is itself an executable, but the CRM114 engine runs the program in mailfilter.crm, which then uses the configuration in mailfilter.cf. This configurability is one of the more powerful (and dangerous) aspects of CRM114. In order to hook CRM114 into your mail flow, create the following Procmail recipe in your .procmailrc file:

```
MAILDIR=$HOME/Maildir
DEFAULT=$MAILDIR/
ORGMAIL=$MAILDIR/
LOGFILE=$MAILDIR/procmail.log

:0fw: .msgid.lock
| /usr/bin/crm -u $HOME/.mailfilter mailfilter.cf

:0:
* ^X-CRM114-Status: SPAM.*
.Spam/
```

The first recipe actually invokes the crm program, and the second one files messages that are considered spam in the folder called .Spam. Remember that we make the following assumptions regarding access to and format of the end-user mailbox:

- Courier IMAP
- Maildir-formatted

SETTING UP .CSS FILES

When preparing CRM114 for use, there are three options for setting up the spam databases (css files):

- Start css files from scratch (empty files)
- Use the distributed css files
- Build and load css files from your own preexisting spam/non-spam messages

The most accurate method over the long term is to build your files from scratch and train CRM114 on errors. Using the included css files will get you up and running more quickly, but it will result in a bigger, slower css database. The third option, building your own css files from preexisting spam and non-spam databases, will result in larger and less accurate databases, to the tune of twice as big and less accurate. We will show all three methods for completeness here.

Each method requires that the css files sit in the directory in which they will be run. Usually, this will be your home directory. However, the css files can go wherever you want (see the —fileprefix=directoryname configure option), but the default is your home directory on the machine on which CRM114 runs.

BUILDING CSS FILES FROM SCRATCH

To build the css files from scratch and train on errors (which will provide the fastest, most accurate result), simply run the following two commands:

```
bash$ cssutil -b -r spam.css
bash$ cssutil -b -r nonspam.css
```

This populates the spam and non-spam database collections for use with CRM114. Remember that you must train the filters after populating the databases. Next, proceed to the section titled "Checking the css Files" later in this chapter.

USING THE CSS FILES DISTRIBUTED WITH CRM114

To use the predefined css files included with the distribution, simply extract the distributed tar files in the directory in which you will run CRM114, like this:

```
bash$ cd CRM114 home
bash$ gunzip /usr/local/src/crm114-20040221-BlameYokohama.css.tar.gz
bash$ tar xvf /usr/local/src/crm114-20040221-BlameYokohama.css.tar
```

Then proceed to the "Checking the css Files" section.

BUILD YOUR OWN CSS FILES FROM SPAM AND NON-SPAM

For this to be as effective as possible (remember that this is not the best method), you need spam archives containing approximately 50% spam and 50% non-spam. First, place the files with spam and non-spam in your home directory with the following associated names:

- `spamtext.txt`
- `nonspamtext.txt`

Make sure that the files contain only straight ASCII text and that they do not contain any base64 encoded attachments (binary data) or "spammus interruptus." If they do contain binary data, decode them by hand before you execute this procedure. Otherwise, the conversion process will stop. Edit the file `scrub_mailfile_rewrites.mfp` located home by default in your home directory to include appropriate values as replacements for the following placeholder values: `wsy`, `merl.com`, and `mail.merl.com`:

- `wsy` to *your username*
- `merl.com` to *your domain*
- `mail.merl.com` to *DNS name of your mail server*

Finally, remove the existing .css files and run the command to make the new ones:

```
bash$ rm -rf spam.css
bash$ rm -rf nonspam.css
bash$ make cssfiles
```

CHECKING THE CSS FILES

CRM114 contains a couple of utilities to check the statistics of your css files. These utilities are

- *cssutil*
- *cssdiff*

cssutil gives you general statistics on the given css data file. An example is as follows:

```
bash$ cssutil -b -r spam.css
```

cssdiff compares two given css files. This tells you how hard it is for CRM114 to discriminate between spam and non-spam.

```
bash$ cssdiff spam.css nonspam.css
```

This command compares the spam and non-spam database files and reports the differences between the two.

TRAINING CRM114

Of course, one of the biggest benefits to Bayesian filtering is the ability to train the filters so that they may catch your spam messages. To do this under CRM114, you have two different options:

- Forward email back to yourself with embedded CRM114 commands
- Save the message as a file and run a command line utility

To use the mail forwarding method, simply forward the message back to yourself and add the following line to the message, starting at column 1 (i.e., no spaces):

```
command your_password spam or notspam
```

So, if you had a piece of mail that should have been classified as spam, and your password was `secret`, you would put this as the first line of the message:

```
command secret spam
```

The second method is a two-step process. First, save the incorrectly classified spam message to a file by itself. Then, from the Unix command line, run mailfilter.crm like this:

```
bash$ mailfilter.crm --learnspam < spam.txt
```

If the message was incorrectly classified as non-spam, run the command as follows:

```
bash$ mailfilter.crm --learnnonspam < nonspam.txt
```

Occasionally, CRM114 may indicate that no training is necessary; in this case, training may be forced by adding the `--force` operator on the command line or by putting `force` on the mail-to-myself password line.

If you make a mistake, you can "unlearn" things from the CRM114 system by putting `--unlearn` on the command line or `unlearn` on the mail-to-myself password line.

WHITELISTING/BLACKLISTING

CRM114 has the ability to whitelist/blacklist addresses. At a minimum, you must create the blacklist files; otherwise, the command will fail.

Simply edit the appropriate file:

- `priolist.mfp` (priority list)

- `whitelist.mfp` (whitelist)
- `blacklist.mfp` (blacklist)

Add the appropriate regular expressions that you want to the appropriate file. `priolist.mfp` is run first, then `whitelist.mfp`, and finally `blacklist.mfp`. A few important notes:

- If the regex appears *anywhere* in the message, it will produce a match.
- Liberal use of beginning and ending anchors (^ and $) is recommended so that your results are correct.
- The priority list uses + and - at the beginning of the line to indicate whitelist and blacklist regular expressions, respectively.

BOGOFILTER

bogofilter is a Bayesian classifier originally written by Eric S. Raymond. It is designed to take messages on the command line and compare them against a database (BerkeleyDB required) of known spam. It is written for speed and efficiency. These instructions assume that BerkeleyDB 4.2 is installed in `/usr/local/BerkeleyDB.4.2`.

INSTALLATION

Download the sources from the bogofilter home page: (*http://bogofilter.sourceforge.net*) *http://sourceforge.net/project/showfiles.php?group_id=62265*. When downloaded, place the sources in `/usr/local/src` and unpack and install like this:

```
bash$ gunzip bogofilter-0.17.2.tar.gz
bash$ tar xvf bogofilter-0.17.2.tar
bash$ cd bogofilter-0.17.2
bash$ ./configure --sysconfdir=/etc/bogofilter \
--with-libdb-prefix=/usr/local/BerkeleyDB.4.2
bash$ make
bash$ sudo make install
```

CONFIGURATION

bogofilter uses the following files to specify its configuration:

- `/etc/bogofilter/bogofilter.cf` is the default location for the system-wide configuration file.

- `~/bogofilter.cf` is the per-user configuration file default name and location
- `~/.bogofilter` is the default directory location for databases

The program itself is called `bogofilter` and is normally run out of `procmail` for per-user invocations, but it can also be called at the MTA level for system-wide filtering.

When installed, you must copy the configuration file over to the proper location, usually `/etc/bogofilter.cf`. The bogofilter configuration allows you to perform several functions. These include

- File locations
- Envelope (header) tag formats and occurrence
- Determining how the data is broken down (tokenized)
- Classification settings

At a minimum, the configuration entries that you will want to activate (by removing the `#`) and perhaps change include

```
#bogofilter_dir=~/.bogofilter
```

This specifies the location of the word count databases.

```
#user_config_file=~/.bogofilter.cf
```

This parameter specifies the location of system-wide settings.

```
#ham_cutoff = 0.10
#spam_cutoff = 0.95
```

These parameters specify what scores determine spam versus non-spam. Three state results (`spam`, `non-spam`, and `unsure`) are enabled if `ham_cutoff` is set to something besides `0.00`.

Components

bogofilter is distributed with the following programs:

- `bogofilter`—This is the command that is used to actually classify messages.
- `bogoutil`—This command manages the spam/non-spam database.
- `db_verify`, `db_recover`, and `db_dump`—Self-explanatory Berkeley database utilities used to manage the spam/non-spam collections.

- contrib—The contrib directory contains a several useful programs:
  - Integration examples (qmail, procmail, milter)
  - Classification utilities
  - Testing
  - Conversion utilities

TRAINING

When using any Bayesian-style analyzer (including bogofilter), the administrator must decide how to deal with training the filters initially as well as when the program makes a mistake. The options mentioned by the bogofilter documentation regarding the area of initial training are as follows:

- Classify a full set of spam and non-spam messages
- Train (repeatedly, if desired) a set of spam and non-spam messages in the order they were received
- Train a random set of spam and non-spam messages
- Classify a set number of spam and non-spam messages and then train on the unsure or misclassified messages

The first option is the quickest but also takes the most space in the database, as does the last option.

EXAMPLE

In this example, we set up a three-folder system of mail classification on a Maildir-formatted mailbox using procmail. This is based upon the bogofilter.cf file settings (see the previous section). The three different classifications are:

- Definitely spam
- Maybe spam
- Definitely not spam

This makes reclassification a little easier, in the sense that only the "maybe spam" messages need to be looked at. This should reduce the amount of time the end user spends going through a lot of spam, as would be the case for false positives in a two-folder setup (spam and non-spam).

There are two scripts and one procmail recipe (see Figure 8.1) to implement this setup.

```
# $Id: procmailrc.example,v 1.6 2003/04/10 20:35:22 m-a Exp $
#
# procmailrc.example
#
#         This is a sample procmail setup file that
#         1 - retains an unprocessed copy of all incoming mail
#         2 - diverts incoming mail with asian character sets
#         3 - runs bogofilter
#         4 - retains a processed copy of all messages identified as spam.
#         5 - retains a processed copy of all messages identified as unsure.
#

### bogofilter - filter & update word lists

MAILDIR=$HOME/Maildir
DEFAULT=$MAILDIR/
ORGMAIL=$MAILDIR/
LOGFILE=$MAILDIR/procmail.log

#BOGOFILTER_DIR=/var/lib/bogofilter

#### testing ####
## MAILDIR=/tmp/mail
## MAILDIR=/home/user/filter/korean.spam/mail
## procmail procmailrc < input.file ; echo $? ; ll -t $MAILDIR | head
#### end testing ####


#### backup ####
:0c:
mail.backup
####


## Silently drop all completely unreadable mail
:0:
* 1^0 ^\/Subject:.*=\?(.*big5|iso-2022-jp|ISO-2022-KR|euc-kr|gb2312|ks_c_5601-1987|
    windows-1251|windows-1256)\?
* 1^0 ^\/Content-Type:.*charset="(.*big5|iso-2022-jp|ISO-2022-KR|euc-kr|gb2312|
    ks_c_5601-1987|windows-1251|windows-1256)
.Spam.Unreadable/
####


#### bogofilter passthrough-update ####

:0fw
| bogofilter -f -p -u -l -e -v
# -f)isher, -p)assthrough -u)pdate, -l)og -e)xitcode 0 for spam and ham
# -v)erbose

#### begin error catcher ####

# m-a 2002-10-28
#     If bogofilter failed, return the mail to the queue.
#     Better put this after _EACH_ delivering recipe (not shown here).
#     Later, the MTA will try again to deliver it.
#     75 is the value for EX_TEMPFAIL in /usr/include/sysexits.h
#
#     Originally published by Philip Guenther on the postfix-users
#     mailing list.

:0e
{
          EXITCODE=75
          HOST
}

#### end error catcher ####


:0c:
* ^X-Bogosity: (Spam|Yes)
.Spam/

# put copy error catcher here to avoid fallthrough

# unnecessary in twostate mode:
:0c:
* ^X-Bogosity: Unsure
.Spam.MaybeSpam/
# put another copy of error catcher here to avoid fallthrough

#### end bogofilter passthrough-update ####
```

Figure 8.1 procmail recipe.

The procmail recipe performs the following steps. First, it copies messages to a backup folder called mail.backup, just in case something happens to the message while processing it. Next, it drops the message if it contains character sets that are unreadable in most email clients. Then procmail processes the message through bogofilter, catches any messages that cause bogofilter to fail, and requeues the message. Next, it copies the message to the appropriate folder, Spam or MaybeSpam, as determined by the call to bogofilter. If the message isn't determined to possibly be spam, it delivers it to the end user's inbox.

```
#! /bin/sh
############################################################
# $Id: reclassify_all_spam.sh,v 1.1 2004/03/25 18:48:01 dale Exp $
#
# reclassify_all_spam.sh
#
# Written by:  Dale Nielsen
# Date:        26 September 2002
#
############################################################
PATH=/usr/local/sbin:/bin:/usr/bin

users=`awk -F: '$6 ~ /^\/home\// && $7 != "/sbin/nologin"{ print $1 }' /etc/passwd`
for user in ${users} ; do
  su ${user} -c reclassify_spam-bogofilter.sh
done
for user in ${users} ; do
  su ${user} -c reclassify_spam-crm114.sh
done
```

Figure 8.2 reclassify_all_spam.sh.

reclassify_all_spam simply invokes reclassify_spam for each user on the system, which classifies messages in their respective inboxes (see Figure 8.2).

reclassify_spam analyzes each message in the user's IsSpam and NotSpam folders and sends them through the bogofilter retraining process appropriately (see Figure 8.3). It then moves the message to the Spam or inbox folders, depending upon whether the message is actually spam or not.

```
#! /bin/sh
###########################################################
# $Id: reclassify_spam-bogofilter.sh,v 1.1 2004/03/25 18:48:01 dale Exp $
#
# reclassify_spam-bogofilter.sh
#
# Written by:  Dale Nielsen
# Date:        11 March 2004
#
###########################################################
PATH=/usr/local/bin:/bin:/usr/bin

mailDir=${HOME}/Maildir
inboxDir=${mailDir}
isSpamDir=${mailDir}/.Spam.IsSpam
notSpamDir=${mailDir}/.Spam.NotSpam
spamDir=${mailDir}/.Spam

bogofilterDir=${HOME}/.bogofilter

if [ -d "${bogofilterDir}" ] ; then

  cd "${bogofilterDir}"

  for dir in new cur ; do
    if [ -d "${isSpamDir}/${dir}" ] ; then
      files=`find "${isSpamDir}/${dir}" -type f -print`
      if [ "${files}" != "" ] ; then
        echo "${files}" | bogofilter -Ns -b
        mv ${files} "${spamDir}/${dir}"
      fi
    fi
  done

  for dir in new cur ; do
    if [ -d "${notSpamDir}/${dir}" ] ; then
      files=`find "${notSpamDir}/${dir}" -type f -print`
      if [ "${files}" != "" ] ; then
        echo "${files}" | bogofilter -Sn -b
        mv ${files} "${inboxDir}/${dir}"
      fi
    fi
  done
fi
```

Figure 8.3 reclassify_spam.sh.

DISCUSSION

The two scripts `reclassify_spam` and `reclassify_all_spam` will take care of reclassifying misclassified emails, assuming that Maildir-formatted mailboxes are being used. The scripts won't work on mail files where the messages are concatenated together, such as mbox-formatted mailboxes. Non-spam messages (ham) go to `Inbox/`; spam goes to `Spam/`.

Users should file emails that need to be reclassified as spam in the `Spam/IsSpam` folder. Messages that need to be reclassifed as non-spam should be filed in the `Spam/NotSpam` folder. `reclassify_all_spam.sh` should be run as often as desired, usually once a night via cron. `reclassify_all_spam.sh` simply runs `reclassify_spam.sh` for each user on the system. The `reclassify_spam.sh` script reclassifies the stuff in `Spam/IsSpam` and moves it to `Spam/`. Messages in `Spam/NotSpam` are reclassified as non-spam and moved to `Inbox/`. Both types of misclassified messages are used to update the bogofilter message filter token databases.

ASSP

ASSP is a Perl program that implements a Bayesian analyzer. The ASSP package is relatively unique for at least two reasons. First of all, ASSP runs as a proxy between your existing mail server and the Internet. This makes installation very easy, although you must have the ability to change the SMTP port on your mail server in order to run ASSP on the same machine as the email server. Second, ASSP has a GUI-based configuration, which makes setup and administration very straightforward.

ASSP is the intermediary between the mail server on the local machine and remote mail systems that want to deliver email to users on the local machine. Utilizing a proxy design makes setup easier because you don't have to touch the email configuration on your installed server. Figure 8.4 illustrates how ASSP can be configured to run as a proxy between your "normal" mail server and the rest of the Internet.

ASSP is also relatively unique in that its configuration is intended to be performed graphically. This is in stark contrast to most other Unix utilities of this sort, which are almost always configured by hand editing a configuration file.

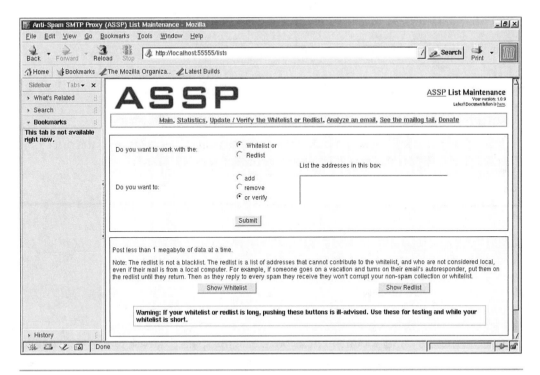

Figure 8.4 ASSP screen to set up proxy functionality.

REQUIREMENTS

To have a successful ASSP installation, you need the following:

- Perl
- Maildir-formatted mailboxes (individual messages rather than one big file such as mbox)
- The ability to change SMTP port (if you want to run ASSP and your SMTP server on the same box)
- 250MB of space for spam databases

Be advised that the program is a Perl script, so it takes extra memory, disk, and CPU. The more users you have, the more resources it will take.

INSTALLATION

To install ASSP, start by making a directory called `/usr/local/assp-1.0.9`:

```
bash$ cd /usr/local/
bash$ mkdir assp-1.0.9
bash$ cd assp-1.0.9
```

Download the ASSP package from *http://sourceforge.net/projects/assp/* to the directory `/usr/local/assp-1.0.9`. Unpack and start up the software as follows:

```
bash$ cd /var
bash$ sudo su
#mkdir assp
#mkdir assp/spam
#mkdir assp/notspam
#mkdir assp/errors
#mkdir assp/errors/spam
#mkdir assp/errors/notspam
# perl assp.pl
```

Contrary to the ASSP documentation, we create the spam database files in `/var` due to the dynamic nature of the databases. Note that a configuration change must be made to change this (see the `Directory Base` setting in the next section).

After executing the preceding steps, you will need to point your browser at *http://127.0.0.1:55555/*. The default username is `admin`, and the password is `nospam4me`. When there, you will see a screen similar to Figure 8.5, which is called the Network Setup screen.

In order to configure ASSP for use with your infrastructure, some configuration settings may need to be changed. These are covered in the next section.

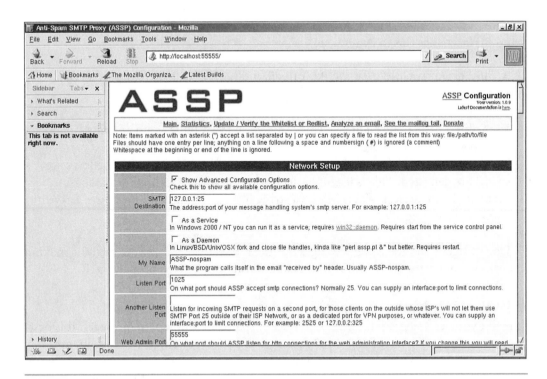

Figure 8.5 Network Setup screen.

Network Setup Screen

The ASSP GUI describes the configuration fields and their meanings. There are a number of settings you should change:

- **As a Daemon**—This enables ASSP to run automatically after system reboot.
- **Listen Port**—Because ASSP works as an SMTP proxy, if you are running ASSP on the same machine as your SMTP server, you will need to change the port on which your SMTP server is listening. Change the value to 1025 or some other available port.
- **Web Admin Password**—It is very important to change the default password!
- **Accept All Mail**—This is the list of IPs that are allowed relay access. This is an important setting, so take care in setting it correctly! Otherwise, your machine might become an "open relay" that spammers can use to send out their garbage.
- **Local Domains**—This is the list of domains you host.
- **Relay Host**—This is the name of the upstream SMTP relay, if any.

- **Directory Base**—This is the location of the spam database files. If you are using our example, change this to /var/assp.

Assuming you are installing ASSP for the first time, you will also want to set these parameters:

- **Use Subject as Maillog Names**—This can help in identifying spam and non-spam messages in your collections.
- **Test Mode**—If this is checked, then all messages (including ones ASSP believes are spam) are delivered. This is useful in the beginning while building the databases.
- **Prepend Spam Subject**—This inserts a string like [SPAM] in the subject line. Leave it blank while testing.

Don't forget to hit the Apply Changes button at the bottom after you are done making changes to your setup. Otherwise, your changes will not be saved or made active.

Initial Training

Initially, you need to provide ASSP with a set of spam and non-spam messages. It is best to work with a collection of 500–1000 messages of each type. There are a number of sources of these messages, but the best way is to use your own email. The messages should be placed in /var/assp/spam and /var/assp/notspam, respectively. When you are happy with the spam in your database, run the following command:

```
bash$ cd /var/assp
bash$ sudo perl /usr/local/assp-1.0.9/rebuildspamdb.pl
```

This generates the ASSP databases for classifying your incoming mail based on your spam and non-spam messages. You also need to set up a cron job to run this command daily in order to reclassify misclassified mail.

After this initial training period, you will probably want to change a few settings. The settings involve what is logged, test mode, and what is prepended to spam identified subject lines:

- **Use Subject as Maillog Names**—Uncheck this box.
- **Test Mode**—Uncheck this box.
- **Prepend Spam Subject**—Change this to something like [SPAM] to identify spam messages.

Training ASSP on bad messages is simple. Just forward the misclassified messages to the appropriate email address, and ASSP will automatically process them, adjusting the statistics database as necessary. The addresses are as follows:

- `assp-white`—Adds an address to the whitelist
- `assp-spam`—Tells ASSP that the message was classified as non-spam when it should have been spam
- `assp-notspam`—Tells ASSP that the message was classified as spam when it should have been ham

Other ASSP Screens

The other screens available on the ASSP are as follows. The Statistics screen gives a nice summary of the ASSP statistics and is shown in Figure 8.6.

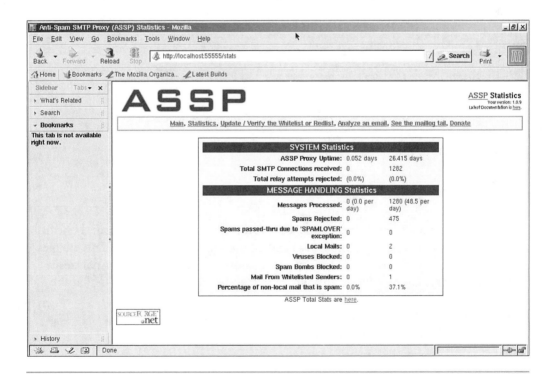

Figure 8.6 ASSP statistics.

The Update/Verify the Whitelist or Redlist screen allows the user to manage the whitelist and redlist (blacklist) as needed (see Figure 8.7).

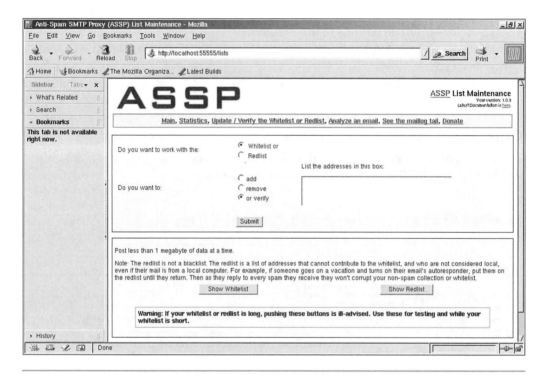

Figure 8.7 Whitelist/blacklist management.

Whereas other Bayesian applications have a training function as a command line utility, ASSP uses a web form to submit misclassified messages instead of emailing the messages to the appropriate addresses (outlined previously). The screen titled Analyze an Email enables users to copy/paste wrongly classified messages into a form so that the Bayesian filters can "learn" from their mistakes.

The screen titled See the maillog Tail enables you to look at the maillog in real time. This enables fast debugging of problems.

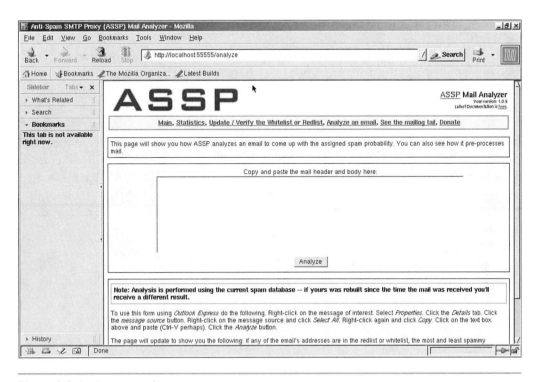

Figure 8.8 Analyze an email.

ASSP Integration with Mail Clients

To have Procmail process the messages tagged by ASSP, this recipe can be used:

```
MAILDIR=$HOME/Maildir
DEFAULT=$MAILDIR/
ORGMAIL=$MAILDIR/
LOGFILE=$MAILDIR/procmail.log

:0
* ^X-Assp-Spam: YES
.Spam/
```

This recipe looks for a subject line containing X-Assp-Spam: YES and, if present, files the message in the Spam folder. Please see Chapter 9, "Email Client Filtering," for more information on integrating ASSP with mail clients such as Outlook and Mozilla Messenger.

CONCLUSION

A number of Bayesian analyzer programs are freely available for download and integration into your email infrastructure. Choosing a Bayesian analyzer program to use on your email infrastructure can be a difficult task. We chose to cover CRM114, bogofilter, and ASSP.

CRM114 is very accurate in identifying spam, and it incorporates its own filtering ruleset, enabling the user to easily define his or her own filters. bogofilter is another very accurate Bayesian classifier. It can easily be set up to handle a three-folder filtering design (spam, maybe spam, inbox), causing fewer problems for the end user. ASSP is a Bayesian analyzer designed as a proxy to sit between your mail server and machines that want to send your users' messages. This proxy design, along with its GUI interface and ease of retraining, makes it a good choice for ease of installation and use.

Email Client Filtering

This chapter covers a few of the tools available to mail clients in the fight against spam. These filtering tools and techniques (with the possible exception of POPFile) are meant to complement the coverage of the anti-spam methods outlined in this book. These tools are meant to show the reader how to use the client-side techniques with the server-side methods covered in other parts of the book. Although the focus of this chapter is on Microsoft Windows, these techniques can also be applied to other platforms where the applications have been ported to run (for example, Mozilla Messenger on Linux).

In this chapter, we cover the following email clients and related software:

- **POPFile v0.21.1**—POPFile is a powerful multi-platform POP3 proxy written in Perl that implements the Bayesian classification algorithm. It works very well, but only with POP3 accounts. (IMAP and other protocols are planned for a future release.)
- **Mozilla Messenger 1.6**—Mozilla has excellent message filtering and a rudimentary Bayesian classification implementation. It enables you to have the benefit of a modern Bayesian anti-spam implementation integrated with an email client.
- **Microsoft Outlook Express 6**—Outlook Express's support for filtering messages is limited to subject line modification. There is no other anti-spam capability within the package.
- **Microsoft Outlook 2003**—Outlook has excellent support for filtering messages and some capability for dealing with spam messages via its Junk E-Mail Filter With Microsoft SmartScreen Technology. Plugins are available that extend Outlook to have integrated Bayesian filtering capability.

The topic of Procmail filtering was covered in Chapter 2, "Procmail," so please refer to that chapter if you are interested in performing filtering "outside" an email client covered here.

The choice of which email client to use is usually a matter of (your or your customer's) personal preference. For the client portions of this chapter, you should pay close attention to the sections of the chapter that cover the clients that you or your customer(s) use. POPFile could be of great use to anyone using any compatible email client (a client that supports the POP3 protocol).

TO FILTER OR NOT TO FILTER

The question of whether or not to filter at the client side is a difficult one. There are benefits and drawbacks to filtering messages at the email client. If you are the email administrator for an enterprise, you should take into account the number and type of users you support. Some questions to ask yourself include

- How sophisticated is my user base?
- Will my users accept a little bit of hassle in exchange for receiving less spam?
- Would my users accept "losing" messages permanently in exchange for no inconvenience?
- Does my organization operate under any regulatory oversight that governs how I must manage email?

Some of the benefits to using a filter on the end-user email client include

- Training Bayesian filters is simplified.
- End users control their own inboxes.
- No off-site, remote "sidelined" email repository for end users or administrators to check.

The biggest downside to filtering is the client support headache that goes along with the approach. In the best environment, your organization would have a help desk that could take some of the support burden. However, this is not always possible.

A hybrid approach could be taken, where users could select the level of nuisance they experience in the fight against spam. This could be on a departmental, geographic, or other level that enables you to identify groups of users. Commercial MTAs such as Microsoft Exchange and Lotus Domino are good at breaking down user populations on certain bases. However, a hybrid approach where different users experience different spam filtering policies will take more time and effort to implement.

POPFILE

POPFile is a Perl-based Bayesian filter written by John Graham-Cummings and licensed under the GPL. It does a very nice job of filtering your email messages at the client side, assuming you access your mail via POP3. (IMAP and other protocols are scheduled for coverage in upcoming versions.) POPFile is platform-independent, meaning that it can be run on any operating system that runs Perl. The platform used in this chapter is Windows 2000.

POPFile can easily be used in conjunction with other anti-spam measures. In fact, it can be used in place of (or in concert with) the filtering capability of an email client such as Mozilla Messenger. By using the filtering capability in POPFile, the email processing stream can usually be simplified. By using a tool such as POPFile, you can achieve a higher level of anti-spam filtering for the end user.

You should think carefully about using POPFile in a mail architecture where another Bayesian-style classifier is in place on the server side. Although possible, it probably makes sense to forego running a Bayesian classifier on the server and simply run POPFile at the client side. However, any of the other non-Bayesian anti-spam tools on the server can be used successfully in conjunction with POPFile. A tool like SpamAssassin can be used as well because it simply scores messages using Bayesian analysis as only part of the score, instead of routing messages directly to your spam filter. You may want to adjust the Bayesian analysis portion of the SpamAssassin score, however.

INSTALLATION

POPFile is provided as a self-installing executable, making it easy to install. The more difficult part is configuring your email client for use with its header or subject modification classification functionality. These topics are the subject of the rest of the chapter.

The most recent version of POPFile can be downloaded from Sourceforge from this URL: *http://sourceforge.net/project/showfiles.php?group_id=63137*. While we use version 0.21.1 here, any recent version should work with these directions. Select the file called `popfile v0.21.1 Windows` under the `POPFile for Windows` heading. When downloaded, save it to your desktop and extract it using your favorite ZIP file extractor or the native Windows XP ZIP utility if you are running under XP.

After it is extracted, run the file called setup. This will guide you through the rest of the installation process. For the most part, the questions the installer asks are self-explanatory. The default settings should be acceptable for most installations. A copy of the release notes is provided in Figure 9.1.

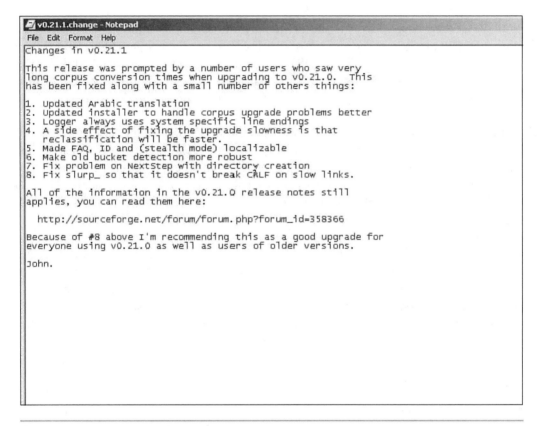

Figure 9.1 POPFile v0.21.1 release notes.

On the POPFile Installation Options page, you may need to adjust the POP3 port (110) and User Interface port (8080) from their defaults if something else on your machine is listening on those ports. Also, you may or may not want to have POPFile start automatically at startup. If you do not check that box, you will need to start it manually. When you are ready to have it run all the time (the recommended mode), you will have to manually put POPFile into your Startup program group. Figure 9.2 shows the POPFile Installation Options screen, with recommended settings.

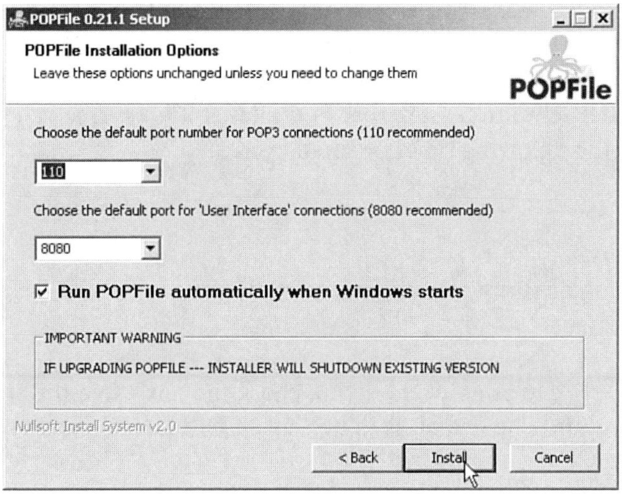

Figure 9.2 POPFile Installation Options.

The next screen, POPFile Classification Bucket Creation, is where you can tell POPFile about the buckets you want to use. The defaults should be fine; they can be adjusted later. However, if you want to use POPFile for classification of email besides spam, the buckets for doing that can be created now. Figure 9.3 shows this screen with the default settings.

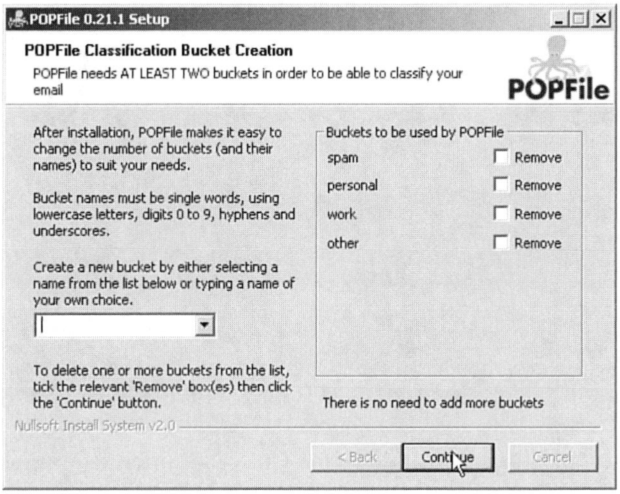

Figure 9.3 POPFile Classification Bucket Creation.

The next set of screens, starting with the one titled POPFile Client Configuration, shows the mail clients POPFile can attempt to automatically set up. POPFile will attempt to set up the email clients that it knows about to work with them. Note that you should go into your client after setup to be sure that POPFile set it up correctly. POPFile can attempt to set up the following types of email clients:

- Eudora
- Microsoft Outlook
- Microsoft Outlook Express
- Mozilla

If you want POPFile to attempt the setup, check the box when the appropriate Reconfigure screen comes up. The default is to not have POPFile attempt to set up your client for you.

When the POPFile Can Now Be Started screen comes up, make sure the radio button marked Run POPFile in Background is set. Otherwise, you will have to manually start POPFile in order to configure or use it.

The final screen is titled Completing the POPFile Setup Wizard. Make sure the box marked POPFile User Interface is checked so that the configuration part can begin. Assuming you checked the box, the screen shown in Figure 9.4 appears.

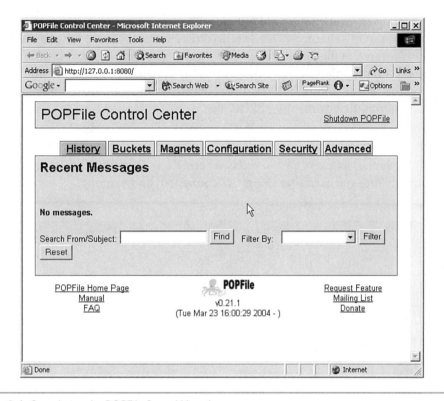

Figure 9.4 Completing the POPFile Setup Wizard.

CONFIGURATION

The six areas of the POPFile User Interface are as follows:

- History
- Buckets
- Magnets
- Configuration
- Security
- Advanced

The configuration settings available are covered in the following sections (see Figures 9.5–9.10).

Please note that the integration of POPFile with your email client is covered in the sub-sequent sections of this chapter. POPFile is no different than many of the other anti-spam applications covered in this book, except that it runs on the email client instead of the server. When you run POPFile, you must still set up the email client to filter the messages based upon the classifications POPFile makes. However, the filtering setup on the email client is often simplified by the use of POPFile.

History

The History screen is where you go to reclassify errors made by POPFile. Initially, you will spend a lot of your time here after things are configured and running.

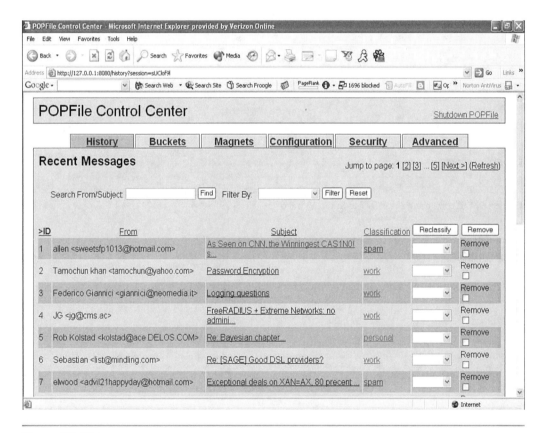

Figure 9.5 History.

You can also view the message itself, complete with the POPFile classification information, by clicking on the subject of the message. You can reclassify messages by clicking the drop-down box, selecting the proper bucket for the message, and then hitting the Reclassify button. Don't forget to click the Reclassify button before selecting another message page or part of the POPFile configuration page. Your changes will be lost and must be reentered if you exit the page without clicking the Reclassify button.

Buckets

The screen titled Buckets is where most user configuration takes place. The term "buckets" is used by POPFile to refer to a particular classification of messages.

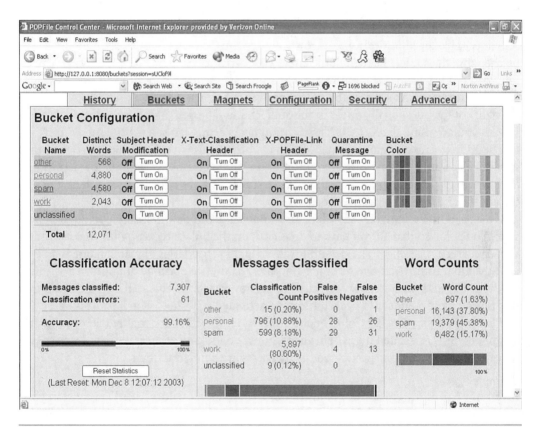

Figure 9.6 Buckets.

You should have one bucket for each type of message you want to classify. In this way, POPFile can be used for much more than classifying spam. It could be used to classify messages from email lists you subscribe to, for example. This screen shows the buckets in use, as well as how they are configured. It also shows a number of statistics and allows you to create, rename, and delete buckets. In addition, you can search buckets for specific words.

Under Bucket Configuration, the following options can be changed:

- Subject Header Modification
- X-Text-Classification Header
- X-POPFile-Link Header
- Quarantine Message
- Bucket Color

Subject Header Modification controls whether you want to identify classified messages by changing the subject header. Some email clients (for example, Outlook Express) can't filter based on arbitrary header lines, so the subject line must be modified to identify how messages are classified. This is a bit of an annoyance because when you reply to a message, the name of the bucket will appear in the Subject line. The default for subject modification is on. If you are using the X-Text-Classification header, this can safely be turned off.

The X-Text-Classification Header option enables the use of the message header by that name. This is probably the easiest method to use when classifying your email, assuming that the email clients in question support filtering based upon arbitrary headers. The default for inserting this header is on.

If the X-POPFile-Link Header selection is enabled, POPFile will insert a link to the message in question so that all you have to do is click on the link to reclassify the message if it's been incorrectly classified. The default for inserting this header of the same name is on.

If the Quarantine Message setting is on, then the message will be quarantined within POPFile. Because extra steps are required to get any misclassified email out of quarantine, this is not recommended. However, it can be activated if desired. The default is off.

The final setting, Bucket Color, enables you to set the color for that particular classification of words or related items. This is useful when looking at message detail under History to quickly determine how words in messages are being classified.

Example

If you want all of the email from your friends to end up in a folder called friends on your email client, you can do this in (at least) two different ways, both using a bucket. Each method is outlined here.

The first method involves setting up a bucket called friends in POPFile. After setting up the friends bucket, your email client must be set up to filter the messages tagged with the POPFile classification friends into a folder called friends-folder. After everything has been set up, you train POPFile by classifying every message that came from your friends to go into the friends bucket. After at least one message comes in from each friend, POPFile will classify messages correctly.

An alternative is to set up a From and CC magnet (see next section) for each friend's email address. The magnet points to the friends bucket, so POPFile automatically classifies every message with your friend's email address on the From line correctly, without manual training.

Magnets

Magnets are words that cause messages to be automatically classified as they are processed.

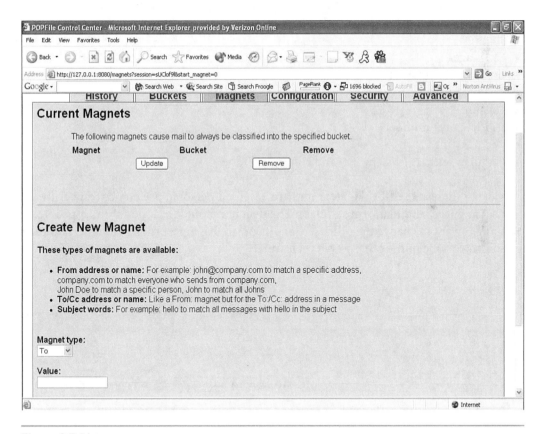

Figure 9.7 Magnets.

Magnets can appear in From, To, Cc, and/or Subject header lines and can be thought of as whitelists/blacklists. Using magnets can reduce the amount of manual reclassifications that you might otherwise have to do.

Example

For example, let's say you want to be sure email from your spouse always ends up in your personal folder. You set a `From` magnet to be his or her email address, `spouse@isp.net`, which points at the `personal` bucket. Then you set up your email client to filter the messages that POPFile classifies as `personal` to be filed in your `personal` folder on your email client.

Configuration

The configuration page lists a number of items not covered anywhere else:

- Skins
- Language
- Connection Timeout
- History Settings
- Logging
- POPFile port number
- POP3 settings
- Platform settings (system tray and console window)

Most of these are self-explanatory and are based on personal preference (especially Skins, Language, and Platform settings). The defaults should be good for most people. You might want to change the other settings if you are having a problem and need to turn on logging or one of the other low-level features.

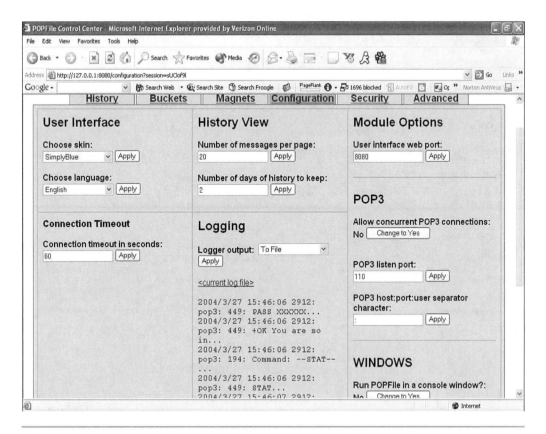

Figure 9.8 Configuration.

Security

The settings on this page manage security-related settings. This page covers the following areas:

- Enabling remote POP3 and HTTP access
- Remote POP3 auth server and port
- User Interface Password
- Automatic Update Checking
- Reporting Statistics

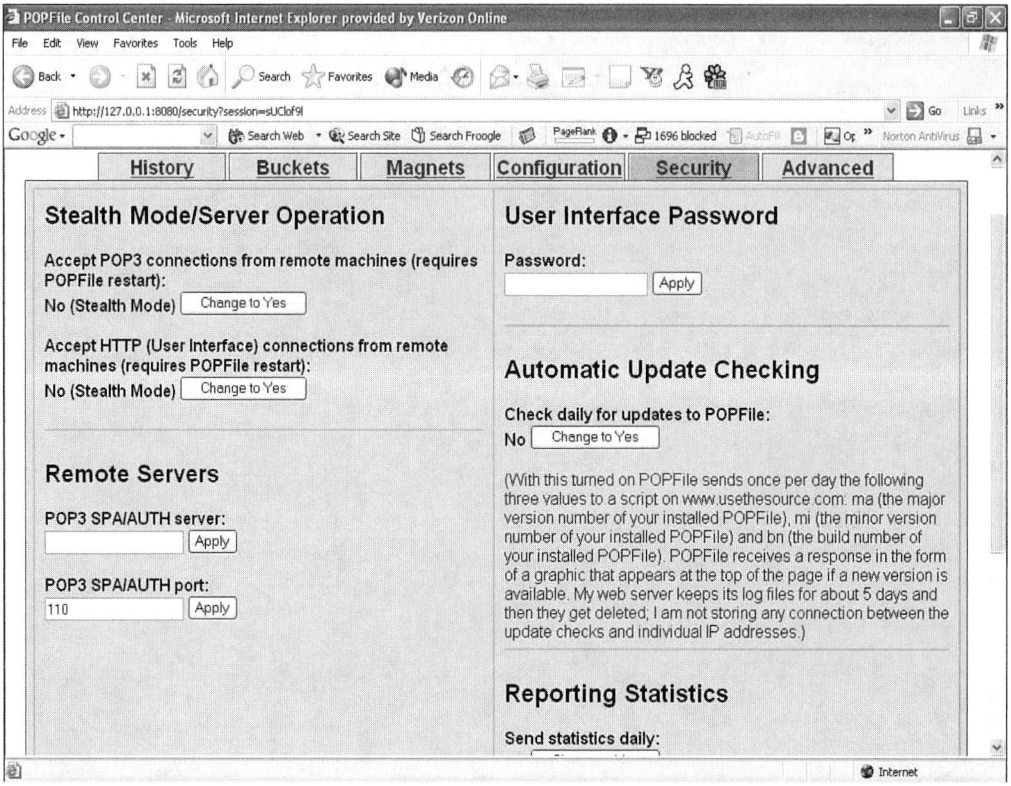

Figure 9.9 Security.

The most dangerous of these settings is the remote POP3 and HTTP access. Be very careful when turning this option on because it could allow anyone to access your POPFile setup. Remote POP3 auth server is used for setups that require two POP3 servers: one for authentication and one from which to retrieve email. The User Interface Password setting enables you to set up passwords for accessing the POPFile UI. This is especially useful if you want to enable remote access to your setup. The Automatic Update Checking enables POPFile to check for program updates, and Reporting Statistics reports statistics back to the POPFile web site for aggregate reporting.

Advanced

The Advanced screen has two areas:

- Ignored Words
- All POPFile Parameters

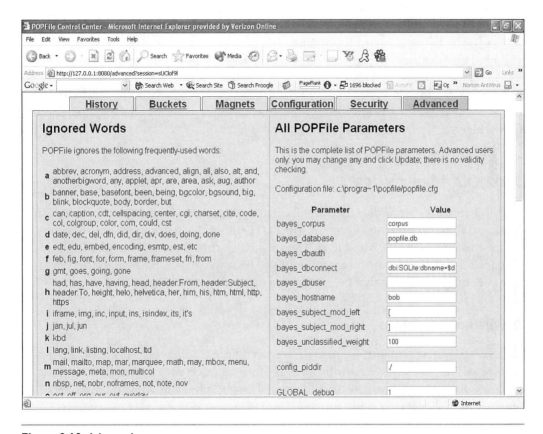

Figure 9.10 Advanced.

Ignored Words lists all of the words that POPFile will not use as part of its processing. Under most circumstances, there is no reason to change this list. The All POPFile Parameters screen lists all POPFile settings. This is for advanced users only, as there is no validity checking of these settings. Under most circumstances, the other screens should be used for making configuration changes.

OPERATION

Initially, you will want to set up your email client to not filter based upon POPFile classifications because POPFile will be wildly inaccurate. After an initial training period of 100 to 200 messages, the filtering capability can be set up in the email client. During the initial training period, you will need to retrain POPFile on every message that is sent through so that the filters can define a base level of filtering. You can enable the email client to filter initially, but you will need to check your spam folder frequently for misclassified messages in order to not miss any legitimate messages.

After POPFile is set up, you only need to go into the History screen and reclassify messages that are not classified properly. POPFile will take care of the other routine tasks for you, such as database maintenance, purging of its history, and so on. If interested, you can view the statistics periodically by going into the Buckets page and viewing the accuracy achieved.

MOZILLA MESSENGER

Mozilla Messenger is a widely used email client available for a large number of platforms. Netscape Messenger is based upon the Mozilla client, so the instructions here may be useful in setting up Netscape Messenger. The version we cover here is 1.6, under Microsoft Windows 2000/XP. Because recent versions of Messenger have a Bayesian implementation, we start by covering that before moving on to filtering messages.

BAYESIAN FILTERING

Mozilla 1.6 contains support for native Bayesian filtering. Although it is useful, it is not as mature and doesn't have as many features as other products such as POPFile. However, it certainly does work and will be useful to people, especially as the Mozilla developers enhance the product over time. You might use the integrated Bayesian classification in Mozilla if you want a simpler client-side solution that requires less setup and that is easier to support for your clients.

To enable Bayesian filtering, simply start classifying messages using the recycle symbol in the message list window. Figure 9.11 shows the location of the column that identifies messages as spam. Clicking on the circle/recycle icon in the Recycle column will toggle the setting of that message from spam (recycle symbol) to not spam (circle).

Recycle Symbol

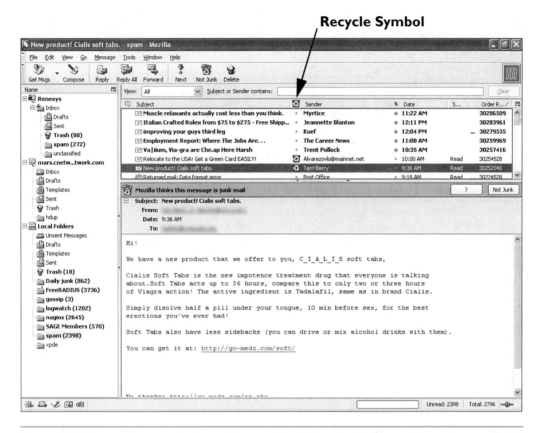

Figure 9.11 The recycle symbol indicates a message Mozilla has identified as spam.

Figure 9.12 shows how to manually reclassify a message as spam. After messages are classified, you can activate Messenger junk controls on the accounts you want, and Messenger will classify messages automatically as they come into your mailbox.

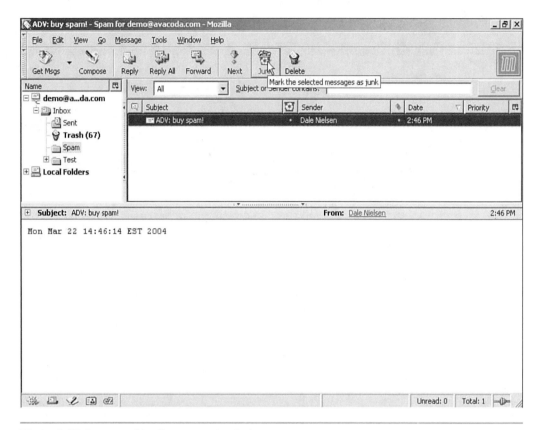

Figure 9.12 Retraining Mozilla on a misclassified spam message.

To activate junk controls, go to `Tools==>Junk Mail Controls`, which brings up the window shown in Figure 9.13.

Simply select the account on which you want to activate junk mail control. You can have Messenger automatically move messages that it thinks are spam, as well as messages that you manually mark as spam, into the appropriate folder(s) by checking the appropriate boxes. You also have the option to whitelist senders who appear in your address book automatically.

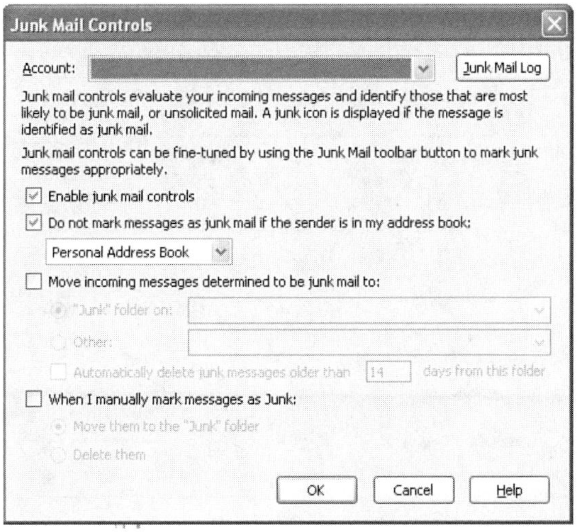

Figure 9.13 Junk Mail Controls screen.

MESSAGE FILTERING

The message filtering capability of Messenger is activated by going to the
`Tools==>Message Filters` option, which brings up the screen in Figure 9.14.

If you then click on the New button, you will see a screen similar to Figure 9.15.
We cover both subject- and custom-based header filtering later in this chapter.

You need to name your filter so that it can be recognized when you activate it. You can
filter based upon several criteria; make the appropriate selection in the corresponding
box. Additional filtering fields can be added by clicking the More button in the middle of
the window.

The filtering pane is broken down into two parts:

- Message selection (top half of window)
- Perform These Actions (bottom half of window)

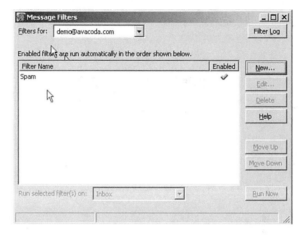

Figure 9.14 Message Filters.

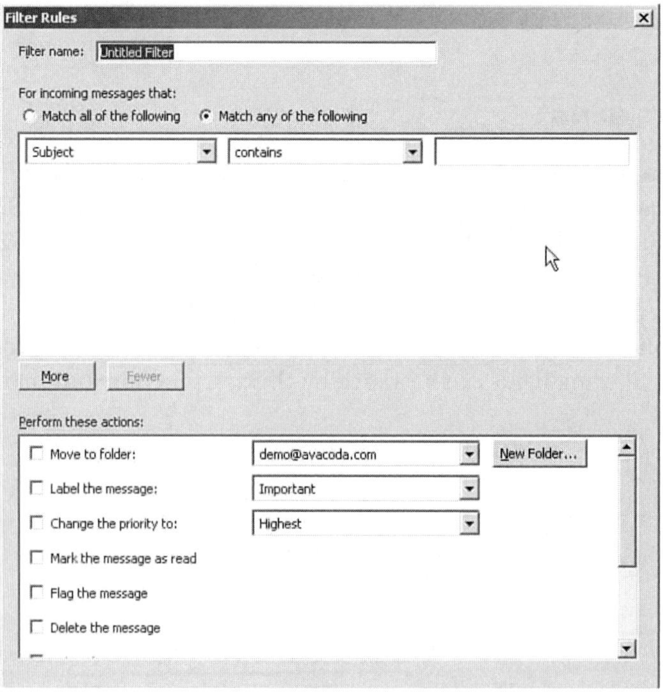

Figure 9.15 Creating a new filter.

Message Selection

The message selection section is broken down into three fields/columns:

- Selection criteria
- Action
- Data

The selection criteria specifies the part of the headers on which to filter, the action part says how to perform the match, and the data part specifies what the value of the header needs to be in order for there to be a match. This is useful for anti-spam programs that assign scores to messages.

Default fields available to filter in the rules section include

- Subject
- Sender
- Body
- Date
- Priority
- Status
- To
- Cc
- To or cc
- Age In Days

This is the standard list of headers available in almost all email messages. If the field you need isn't there, the selection called Customize will create a header for you. It allows you to enter your own unique fields to filter on (see the "Header Based Filter" section later in this chapter).

The action fields (second column) are as follows:

- Contains
- Is
- Begins with
- Ends with

These fields are self-explanatory. Most often, Contains is used. The third field is the actual text/data you are activating the filter on, such as a spam score.

Perform This Action

The lower half of the pane specifies what to do with the message after it is flagged. A number of actions can be taken, including

- Move to Folder
- Label the Message
- Change Priority To
- Mark Message As Read
- Flag Message
- Delete Message
- Delete from POP3 Server

Most often, the Move to Folder option is used. You specify the account and folder to file this message into. Any number of the options can be selected if desired. If you are filtering to a folder, and the folder doesn't exist, the New Folder button can be clicked to bring up a dialog box to create the folder.

Examples

In this section, examples are provided for the subject- and header-based filters under Mozilla Messenger. Depending on the functionality of the particular server-side anti-spam tool(s) implemented, you may need to configure both types of filters.

Subject-Based Filter

If you need to create a Subject line filter, leave Subject in the first column, Contains in the second column, and the string you want to filter on, such as ADV:, in the third column. Figure 9.16 shows an example.

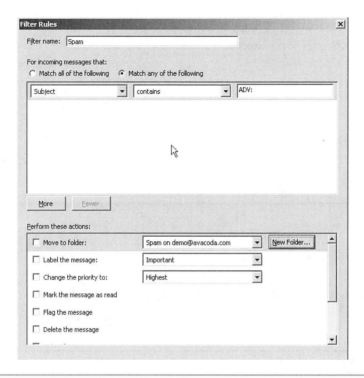

Figure 9.16 Example Filter Rules screen.

Header-Based Filter

If you need to create a customized filter, select Customize from the first column drop-down box and insert the header name you want to filter on. For our example, this is X-Bogosity because we are running bogofilter. Creating a customized header is shown in Figure 9.17.

Figure 9.17 Creating a customized header.

Figure 9.18 lists many of the spam filtering headers used by programs covered in this book. After you have entered the new header, it shows up in the list of available headers to filter on.

Package	Headers	Subject Modifications
ASSP	X-Assp-Spam: YES X-Assp-Spam: NO	Prepend Spam Subject (no default)
Bogofilter	X-Bogosity: Yes X-Bogosity: No X-Bogosity: Unsure	spam_subject_tag=***SPAM***
CRM114	X-CRM114-Status: Good X-CRM114-Status: SPAM	:spam_flag_subject_string: /ADV:/

DCC	"X-DCC-brand-Metrics: chost server-ID;
	    bulk cknm1=count cknm2=count"
	ex: "X-DCC-RHYOLITE-Metrics:
	    calcite.rhyolite.com 101; Body=16
	    Fuz1=16 Fuz2=16"
		none

Vipul's Razor	X-Razor2-Warning: SPAM	uses formail from procmail Subject: Razor Warning: SPAM/UBE/UCE
SpamAssassin	X-Spam-Status: Yes	rewrite_subject 1 *****SPAM*****

Figure 9.18 Selected spam filtering keywords.

Figure 9.19 shows selecting the new X-Bogosity filter we just created.

Figure 9.19 Selecting customized header.

Next, make sure the second field is set to the appropriate action, in our case Contains. Finally, make sure that the data field (third field) is set to the correct value (in our example, Yes) so that proper messages are selected.

Perform These Actions

Continuing with our example, under the Perform These Actions portion of the filtering window, we select Move to Folder with a drop-down box value of Spam on demo@avacoda.com, as shown in Figure 9.20.

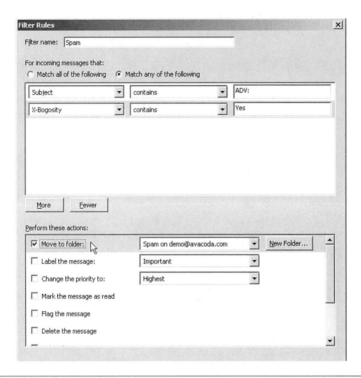

Figure 9.20 Move message to folder.

Running Filters

After the OK button is pressed, you are brought back to the Message Filters pane with the name of our filter, spam, as the only filter entered. If desired, this filter can be run now to filter mail in the inbox into the spam folder. This is done by selecting the filter (in our example called spam) and the appropriate message store (for example, Inbox) and clicking the Run Now button. If this step isn't performed, messages will be filtered as they come into the configured mail folder.

MICROSOFT OUTLOOK EXPRESS

Microsoft Outlook Express contains only limited support for filtering (subject line) and only blacklist anti-spam support. Each is covered in the following sections.

FILTERING

Filtering is a two-step process. First, define the filter(s) you want and then activate them. We will set up a rule to filter messages with ADV in the subject line to our spam folder.

To set up subject line filtering, go to Tools==>Message Filters==>Mail. A screen similar to Figure 9.21 should appear, which shows the selection called Where the Subject Line Contains Specific Words is checked.

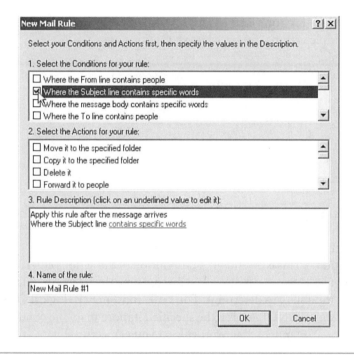

Figure 9.21 New Mail Rule.

Before continuing with our example, we'll cover the filtering panel itself. There are four fields on the New Mail Rule panel, and they are numbered as follows:

1. **Select the Conditions for Your Rule**—This defines the selection criteria available for your filter. Multiple criteria can be selected. Options are
   - From
   - Subject
   - Message body

- To
- CC
- To or CC
- Priority
- More than certain size
- Existence of attachment
- Secure
- All messages

2. **Select the Actions for Your Rule**—This setting indicates what should happen to your message. Multiple actions can be selected. Options are
   - Move to folder
   - Copy to folder
   - Delete
   - Forward
   - Highlight
   - Flag
   - Mark as read
   - Mark as watched or ignored
   - Reply
   - Stop processing more rules
   - Don't download from server
   - Delete from server

3. **Rule Description**—This is essentially a description of the actions entered in boxes 1 or 2, along with hot links that must be clicked on to define the selection criteria or needed actions. Also, the ability to determine if one rule must match (logical OR) or all rules must match (logical AND) needs to be specified if more than one condition is defined.

4. **Name of Rule**—You must name your rule so you can activate it.

Continuing with our example, select the following options for each box of the New Mail Rule panel:

1. Where the subject line contains specific words
2. Move it to the specified folder
3. This box will contain the following text:

```
Apply this rule after the message arrives
Where the Subject line contains specific words
Move it to the specified folder
```

4. Spam with ADV in subject line

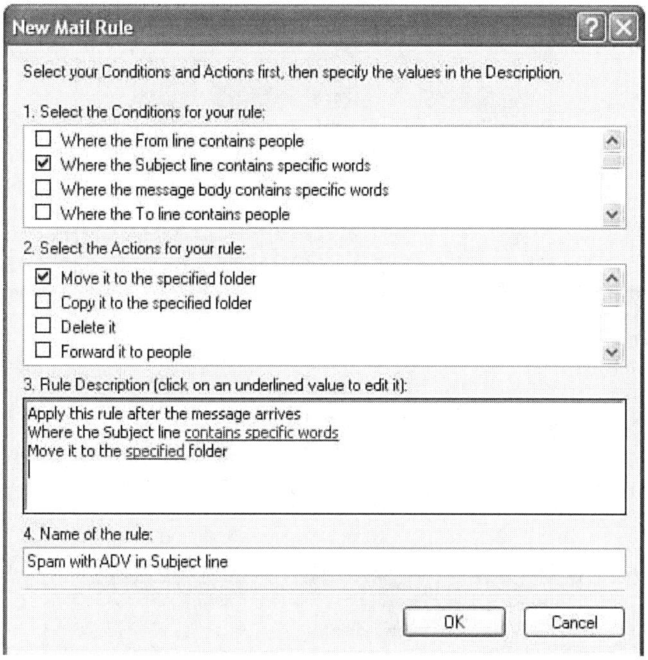

Figure 9.22 Make a new mail rule (completed).

At this point, we need to define the rule-matching criteria, as well as what action to take. By clicking on the `contains specific words` hot link, a dialog box comes up. Enter the text you want to match on (in our case ADV) in the top field and click Add. Figure 9.23 shows the rule setup completed.

Figure 9.23 Selecting words or a phrase to filter on.

Now click OK to go back to the New Mail Rule panel. Next, click on the specified hot link, which brings you to another dialog box where you can specify the folder to move the message to if it matches. This is shown in Figure 9.24.

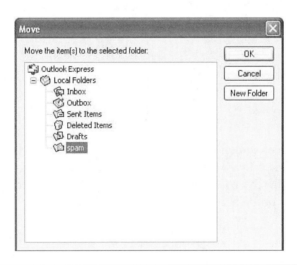

Figure 9.24 Selecting target folder for filing message.

By default, your rule should be activated. This is shown by a checkmark next to the rule in the listing, as shown in Figure 9.25.

Figure 9.25 Activating/selecting a rule.

If multiple rules are defined, the order in which they are run can be defined by the Move Up and Move Down buttons.

BLACKLISTING

Blacklisting can be achieved by appropriate use of filters as shown before, or by specific Blocked Senders functionality provided by Outlook. This can be accessed by going to Tools==>Message Rules==>Blocked Sender Lists. There, addresses to be blocked are defined by clicking the Add button and entering an address (or domain) to be blocked, as shown in Figure 9.26.

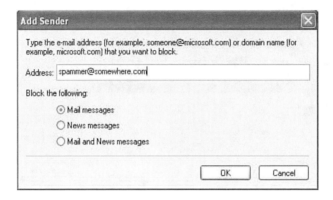

Figure 9.26 Selecting sender for blacklisting.

After clicking OK, the list of blocked addresses is shown in Figure 9.27.

Figure 9.27 List of blocked (blacklisted) senders.

MICROSOFT OUTLOOK

Microsoft Outlook is an email client available commercially as a standalone product or as part of Microsoft Office 2003. It contains the anti-spam capabilities you would expect in a commercial product, including

- Whitelisting
- Blacklisting
- Filter by subject
- Filter by arbitrary header

Outlook does not include a native Bayesian analyzer, although it does have Junk E-Mail Filter with Microsoft SmartScreen Technology. In order to get Bayesian-style content filtering, one of the following packages can be used:

- Outclass (*http://www.vargonsoft.com/Outclass/*)
- K9 (*http://www.keir.net/k9.html*)
- Spamihilator (*http://www.spamihilator.com/*)

JUNK E-MAIL FILTER WITH MICROSOFT SMARTSCREEN TECHNOLOGY

Microsoft Research has developed its patented Junk E-Mail Filter with Microsoft Smart-Screen Technology in order to fight spam. Although it appears to be very similar to Bayesian-style filtering, the Junk E-Mail Filter does not give the Outlook 2003 user the ability to train the filters like POPFile and Mozilla Messenger do.

The Microsoft Research filtering approach has three goals:

- Proactive prevention against spam
- Comprehensive protection from spam
- Automated intelligence

The filter works by taking a broader approach than many other anti-spam solutions. Rather than identifying specific words, the filter identifies the characteristics of spam messages themselves. It works by integrating with the other built-in anti-spam features in Outlook 2003 such as Safe Senders, Safe Recipients, and Blocked Senders (what we call whitelists and blacklists). In addition, Microsoft updates the filter periodically so that the latest and greatest anti-spam innovations are used in the fight against spam.

JUNK E-MAIL TOOLS

Outlook's whitelisting and blacklisting tools can be accessed in several ways. The easiest way to add something to the Outlook whitelist or blacklist is by going to Actions==>Junk E-mail, which brings up the following options (shown in Figure 9.28):

- Add Sender to Blocked Senders List
- Add Sender to Safe Senders List
- Add Sender's Domain to Safe Senders List
- Add Recipient to Safe Recipients List

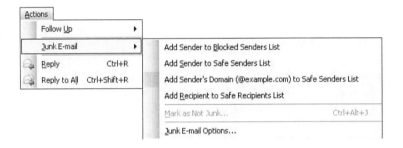

Figure 9.28 Blacklisting/whitelisting menu options.

Blocked Senders List is analogous to a blacklist, and Safe Senders List is Outlook's term for a whitelist. Another way to access the lists is by selecting the Junk E-Mail options on the Junk E-Mail page. This brings up a window similar to Figure 9.29.

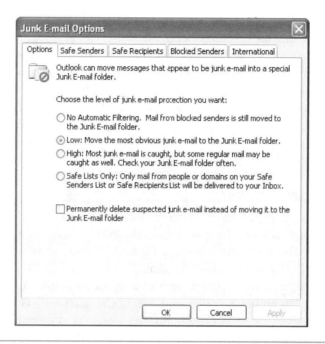

Figure 9.29 Junk E-Mail Options.

Configuring Junk E-Mail Filter with Microsoft SmartScreen Technology

The Junk E-Mail Options screen is how you enable MS Research's anti-spam filtering technology. It allows the user to specify varying levels of anti-spam filtering, including

- No Automatic Filtering
- Low
- High
- Safe Lists Only

The Options tab enables you to select the desired level of filtering. The No Automatic Filtering setting turns the advanced filtering off completely and would be used if another anti-spam solution were being used on the client end.

Setting the level to Low causes Outlook to move the most blatant spam, which should result in the lowest number of false positives. The High setting causes the anti-spam filters to be more aggressive, which may cause some legitimate messages (false positives) to end up in the spam folder. If the High setting is used, you should check the `Junk E-mail` folder very often for misclassified messages.

The Safe Lists Only setting is for the truly paranoid and will allow messages *only* from senders on your whitelists (Safe Lists) to come through. Messages from senders not on your Safe Lists will be routed to the `Junk E-mail` folder. Finally, the Permanently Delete Suspected Junk E-mail setting should be used with caution. It will cause Outlook 2003 to automatically delete messages it determines to be spam, rather than simply moving them to the junk folder. It is not recommended that this option be used, as legitimate messages will undoubtedly get deleted by mistake.

Other Anti-Spam Settings

Three other tabs on this page enable you to manually enter senders and recipients on the appropriate whitelist/blacklists. The Safe Senders screen is the list of whitelisted senders, the Safe Recipients tab allows you to manage the collection of whitelisted recipients, and Blocked Senders is the list of blacklisted senders.

The tab marked International allows the user to block messages from particular top-level domains as well as messages containing certain character sets. This can be useful for blocking certain types of messages (and spam) that come from foreign countries.

For example, you may never receive messages from the top-level domain `cn` (China). That domain could be added to the list of blocked domain, and all messages (including spam and non-spam messages) will be blocked. In a similar fashion, if you never receive messages in Chinese, Chinese Simplified and Chinese Traditional could be selected in the Blocked Encodings List. However, if you communicate with people internationally, these settings can cause problems and should be avoided. The default is no domain or character set filtering.

FILTERING

In order to work with many of the anti-spam packages in this book, Outlook can be configured to filter based upon subject lines as well as arbitrary headers. Each is covered in this section.

Filter by Subject

In order to set up a filter by subject, go to `Tools==>Rules and Alerts==>E-mail Rules` tab, which brings up a window similar to Figure 9.30. Click on the New Rule button to start the wizard.

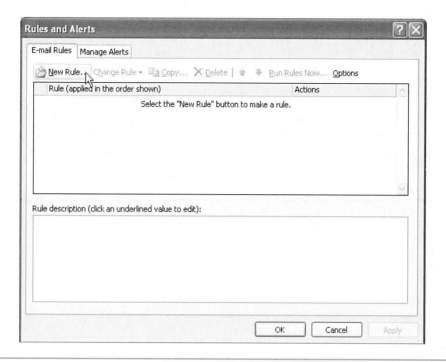

Figure 9.30 Creating a new email filtering rule.

Under the Stay Organized portion of the window, select the Move Messages with Specific Words In the Subject To a Specific Folder option. Then click the `specific words` link in the dialog box to enter the keywords used to select messages, as shown in Figure 9.31.

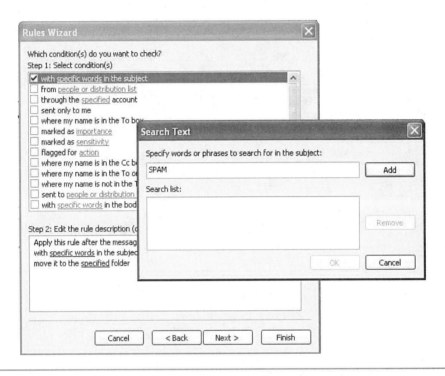

Figure 9.31 Specifying words to filter upon.

Subject lines for certain covered anti-spam packages can be found in Figure 9.18. Because the desired end action is to move the message into a folder, the target folder needs to be specified. This is accomplished by clicking on the `specified` link. Clicking on the link brings up a screen similar to Figure 9.32 where the destination folder can be input.

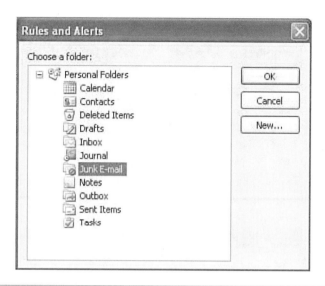

Figure 9.32 Specify target folder for filtered message.

Filter by Header

Filtering by header is similar to subject. Start by going to Tools==>Rules and Alerts==>
E-mail Rules tab and, when there, click on Start From a Blank Rule. This will bring up a
screen similar to Figure 9.33.

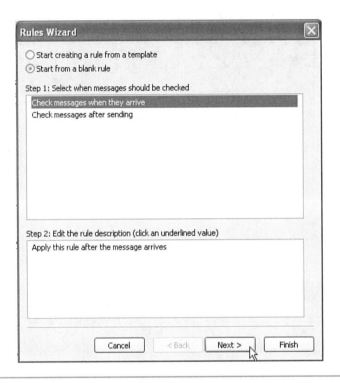

Figure 9.33 Blank email filtering rule.

After clicking Next, a screen similar to Figure 9.34 is displayed where the option called With Specific Words in the Message Header needs to be selected (checked).

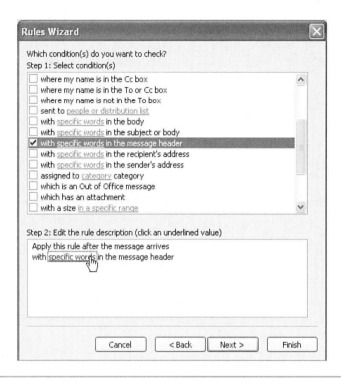

Figure 9.34 Select condition for rule.

Next, the specific words hot link needs to be clicked so that the message headers to be filtered on can be input. Figure 9.35 illustrates an example.

Now the folder where the message gets moved to needs to be specified. Check the checkbox in front of the option called Move It to the Specified Folder and click the specified link, which brings up a dialog box similar to the one shown in Figure 9.32 where the folder can be entered.

Figure 9.35 Specify phrase to filter upon.

Filter Activation and Order

In Outlook, filters are activated by default, so no activation is required. The order of the filter can be adjusted by going to the `Tools==>Rules and Alerts==>E-mail Rules` tab. When there, select the rule and press the up arrow or down arrow to move the selected rule up or down in the run order. To not run a rule but leave it in place, uncheck it.

CONCLUSION

Email clients such as Microsoft Outlook, Mozilla Messenger, and Microsoft Outlook Express have varying degrees of functionality in the area of filtering messages. Filtering messages at the email client level is not for every organization, as it can be confusing for users and time-consuming to set up and can cause an increased support burden. However, filtering at the client level enables the most functionality. In many cases, other anti-spam solutions covered in this book depend upon email client filtering in order to work.

POPFile is an excellent Bayesian classifier that runs natively on any POP3-capable client. POPFile also has front ends for Microsoft Outlook. Mozilla Messenger 1.6 has a native Bayesian analyzer in the early stages of development that will likely get better over time. Messenger has the best email message filtering—both arbitrary header filtering and subject line filtering.

Microsoft Outlook 2003 has Microsoft Research's Junk E-mail Filter with Smartscreen Technology, which is an advanced filtering mechanism similar to Bayesian analysis, though without user training. Outlook 2003 also has arbitrary header filtering and subject line filtering. Microsoft Outlook Express has the most limited set of email filtering options, containing only subject line filtering.

Microsoft Exchange 10

In this chapter, we cover the Microsoft Exchange Server 2003 mail server's functionality as it relates to stopping spam. This chapter is not meant to be a thorough treatment of Exchange; it only covers those pieces that help administrators use Exchange in their fight against spam. For pointers to Microsoft Exchange resources, please see Appendix G, "References."

Microsoft has released an Exchange plugin called Intelligent Message Filter (IMF), which enables a high level of spam fighting capability. Specifically, IMF appears to use a Bayesian-style classifier that uses the characteristics of spam and non-spam messages to classify messages that go through the Exchange server. Exchange then uses IMF and the statistical information to assist Outlook 2003 clients in determining whether a given message is spam or not and gives you the ability to block it, delete it, or deliver it to the junk email folder.

Regarding more traditional mail transfer agent (MTA) style controls, Exchange gives the administrator the ability to filter incoming messages based upon the following criteria:

- Connection
- Recipient
- Sender

Blocking at the connection level is the best, as it rejects the message before too many resources are consumed. An example of connection-level blocking would be a blackhole listing service such as DNSBL. Of course, blocking at the connection level also means that some false positives may be blocked without your knowledge (unless you dig through Exchange logs). Blocking (blacklisting) the recipient or sender is more accurate, though the message will be stopped after consuming more machine resources.

On the sending side, Exchange controls sending email messages based upon these areas:

- Access Control
- Connection Control
- Relay Restrictions

Each of these areas is covered in this chapter. Exchange is started by going to Start==>Programs==>Microsoft Exchange==>System Manager. The main Exchange screen is shown in Figure 10.1.

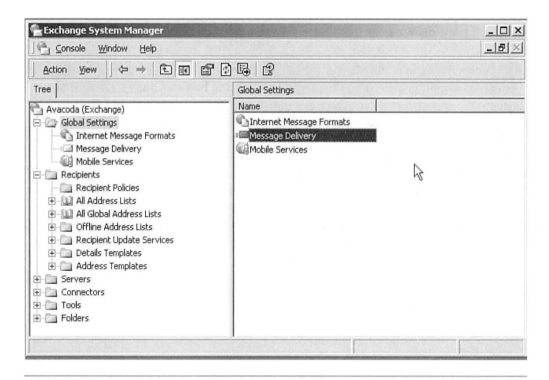

Figure 10.1 Main Microsoft Exchange screen.

Note that there are two areas of the Exchange System Manger window: the Tree view pane on the left and the "expanded" view pane of the selected item on the right. It doesn't matter which way you use to get into the particular function, but in this chapter we will use the Tree view.

This chapter also covers McAfee SpamKiller for Exchange 2.1.1, a SpamAssassin-based plugin for MS Exchange. SpamKiller has a number of features, including

- Policy-based rules
- Hierarchical server-based whitelists/blacklists controlled by administrator via separate client software available from McAfee
- Integrated Bayesian-style analysis
- Content filtering
- Message scoring

INTELLIGENT MESSAGE FILTER

IMF is a plugin provided by Microsoft that greatly improves Exchange 2003's spam fighting capability. Microsoft doesn't give the administrator the ability to allow users to retrain the filters like you can in CRM114 or bogofilter, but IMF is still very useful.

Microsoft uses a concept known as the Spam Confidence Level (SCL) to determine whether or not a particular message is spam. Each message is scored with an integer value from 0 to 9, with 0 indicating a non-spam message. Values from 1 to 9 indicates a spam message, with a lower number indicating that a message is likely not spam and a higher number indicating that a message is probably spam. Each message is scored, and then depending upon its score, the message can be rejected, deleted, or moved to a junk email folder, which is UceArchive at the system level or Junk Email for individual users.

Unfortunately, Microsoft doesn't enable the administrator to easily view SCL scores for messages. However, the References contain links to web pages that step you through the process of viewing SCL scores for both Outlook messages and spam messages, which end up in the UceArchive folder.

INSTALLATION

In a large Exchange installation with many servers, IMF should be run on the machines we call the email relay machines. These are MS Exchange servers that process email messages between the Internet (or non-Exchange servers) and the Exchange mailbox servers your users login to in order to read their messages. Microsoft refers to the machines that IMF is to be installed on as *bridgehead* machines. In smaller shops where there is no email relay, IMF can be installed directly on the MS Exchange mailbox servers.

The IMF update must be downloaded from the MS Exchange IMF site, *http://www.microsoft.com/exchange/downloads/2003/IMF/default.asp*, under the link called `Exchange Intelligent Message Filter`.

After you've downloaded the update, install the package. The only options available during install are checkboxes called Management Tools for Intelligent Message Filter and Intelligence Message Filter Functionality, which are both enabled by default.

CONFIGURATION

The main IMF configuration screen is available by going to `Global Settings==>Message Delivery==>(right-click)==>properties==>Intelligent Message Filtering`, which should bring up a screen similar to Figure 10.2.

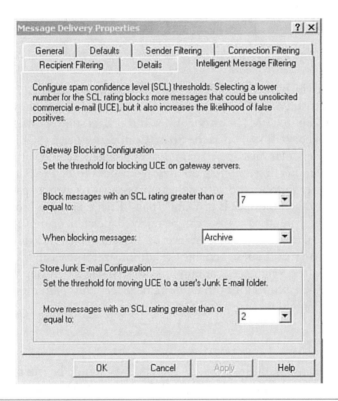

Figure 10.2 Intelligent Message Filtering tab.

The IMF default values need to be changed because the software ships with values that won't work correctly in a production environment. There are two thresholds, which can be set within the IMF configuration. The first is at the server level and is located at the top of the IMF screen, titled Gateway Blocking Configuration. The second is at the bottom of the IMF setup tab and is called Store Junk Email Configuration; it is processed when the message enters a user's email box.

After the configuration has been set up via the IMF screen, the filter must then be made active, which is covered in the *Enabling IMF* section of this chapter.

Gateway Blocking Configuration

When a message is presented to the Exchange server by a remote MTA, the Gateway Blocking Configuration defines what the IMF system will do with the message after it is scored. The field named Block Messages with an SCL Rating Greater Than or Equal To: specifies the score to match or exceed. We suggest setting this value to 8 initially and adjusting it as necessary. If an SCL of a message is at or above this score, the action on the message can be one of the following:

Archive

Delete

No Action

Reject

Archive causes the messages to be filed in the UceArchive folder (see the "UceArchive" section later). The Delete action causes the message to be accepted by the server and then deleted. This setting should be used with caution, as messages are irretrievably lost when this option is selected. The No Action setting allows you to see how the IMF system would score messages without causing anything to happen to them. This setting is good for the paranoid administrator who would like to see how IMF scores messages before implementing IMF on real clients.

Finally, the Reject setting causes the server to reject the message back to the originating MTA when the SCL score meets the criteria. Like the Delete setting, this action should be used with caution because messages are essentially lost when the Reject action is performed.

Store Junk E-mail Configuration

The Store Junk E-mail Configuration setting is what IMF should do with messages as they are being delivered into the recipient's email box. This score defines the threshold at which messages should be delivered into a user's junk email folder rather than his or her inbox. The field is called Move Messages with an SCL Rating Greater Than or Equal To, and a good value to start off with is 4. If you are afraid your users will not go into their junk email boxes to view false positives, then set this value to a higher number. However, more spam will likely end up in your user's inbox.

Enabling IMF

After configuring the IMF values, you must activate filtering. This is accomplished by going to the following click chain: *root*==>servers==>*name of server*==>SMTP==> Intelligent Message Filtering==>*(right-click)*==>properties, which should bring up a screen similar to the one shown in Figure 10.3.

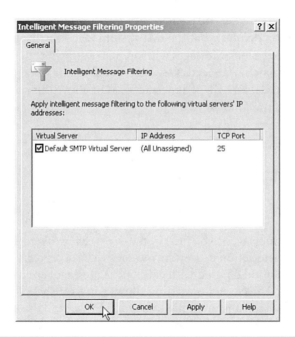

Figure 10.3 Enabling IMF.

Click the Default SMTP Virtual Server checkbox and click the OK button. Your server is now running with IMF enabled.

ONGOING MAINTENANCE

A couple of ongoing tasks need to be performed. One task is viewing the UceArchive folder, and another is viewing the performance statistics of the IMF system.

UceArchive

When the Gateway Blocking Configuration item called When Blocking Messages is set to Archive, messages above the SCL are placed in a folder called UceArchive. The administrator should view this folder periodically to be sure that no legitimate email messages have slipped past the filters.

Unfortunately, Microsoft doesn't provide an easy way to view message scores. Appendix G contains a link to a program called IMF Archive Manager, which enables the administrator to easily view messages in the UceArchive along with their scores.

The UceArchive folder can be viewed by viewing the following directory path: *drive letter*:\Program Files\Exchsrvr\Mailroot\vsi 1\UceArchive. In the UceArchive folder, each message that has been archived is saved as an email message. A message is viewed by double-clicking on it, which should bring up Outlook so that the message can be forwarded if necessary.

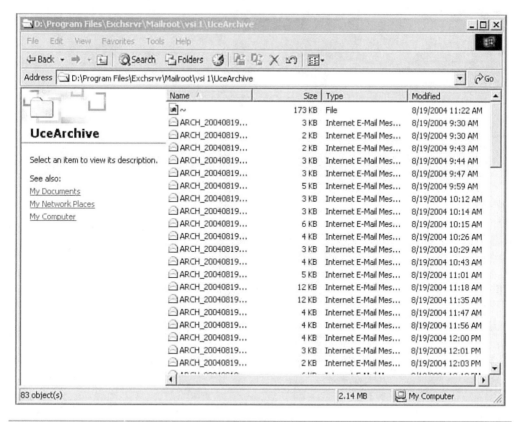

Figure 10.4 UceArchive folder.

Be sure to delete the confirmed spam messages on a regular basis to prevent your disk from filling up.

Performance Data

If you would like to view statistics on how IMF is running, the IMF utility includes data for the built-in Windows performance monitor. To view IMF data, bring up the Windows monitor by clicking on the following path: Start==>Programs==>Administrative Tools==>Performance. When on the Performance screen, click the + (add) button in the toolbar. On the Add Counters screen, make sure the All Counters and All Instances radio buttons are active, and select MSExchange Intelligent Message Filter in the Performance Object drop-down box. Then click the Add button and the Close button. The real-time display of all of the performance variables related to IMF should start, similar to Figure 10.5.

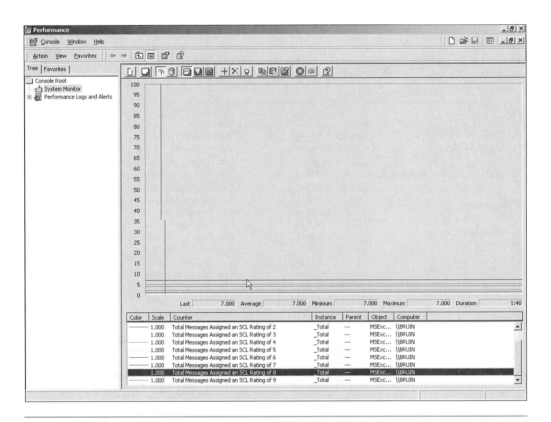

Figure 10.5 IMF performance monitoring.

This is useful for determining how busy your server is and for troubleshooting problems. The individual performance characteristics or variables can be selected as needed.

INCOMING MESSAGE FILTERING

Message/connection filtering on the inbound side is controlled by going to this window: `Global Settings==>Message Delivery` *(right-click)*`==>Properties`. Please note that to activate any of the filtering options on this page, the respective filter must be applied under the Default SMTP Virtual Server. See the section "Activating Filtering" in order to accomplish this.

CONNECTION FILTERING

Connection filtering enables the administrator to control what servers are allowed to connect to an Exchange mail server. To view the connection filtering control page, go to the following Connection Filtering tab. The Connection Filtering pane that comes up is shown in Figure 10.6.

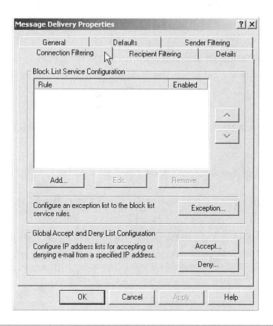

Figure 10.6 Connection Filtering.

Exchange makes the following functions available in the Connection Filtering pane:

- Block list service configuration
- Exception to block list
- Global Accept list
- Global Deny list

Microsoft's term for blackhole listing service (BLS) is "block list." As you may recall from Chapter 4, "Native MTA Anti-Spam Features," blackhole listing services are DNS-based systems that list IP addresses of known sources of spam. The exception lists enable the administrator to allow connections from certain IP addresses that have made their way onto a DNS blacklist. The Global Accept/Deny lists are static whitelists and blacklists, respectively. (See Chapter 4 for more information on whitelists/blacklists.) These lists enable the administrator to always enable connections from good servers (accept/whitelists) and block connections from bad servers (deny/blacklists).

Block List Service Definition

In order to activate BLS lookup in the Exchange server, go to the Connection Filtering tab and click on the Add button. A window titled Message Delivery Properties is displayed (see Figure 10.7), which allows you to enter the following information:

- **Display Name**—The name of the BLS filter
- **DNS suffix of provider**—The DNS name for the BLS used
- **Custom error message**—An optional SMTP error message

If no custom error message is defined, and the name of the BLS filter is Demo Blacklist, then the code returned by the server is

```
550 5.7.1 ip address has been blocked by Demo Blacklist
```

Exceptions to the block list can be made by clicking on the button marked Exception... and entering the IP address that should be allowed to connect to your server, even if it is listed on one or more of the block lists. Besides changing the name of the list (in our example, Demo Blacklist), there is no other way to modify the message that Exchange outputs.

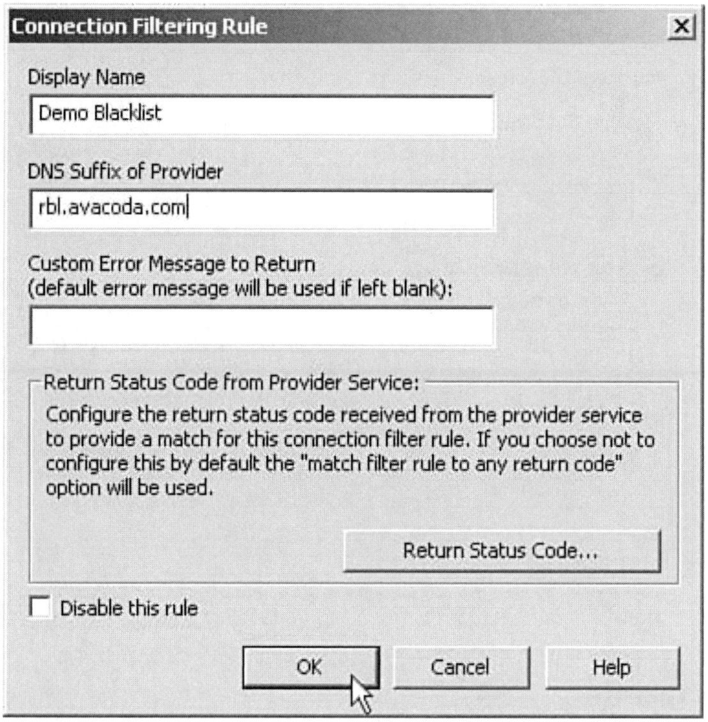

Figure 10.7 Message Delivery Properties.

Global Accept/Deny

The Global Accept/Deny lists are a way to whitelist or blacklist connections from certain IP addresses. Clicking on the appropriate button accesses these lists, which show you the existing lists of IP addresses and networks that are allowed or disallowed.

By pressing the Add button on this page, a new IP address or network can be added to the appropriate list. Figure 10.8 shows an example of a network (the entire 192.168 network) being added to the deny list. In this case, spam generated by an internal 192.168 network is rejected by the Exchange Server.

When a machine on the deny list attempts to connect to the server, it receives the following SMTP message:

```
550 5.7.0 Access Denied
```

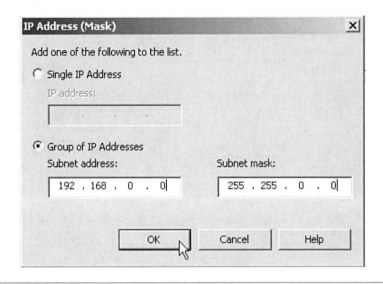

Figure 10.8 Deny List IP entry.

SENDER FILTERING

Sender filtering enables the administrator to control what senders can send messages to this server. The Sender Filtering tab is shown in Figure 10.9.

The top half of the window lists the senders who are blocked. There are three buttons on this page:

- **Add**—Adds a sender to the list
- **Edit**—Enables editing of an existing filter
- **Remove**—Deletes the highlighted filter

To add a sender to the list, click on the Add button and type in the email address of the sender you want to block. An asterisk (*) can be used to indicate that all users in that domain should be blocked.

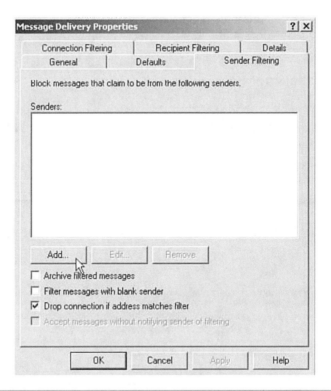

Figure 10.9 Sender Filtering tab.

The checkboxes on this page are

- **Archive Filtered Messages**—This setting causes Exchange to archive messages that are filtered. The messages can be viewed by looking in the `<root>\Exchsrvr\Mailroot\vsi #\Filter` directory, where `vsi #` is the SMTP virtual server and is usually 1.
- **Filter Messages with Blank Sender**—This causes messages that contain an envelope From: of <> to be automatically filtered at the time the message is offered from the remote SMTP server. This can be useful for blocking some types of spam, but it may block legitimate messages as well.
- **Drop Connection if Address Matches Filter**—Checking this box causes Exchange to drop the connection immediately rather than simply letting it time out. The benefit of dropping the connection (rather than allowing the message to be delivered) is that disallowing the session uses fewer resources on your Exchange server.

Don't forget to activate these filters after they are created. Otherwise, the filters won't block potential spammers! Enabling filters is covered in the section "Activating Filters."

RECIPIENT FILTERING

Recipient filtering enables the administrator to control which recipients can receive email. This might be used to block spam messages sent to old unused email accounts, for example. The Recipient Filtering screen is shown in Figure 10.10.

The top half of the window lists the addresses that are filtered. The checkbox labeled Filter Recipients Who Are Not in the Directory enables the administrator to globally filter email for recipients whose accounts have been deleted or that never existed in the first place.

As with the other options, don't forget to activate these filters. This topic is covered in the next section.

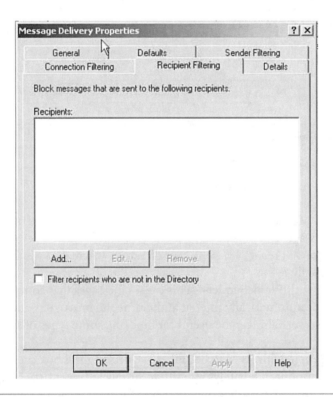

Figure 10.10 Recipient Filtering.

ACTIVATING FILTERS

In order to activate the filters that you have defined, an additional setup step is required. From the main Exchange screen, navigate to Servers==>*server name*==>Protocols ==>SMTP==>Default SMTP Virtual Server *(right-click)*==>Properties==>General tab==>Advanced, which brings up a screen titled Default SMTP Virtual Server Properties.

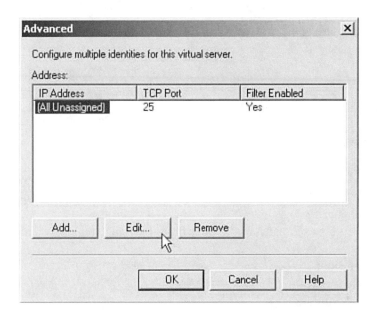

Figure 10.11 Default SMTP Virtual Server Properties.

The top portion of this screen lists the defined filters. The buttons are as follows:

- **Add**—Adds a new ruleset for the given server.
- **Edit**—Edits the selected ruleset.
- **Remove**—Deletes the selected ruleset.

There should be one listed port by default, namely 25. Highlight the preexisting ruleset and click the Edit button, which should display a window similar to Figure 10.12.

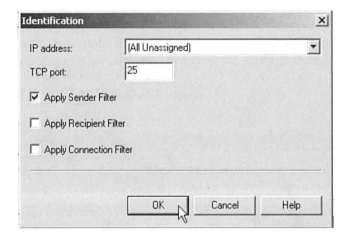

Figure 10.12 Apply Sender Filter.

The line labeled IP Address: should be left as the default, unless you have a special configuration. TCP Port: should be left as 25, unless you have Exchange listening on a nonstandard SMTP port.

There are checkboxes for each of the filter types Exchange makes available:

- Apply Sender Filter
- Apply Recipient Filter
- Apply Connection Filter

Make sure that each checkbox is activated for each filter you want to activate. After saving your changes, your filters have been enabled.

LOGS

Exchange logs are available by default in *root*\Exchsrvr*host*.log. Inspecting the log file is useful to help troubleshoot filtering or other setup issues. It also will tell you what messages are being rejected or blocked that you otherwise might not find out about.

By default, Exchange does not log the DNS name of hosts that connect to it. In order to turn this functionality on, click on the Perform DNS Lookup on Incoming Messages checkbox available from the following path: Servers==>*server name*==>Protocols ==>SMTP==>Default SMTP Virtual Server *(right-click)*==>Properties==>Delivery tab==>Advanced.

Enabling DNS lookups will make reading the logs and troubleshooting easier, although there is a small performance penalty when performing DNS lookups (see Figure 10.13).

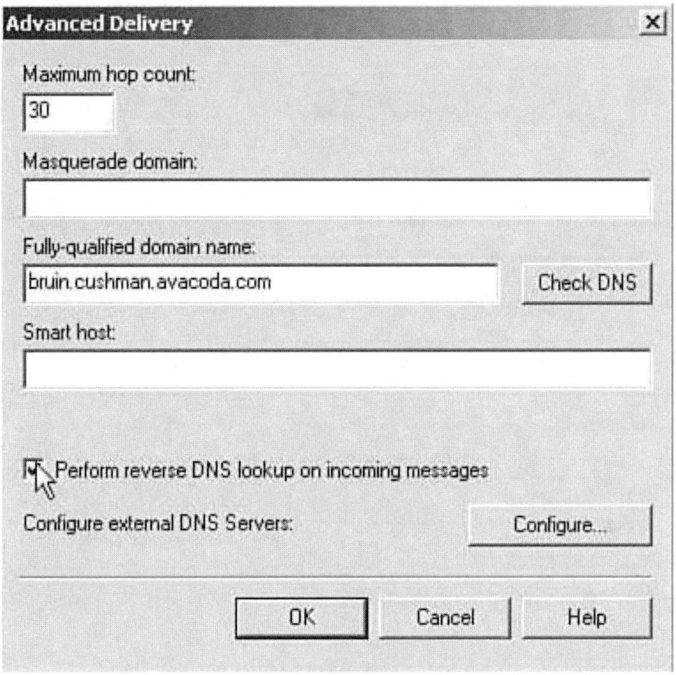

Figure 10.13 Enabling DNS lookups on incoming messages.

OUTBOUND MESSAGE CONTROL

This section covers the parts of Exchange that manage sending messages. The topics covered here include

- Access Control
- Connection Control
- Relay Restrictions

The main screen can be accessed by navigating the following path: `Servers==>server name==>Protocols==>SMTP==>Default SMTP Virtual Server (right-click)==> Properties==>Access` tab. This screen is shown in Figure 10.14.

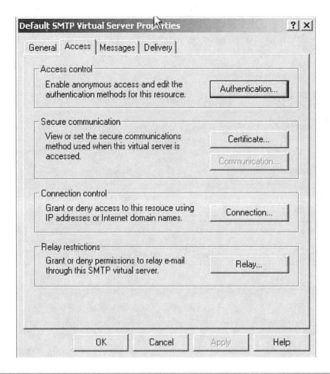

Figure 10.14 Access tab.

The options available on the Access tab are as follows:

- **Access Control**—Controls what methods must be used to access the Exchange SMTP server
- **Secure Communications**—Defines certificates for encrypted communications between the client and Exchange server
- **Connection Control**—Controls which IP/networks can access the server
- **Relay Restrictions**—Controls which IP/networks can send email through the server for recipients not located on this machine

Access Control

This screen controls what Exchange requires in the way of SMTP AUTH, TLS, and other related security settings. (Refer to Chapter 5, "SMTP AUTH and STARTTLS," for more information on the topics presented in this section.) Clicking on the Authentication... button on the Access tab (shown in Figure 10.14) brings up a window titled Authentication (see Figure 10.15).

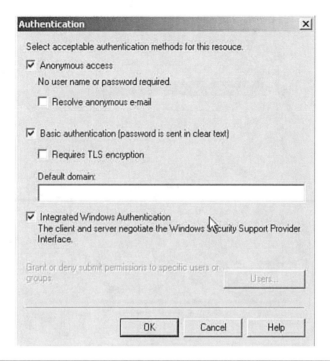

Figure 10.15 Authentication panel.

Within the Authentication window, you have the following options:

- **Anonymous Access**—Enables anyone to connect to the Exchange SMTP server to send messages out; unchecking it will cause Exchange to use the SMTP AUTH sending mechanism. Unchecking this box enables the Users button to be available.
- **Resolve Anonymous E-mail**—Displays email addresses from Exchange email to name mappings. This feature typically shouldn't be enabled, as this would make it possible for unauthorized users to send email messages with the forged address of a legitimate user (also known as spoofing).
- **Basic Authentication**—Permits SMTP AUTH for connections.
- **Requires TLS Encryption**—Requires TLS encryption for connections.
- **Integrated Windows Authentication**—Checking this box requires all users to have valid MS Windows user accounts.
- **Users button**—Clicking this button brings up a screen titled Permissions for Submit and Relay similar to Figure 10.16.

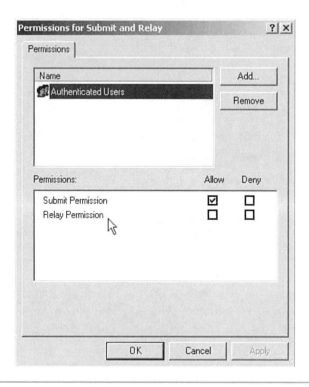

Figure 10.16 Permissions for Submit and Relay.

This screen has two parts. The upper part allows the administrator to list classes of users; the lower part enables the administrator to specify Submit and Relay permissions for each class of users.

Secure Communication

The Secure Communication section is for managing certificates. Clicking on the Certificate... button brings up the Welcome to the Web Server Certificate Wizard. The Communication... button enables TLS (Transport Layer Security) encryption after a certificate has been installed on the server.

Connection Control

This section enables IP addresses that are allowed to connect to the SMTP server. Pressing Connection... on the Access screen shown in Figure 10.14 brings up a window similar to Figure 10.17.

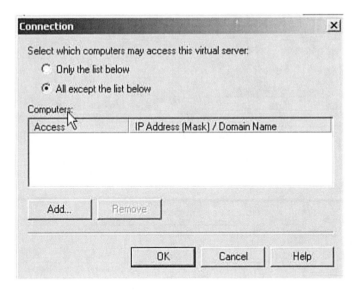

Figure 10.17 Connection panel.

The radio buttons marked Only the List Below and All Except the List Below control whether the IP addresses input are added to the Granted or Denied lists, respectively. After selecting the list via the radio button, pressing the Add... button brings up a screen titled Computer similar to Figure 10.18.

This screen allows the administrator to add IP addresses of the following types:

- Single Computer
- Networks (labeled as `Group of computers` on this screen)
- Domain

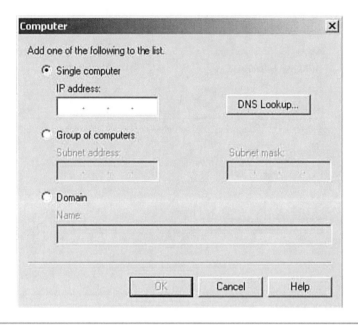

Figure 10.18 Adding IP address restrictions.

Relay Restrictions

This section defines IP addresses that are allowed to send messages to domains outside the one(s) Exchange is hosting. The screens for Relay Restrictions work very similarly to the Connection Control restrictions, as outlined in that section. The Relay Restrictions button is shown at the bottom of Figure 10.14.

The checkbox marked Allow All Computers Which Successfully Authenticate To Relay is checked by default. Unchecking this box causes the Users button to be made available. Pressing this button brings up the screen titled Permissions for Submit and Relay, which is outlined in the Users button in the earlier section, "Access Control."

MCAFEE SPAMKILLER FOR EXCHANGE

McAfee SpamKiller for Exchange 2.1.1 is the second generation of the product originally based upon the SpamAssassin open source software. The biggest change from the first iteration is the addition of a policy framework in managing rulesets. This functionality allows the mail administrator to control objectionable content as it enters the mail server.

Policy groups, as they are known, can be applied at the following levels:

- Global
- Geographic area
- Business function
- Domain
- Department
- Mailbox

An administrator could easily apply a policy to all users by activating it at the global level, or to particular email groups by virtue of the policy group framework. Some of the ruleset types that can be utilized with SpamKiller for Exchange include

- Content and headers
- Existence (and size) of attachments
- Types of files attached (for example, `.jpg`)
- Source/destination email addresses

Unfortunately, the current version of SpamKiller for Exchange does not support distributed collaborative filter checks against such services as DCC and Razor. (See Chapter 6, "Distributed Checksum Filtering," for more information on DCC and Razor.) SpamKiller for Exchange does contain embedded Bayesian-style statistical analysis, although it doesn't give the administrator control over settings, nor does it allow "training" of the Bayesian filters as SpamAssassin does. Also, SpamKiller for Exchange 2.1.1 does not allow direct manipulation of the anti-spam rules and policies, although it is possible to do this with advanced knowledge. McAfee, Inc. does not recommend making changes to the anti-spam rulesets, though.

It is interesting to note that SpamKiller only analyzes messages that are less than 250K bytes (by default) in size. The assumption the developers make is that spammers' messages are always small in size. McAfee allows the administrator to adjust the scanned message size, so if spammers adjust their tactics, the administrator can adjust the message scan size threshold accordingly. Although McAfee SpamKiller for Exchange covers a wide range of email filtering capabilities, we only cover the SpamKiller functionality as it directly relates to the fight against spam.

INSTALLATION

Installation is provided through a self-install executable as part of the zip file. In most cases, the optional components `Alert Manager 4.7` and `User Level Black and White List Server` should be selected. These provide additional functionality that is useful in certain configurations. The alert manager enables SNMP, email, and other types of notifications on SpamKiller events. The Black/Whitelist server is a nice hierarchical blacklist/whitelist manager, enabling the administrator to have some degree of control over what users put in their whitelists/blacklists.

The installer places two items in the program menu item for SpamKiller. One is Spam-Killer itself (identified as `McAfee SpamKiller`), and the other is `McAfee SpamKiller Access Control`. The access control link simply brings up the MS Access Control page for the SpamKiller program itself. This can be used to control which users on the Exchange server are allowed to run the SpamKiller application. The defaults should be good for most people. Larger enterprises will want to adjust the controls for administrative accounts according to their security policies.

USING SPAMKILLER

To run SpamKiller for Exchange, go to `Start==>Programs==>Network Associates==> McAfee SpamKiller`, which brings up the main administrative screen (see Figure 10.19).

This screen provides the main access to all SpamKiller functions. Under the View heading, the options are as follows:

- **Detected Items**—Shows a log of all messages flagged by SpamKiller as spam and their disposition
- **Scheduled Tasks**—Enables the administrator to schedule routine maintenance and other types of tasks
- **Product Log**—Presents a log of all application events, useful for troubleshooting

Under the Schedule heading, choices are as follows:

- **Product Update**—Enables the administrator to have SpamKiller automatically download and install updates to the software
- **Status Report**—Allows the administrator to automatically send email updates of the status of spam and other unwanted messages.

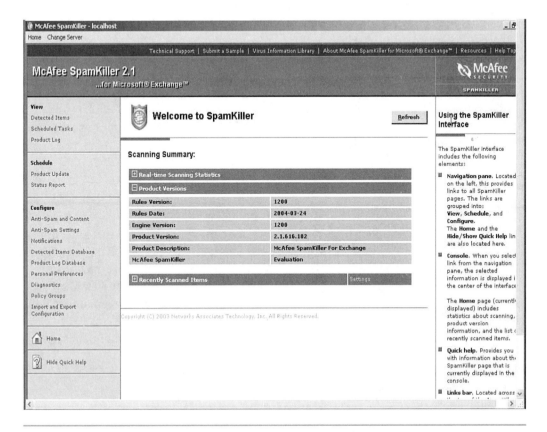

Figure 10.19 McAfee SpamKiller for Exchange main screen.

Most of the often-used options are under the Configure menu, which are as follows:

- **Anti-Spam and Content**—Enables the administrator to manage policies, rules, and rule groups
- **Anti-Spam Settings**—Contains system-wide settings such as blacklists, junk mail folders, and related settings
- **Notifications**—Allows the administrator to define the format of SpamKiller system notification messages for detected spam
- **Detected Items Database**—Enables the administrator to define settings for the detected items database
- **Product Log Database**—Contains administrator settings for defining what is logged, how long log messages are kept, etc.

- **Personal Preferences**—Includes settings for changing how SpamKiller displays various pieces of the application itself
- **Diagnostics**—Allows the administrator to set logging preferences and other trouble-shooting parameters
- **Policy Groups**—Enables an administrator to set up policy groups for arbitrary groups of users (departments, functions, etc.)
- **Import and Export Configuration**—Facilitates the moving of configurations from one SpamKiller server to another

ANTI-SPAM SETUP

Although McAfee gives you the ability to create policies under separate policy groups, we cover the default Global policy here. A separate anti-spam policy other than Global might be useful in certain cases where messages inadvertently caught by the Global policy could be allowed through by setting a separate policy for a certain sub group of email boxes.

To bring up the anti-spam configuration screen, click on Anti-Spam and Content under Configuration on the left side of the screen. On the subsequent screen, under Policies, make sure Global is highlighted and right-click on it.

Select Anti-Spam, right-click on it, and select Edit Settings, which brings up a screen similar to Figure 10.20.

The fields on the screen are as follows:

- **Enable Anti-Spam Scanning**—Enables/Disables anti-spam scanning for this policy (default is on).
- **Properties Summary**—This part of the screen has three areas, from top to bottom:
  - Three separate actions, for three ranges of scores
  - Blacklists/whitelist management
  - Disable rules

  More on this option is presented in the respective sections later.
- **Spam Reporting Threshold Is**—This can be one of High, Medium, Low, and Custom, which represent the following score thresholds from the spam scoring engine:

High	15
Medium	10
Low	5
Custom	Specified by the administrator

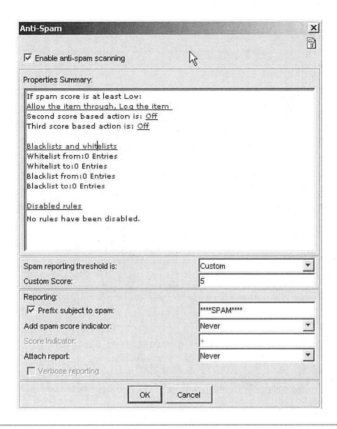

Figure 10.20 Anti-Spam configuration panel.

- **Prefix Subject to Spam**—Enables/disables the listed prefix on subject lines for spam messages identified by McAfee SpamKiller. Defaults to Enabled, with a subject prefix of ****SPAM****.
- **Add Spam Score Indicator**—Controls whether the spam score header is added to messages. Useful for certain email clients for helping the client determine how certain the spam designation is.
- **Score Indicator**—The character used by the spam score indicator header; defaults to ±.
- **Attach Report**—Enables the display of the exact rules that were triggered in the spam processing engine; defaults to off.

  Here is an example of the report that is added when Attach Report is enabled, showing the tests that were triggered and the scores:

```
X-NAI-Spam-Flag: YES
X-NAI-Spam-Level:
+++++++++++++++++++++++++++++++++++++++++++++++++++++++++++++++++++++++++
X-NAI-Spam-Score: 997.6
X-NAI-Spam-Threshold: 5
X-NAI-Spam-Rules: 3 Rules triggered
      GTUBE=1000, BAYES_00=-4.9, DATE_IN_PAST_96_XX=2.5
X-NAI-Spam-Checker-Version: NAI SpamAssassin 1.2 (core version 2.70
date 20031104 serial 1200)
```

- **Verbose Reporting**—Displays more information in the spam report.
  Here is an example of the headers added with Verbose Reporting turned on, which, in
  addition to the Attach Report headers, gives additional information regarding the rules
  that were triggered:

```
X-NAI-Spam-Flag: YES
X-NAI-Spam-Level:
+++++++++++++++++++++++++++++++++++++++++++++++++++++++++++++++++++++++++++++
X-NAI-Spam-Score: 997.6
X-NAI-Spam-Threshold: 5
X-NAI-Spam-Report: 3 Rules triggered
     *  1000 -- GTUBE -- Generic Test for Unsolicited Bulk Email
     *  -4.9 -- BAYES_00 -- Bayesian spam probability is 0 to 1%
     *  2.5 -- DATE_IN_PAST_96_XX -- Date: is 96 hours or more before Received: date
X-NAI-Spam-Checker-Version: NAI SpamAssassin 1.2 (core version 2.70
date 20031104 serial 1200)
```

Actions

As we mentioned earlier, this is the first part of the Properties Summary section of the
Anti-Spam window (refer to Figure 10.20). This section specifies what course to take
when SpamKiller encounters a potential spam message. Up to three actions can be specified by the administrator per policy. Enabling an action results in a small window appearing and asking for the following bits of information:

- **When the Score Is At Least**—When not checked, this will result in the action being dis-
  played as Off at the previous screen. If enabled, can be High, Medium, Low, or Custom.
- **Take the Following Action**—Can be set to the following dispositions:
  - Allow the item through—Processes message but tags it as defined in previous
    screen; this is the default.
  - Route to system junk folder—Message goes to server junk email folder.
  - Route to user junk folder—Message is placed in the user's email client junk folder.

- Reject—SpamKiller does not accept the message for further processing.
- Delete— SpamKiller automatically deletes message; use with caution, as any message deleted in error is non-recoverable.
- **And Also**—Three additional actions can be taken:
  - Log the item—Logs item for later inspection by administrator.
  - Quarantine the item—Places the message into the quarantine folder.
  - Notify Administrator—Sends an email message to the administrator. This should not be used under normal production, as this will quickly fill the administrator mailbox on a busy server.

Blacklists and Whitelists

The second area in the Properties Summary section of the Anti-Spam window is the blacklist and whitelist area. This area allows you to manage blacklists and whitelists. McAfee SpamKiller also gives the administrator the ability to import or export lists using this mechanism.

Disabled Rules

This is the third area of the Properties Summary section. Any of the rules that SpamKiller provides can be disabled here. Simply select the rules that conflict with the organization's business, and they will not be run under the selected policy.

ANTI-SPAM SETTINGS

System-wide anti-spam configuration information is stored on the Anti-Spam Settings screen, available from the left menu under configuration (see Figure 10.21).

This screen has several options that must be modified if the administrator plans on forwarding email to system or user junk email folders or to use the McAfee user-level whitelist/blacklist client add-on software.

- **System Junk Folder Address**—The Exchange mailbox to receive messages routed to the system junk email folder. This must be changed from its default, `junkmail@example.org`, if the administrator wants to route messages there.
- **User Junk Folder Routing**—In order to move messages into user junk email boxes, this option must be changed from disabled (the default) to enabled.
- **Enable User-Level Blacklist/Whitelists On This Server**—To use the additional client software for managing user whitelists/blacklists, this option must be enabled. The default is disabled.

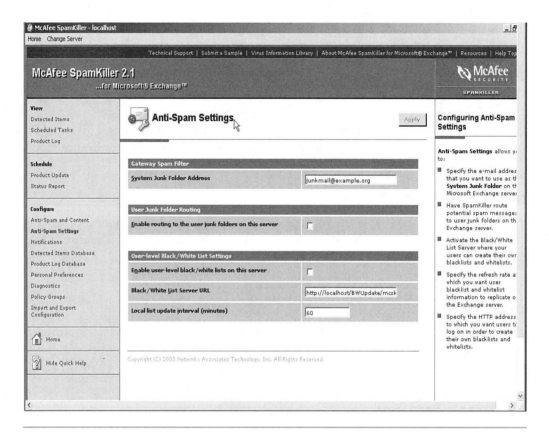

Figure 10.21 Anti-Spam Settings.

- **Black/Whitelist Server URL**—Specifies the URL for updating client whitelists/blacklists.
- **Local List Update Interval**—The number of minutes between client checks for whitelist/blacklist updates.

CONCLUSION

Microsoft Exchange contains many of the usual anti-spam features found in most modern mail transfer agents. Microsoft Research has developed a plugin called Intelligent Message Filter, which appears to work like a Bayesian-style classifier, although without the capability for user training of the filter. Exchange has many traditional anti-spam-related features, including blackhole listing service blocking, filtering, and whitelists/

blacklists. Microsoft Exchange can be set up as an outbound mail relay with SMTP AUTH/STARTTLS. For many organizations, the anti-spam features in Microsoft Exchange might need to be augmented.

In order to improve Microsoft Exchange's ability to handle spam, we covered McAfee SpamKiller for Exchange 2.1.1. This software integrates directly into Exchange and provides a number of spam-stopping features, including message scoring, Bayesian analysis, and administrator-controlled user-level white lists.

Lotus Domino and Lotus Notes

Lotus Domino is an enterprise-level mail server (and more) that runs on Microsoft and Unix operating systems. Domino contains many server functions, including SMTP, POP3/IMAP, web, and instant messaging, among others. Lotus Notes is an email client that is often used to access a Domino server, though in theory it can be set up to access any POP3-compliant server. In this chapter, we cover the basic anti-spam capabilities incorporated into the server and client level as they are shipped in version 6.5.1. Domino has a very easy-to-manage filtering capability at the server level, which is rare among the MTAs that are available today.

In addition to the basic coverage in Lotus, we also cover McAfee SpamKiller for Lotus 2.1. SpamKiller (SK) enables a higher degree of anti-spam filtering for those organizations that don't want to deploy a separate spam filtering mechanism outside of Lotus (see Chapter 1, "Introduction"). SK is based upon SpamAssassin, although with less control than the native open source version. SpamKiller also has software that runs at the client machine (with Notes) that enables specialized whitelisting/blacklisting. Although Notes has native whitelisting/blacklisting, the SK client software allows a hierarchical approach to whitelisting/blacklisting. For example, a whitelisted domain on the administrator-specified list would override a domain a particular user might have on his or her blacklist.

Finally, configuring Domino for SMTP AUTH and STARTTLS support is covered. These protocols can be used to control relaying through Domino by requiring a user-name/password and SSL encryption between the server and Notes client. More information on these topics can be found in Chapter 5, "SMTP AUTH and STARTTLS."

LOTUS DOMINO

Lotus Domino has the anti-spam controls you would expect to see in a modern commercial MTA. These controls include

- Relaying
- Whitelisting/blacklisting
- Filtering
- DNS Blackhole Listing

Relaying controls include the ability to specify users who are allowed to relay messages through the server and STARTTLS and SMTP AUTH support. Server-level whitelists and blacklists are available on both the SMTP inbound and outbound side on both sender and recipient, enabling very fine-grained control of email flow. In an unusual feature for an email server, Domino has easy filtering at the server level, making it much easier to enforce policies that an organization might have regarding email. For more information on the underlying topics presented in this chapter, please see Chapters 4 and 5.

GETTING STARTED

The Lotus Domino anti-spam configuration parameters are contained in the following location: *domain (in our case, AVACODA)*`==>Server==>Configurations==>Edit configuration==>Router/SMTP==>Restrictions and Controls`. The Restrictions and Controls screen contains the following two tabs, which are covered here:

- **SMTP Inbound Controls**—Includes the following areas on the incoming message:
  - Relay controls
  - Enabling blackhole listing services (Domino calls them DNS Blacklist Filters)
  - Connection controls
  - Sender controls
  - Recipient controls
- **Rules**—Enables messages to be filtered at the server level.

SMTP INBOUND CONTROLS

The following areas control inbound mail SMTP connections to Lotus Domino. Each tab is covered in the section with the corresponding name.

Inbound Relay Controls

Inbound Relay Controls gives the administrator the ability to control incoming SMTP messages that are not destined for users on this system (see Figure 11.1). These relay controls are identified as follows:

- **Allow Messages To Be Sent Only to the Following External Internet Domains**—Whitelisted domains.
- **Deny Messages To Be Sent to the Following External Internet Domains**—Blacklisted domains.
- **Allow Messages Only from the Following Internet Hosts To Be Sent to External Internet Domains**—Whitelisted hosts.
- **Deny Messages from the Following Internet Hosts To Be Sent to External Internet Domains**—Blacklisted hosts.

In the case of blacklists, an asterisk (*) can be entered to indicate all hosts should be blocked. Domains beginning with @ indicate an exact domain match, and no @ indicates a match on the end of the domain—for example:

@spamalot.com would match spammer@spamalot.com but not spammer@ham.spamalot.com

spamalot.com would match spammer@spamalot.com and spammer@ham.spamalot.com.

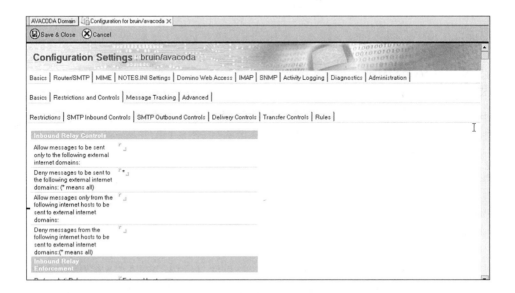

Figure 11.1 SMTP Inbound Relay Controls.

Inbound Relay Enforcement

This subsection specifies the parameters for the connections that are allowed to relay mail. Under the Inbound Relay Enforcement subsection, the following options are available:

- **Perform Anti-Relay Enforcement for These Connecting Hosts**—Define what connections are processed through anti-relay checks. There are three options for this setting:
  - External Hosts (default)—Hosts that fall outside the local domain (as defined by the Global Domain document or the domain of the server).
  - All Hosts—Any connecting host must go through anti-spam checks.
  - None—All hosts can relay. This setting should be used with extreme care, as it makes the server an "open relay," which anyone can use to send email without appropriate checks.
- **Exclude These Connecting Hosts from Anti-Relay Checks**—Hosts listed here are allowed to skip anti-relay checks. Hosts can be listed as names or IP addresses. If IP addresses are listed, they must be entered in square brackets, and * can be used to indicate an entire subnet. For example, entering `192.168.0.*` here would exclude addresses from 192.168.0.1 to 192.168.0.255.
- **Exceptions for Authenticated Users**—Domino POP3 or IMAP users who have authenticated can be allowed to relay email. Options are as follows:
  - Perform anti-relay checks for authenticated users—The server does not allow exceptions for authenticated users.
  - Allow all authenticated users to relay—Any authenticated user is allowed to relay email without checks.

DNS Blacklist Filters

Domino allows the administrator to enable what we call blackhole listing service (BLS) lookups on incoming connections. (More information on this topic is presented in Chapter 4). Be careful when selecting blackhole listing services, as selecting an overly restrictive service will result in false positives.

- **DNS Blacklist Filters**—When set to Enabled, additional settings (next) appear.
- **DNS Blacklist Sites**—Enter names of the BLS sites to check (see Chapter 4).
- **Desired Action When a Connecting Host Is Found in a DNS Blacklist**—Function to perform when a connection matches a host on the BLS site:
  - Log Only—The message is accepted, and Domino logs the hostname and IP address of the server along with the name of the BLS list it came from. For example:

```
05/30/2004 07:37:37 PM SMTP Server: Remote host 192.168.16.7
(bonzo.cushman.avacoda.com) found in DNS blacklist at rbl.avacoda.com
```

- Log and Tag Message—Logs message (as previous) and adds the Note item, $DNS-BLSite, which enables the administrator to custom route messages that are from sites listed in the BLS.

- Log and Reject Message—Logs message (as previous) and rejects message with the following message (by default):

```
554 Connection from ip addr rejected for policy reasons. Host found in DNS blacklist at list name
```

- **Custom SMTP Error Response for Rejected Messages**—If desired, the administrator can specify a custom message when rejecting messages for matching a host on the BLS. The first %s is replaced with the IP address of the blocked host and the second %s with the name of the BLS-listed host.

Inbound Connection Controls

Inbound connection controls enable the administrator to manage connections to the server (see Figure 11.2). By controlling what SMTP connections are processed by the server, the system can filter mail at the earliest point possible.

The settings here include:

- **Verify Connecting Hostname in DNS**—Enabling this setting causes the server to perform reverse DNS lookups on all incoming connections and verify that they exist. This process consumes additional resources on the server and may cause legitimate email to be blocked.
- **Allow Connections Only from the Following SMTP Internet Hostnames/IP Addresses**—This creates a whitelist at the server inbound connection level, severely restricting what servers are allowed to send mail to this Lotus Domino machine. This might be useful if the Domino machine was strictly a mailbox server, and another machine was the email relay to the Internet.
- **Deny Connections from the Following SMTP Internet Hostnames/IP Addresses**—Inputting IP addresses here creates a blacklist, which blocks SMTP connections from the listed machines.

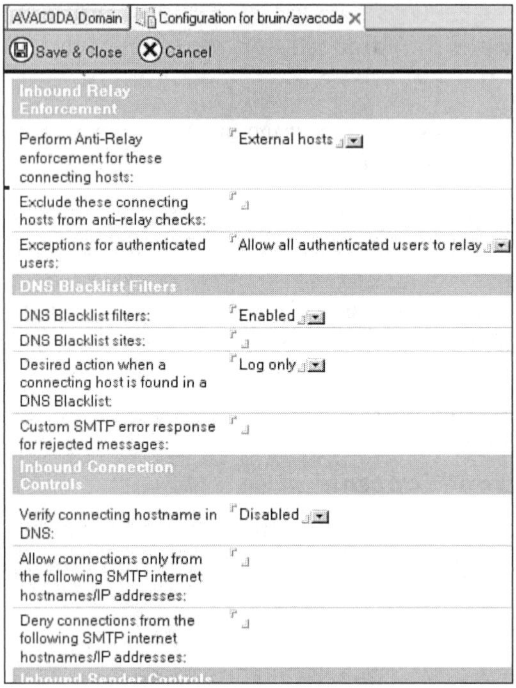

Figure 11.2 Inbound Relay Enforcement, DNS Blacklist Filters, and Inbound Connection controls.

Inbound Sender Controls

These settings are identical to the Inbound Connection Controls, except that they occur at a higher level in the process. Instead of being enforced at the connection level, the controls are checked after the connection has been established on the envelope (header) part of the message.

Inbound Intended Recipient Controls

The intended recipient controls are similar to the inbound sender/connection controls, except that they happen on the recipient envelope part of the message (see Figure 11.3). The controls are as follows:

- **Verify Local Domain Recipients Exist in the Domino Directory**—The message will only be delivered if the recipient exists as a Domino user.

- **Allow Messages Intended Only for the Following Internet Addresses**—This will create a recipient whitelist, forcing every Domino user who wishes to receive email to be on this list.
- **Deny Messages Intended Only for the Following Internet Addresses**—Placing an email address will create a recipient blacklist, blocking messages destined for the recipients listed here.

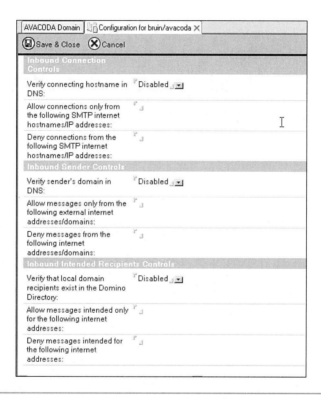

Figure 11.3 Inbound Connection Controls, Inbound Sender Controls, and Inbound Intended Recipient Controls.

RULES

Lotus Domino gives the administrator the ability to filter at the server level. This is something that is relatively unique to Domino, as most MTAs only have rudimentary (if any) filtering at this point in the mail transfer process. If the capability even exists to filter in other MTAs, filtering is usually more difficult to set up and configure on other platforms when compared to Domino.

After clicking on the Rules tab (from the Restrictions and Controls tab), a two-part screen comes up that is similar to Figure 11.4. Fields that can be filtered on include the following:

Sender	Body or Subject
Subject	Internet Domain
Body	Size (in bytes)
Importance	All Documents
Delivery Priority	Any Attachment Name
To	Number of Attachments
CC	Form
BCC	Recipient Count
To or CC	Any Recipient

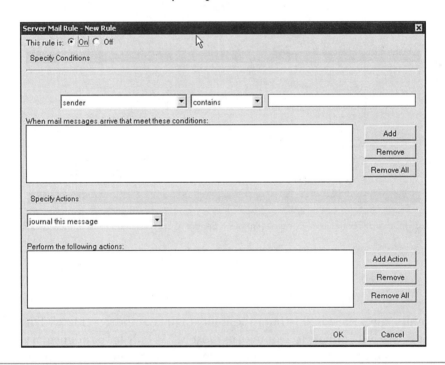

Figure 11.4 Blocked sender list.

Note there is no way to add arbitrary fields to filter upon. As a result, the anti-spam tool must use the subject modification method in order to filter messages. (See Figure 9.18 for a list of subject lines and the anti-spam applications that use them.)

The Specify Actions field can be set to the following:

Journal This Message

Move to Database

Don't Accept Message

Don't Deliver Message

Change Routing State

The appropriate action should be selected. Dropping and not accepting messages are very severe solutions, so they should be used with appropriate care.

Examples

These rules can be used as whitelists or blacklists at the server level, blocking on any field that is available in the list. This rules-based blocking is very good for blocking certain types of spam as well as viruses (malware).

For example, if you want to send all messages that have a From: address of @spamalot.com to the "bit bucket," a rule can be set up to easily filter those messages. From the Add Rules screen, click on the drop-down labeled Sender and select the item called Internet Domain. Keep the middle column at the default, Contains. Input the name of the domain on which you want to filter in the right field (we are using spamalot.com). On the Specify Actions part of the window, select Don't Accept Message as the action, and the message will be dropped when the sending system offers it to the Domino server.

Another use for the rules is to filter messages based upon subject lines. In this case, you select Subject in the top left drop-down of the Specify Conditions pane, leave the middle column at Contains, and input the string the anti-spam tool inserts into the Subject line in the right box. Figure 9.18 contains a list of the subject modifications for the anti-spam facilities covered in this book. Finally, in the bottom pane labeled Specify Actions, you select the desired action.

LOTUS NOTES

Notes has support for subject line-based filtering and blacklisting senders of messages. Both are available from the Rules menu of the main Notes screen and are covered next. Note that, similar to Domino, there is no way to filter on arbitrary headers. As a result, subject line modification must be used when deploying external anti-spam mechanisms.

SUBJECT LINE FILTERING

Filtering in Notes is available by going to `Tools==>Mail Rules`. You can also use the Quick Rule screen, which is essentially a subset of the Mail Rules functionality, or open the Rules folder directly.

Clicking on the New Rule button brings up a screen very similar to the one available under Domino. On the top portion of the window drop-down (which defaults to Sender), the following fields to filter on are available:

Sender
Subject
Body
Importance
Delivery Priority
To
CC
BCC
To or CC
Body or Subject
Internet Domain
Size (in bytes)
All Documents

The middle box defines the comparison action (which defaults to Contains) and has four possible values:

Contains
Does Not Contain

Is

Is Not

The right box is where the keyword you wanted to filter on would go. When filled in, simply press the Add button, and the rule will be added to the defined list. Now, the bottom part of the screen (what action to take) must be defined.

The left box (which defaults to Move To Folder) can be set to the following values:

Move To Folder

Copy To Folder

Send Copy To

Set Expire Date

Change Importance To

Delete

The Delete option should be used with care. After a message has been deleted, there is no getting it back. For our examples here, the default Move To Folder works fine. The right box is where the action parameter is input. In our example, this is `Junk Mail`. A new folder can also be selected via a dialog box by clicking the Select... button. This button also allows the creation of a new Notes folder to file messages in if the folder desired hasn't been created.

By default, any newly defined rule is on. If you need to turn the rule off, simply check the Off radio button at the top of the New Rule screen before saving.

SUBJECT LINE FILTERING EXAMPLE

To illustrate how a filter would be set up to route all messages with the string `***Spam***` in the subject line to a folder called `Junk Email`, consider the following example. First, the `New Rule` screen is brought up by going to `Tools==>Mail Rules==>New Rule`. At the top of the screen in the drop-down box under Create Condition that defaults to Sender, select Subject instead. Leave the middle drop-down selection Contains and put the string `***Spam***` in the right box.

After clicking the Add button, the Specify Action area at the bottom of the window must be completed. Leave the left drop-down box at the default Move To Folder and click the Select... button to bring up a dialog box where the `Junk Mail` folder can be created if it doesn't already exist.

Blacklisting From: Addresses

Notes contains rudimentary support for blacklisting From: addresses. Although not widely useful, this capability could be used for certain types of spam. Both senders (`user@spammer.com`) as well as whole domains (`@spammer.com`) can be blocked with this support.

The blacklisting functionality is accessed by clicking on the Tools... button and then selecting the Block Mail from Sender option. Doing so brings up a screen that has two radio buttons that enable one of the following options to be selected:

Block Mail from This Sender: *sender*

Block Mail from Any Address That Ends with: *domain*

Any message originating from the selected sender or domain will end up in the `Junk Mail` folder. Figure 11.5 shows an example screen for blocking senders.

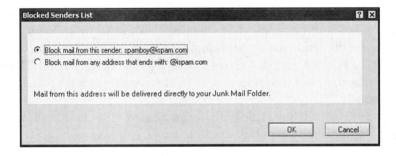

Figure 11.5 Block Sender.

McAfee SpamKiller for Lotus Domino v2.1

McAfee SpamKiller for Lotus Domino v2.1 is an anti-spam plugin based upon SpamAssassin available for Lotus Domino. Some of its features include

- Rules-based scoring engine
- Quarantine flagged messages
- Statistical (Bayesian) analysis
- Heuristic and content analysis

- Whitelist/blacklist at both administrator and user levels
- Automatic update of rulesets

The biggest downside to SpamKiller is the fact that many of the native SpamAssassin features are not accessible via its graphical user interface. For example, you cannot provide feedback to the Bayesian analyzer to improve its "learning" of what you (or your users) consider to be spam. Also, it doesn't have as fine-grained control over the configuration and rules that SpamAssassin allows you. The rules downloaded from McAfee can only be disabled (or reenabled). In particular, the administrator cannot add his or her own rules easily via the GUI. Rules can only be added via direct manipulation of the underlying Lotus database, which is not recommended unless you are an expert.

INSTALLATION

McAfee SpamKiller for Lotus Domino version 2.1 can be downloaded from the McAfee, Inc. web site. It requires approximately 13MB of space, not including quarantine space for messages that are designated as spam. The defaults in the installation program create an acceptable SpamKiller installation for use with Lotus.

CONFIGURATION

Out of the box, SpamKiller doesn't require much configuring. To access the SpamKiller configuration screens from the main Domino screen, go to `File==>Database==>Open`. Select the name of your server in the Server drop-down box and McAfee in the Database window, as shown in Figure 11.6.

Clicking the Open button brings you to a screen where you can select one of the following options:

- SpamKiller for Lotus Domino Help
- SpamKiller for Lotus Domino
- SpamKiller for Lotus Domino Repository

Select the SpamKiller for Lotus Domino option and click on the Open button. This is the main SpamKiller configuration screen, which allows you to manage the installation; view the log, quarantine, and other files; and perform other administrative tasks.

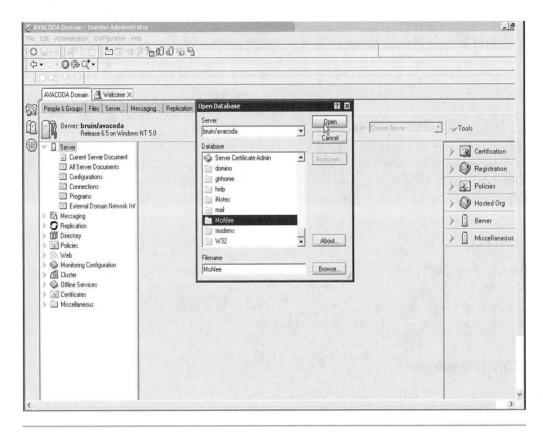

Figure 11.6 Open McAfee Configuration.

The left side contains the functions, which consist of the following options under the Tasks heading:

- View Scanning Information
- Configure Anti-Spam Settings
- Configure Update Schedule
- View Scanning History
- View Quarantined Mail

(These selections are available on most SpamKiller screens on the left hand side. Figure 11.7 shows these options.) The following options are available under the Advanced Tasks heading:

- View Anti-Spam Rules List
- View Repository Database
- Select Server

Each area is described next.

View Scanning Information

This screen contains a summary of the results to date for the McAfee SpamKiller scanner. Information presented here includes scanned items, marked items, quarantined items, discarded items, and average scan time.

Configure Anti-Spam Settings

This screen contains most of the ways to customize the software to work with your environment. Figure 11.7 shows an example configure screen.

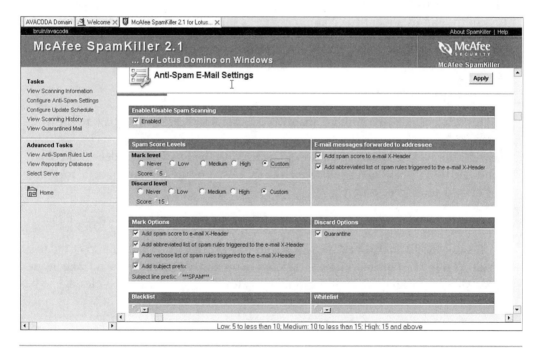

Figure 11.7 Configure Anti-Spam Settings.

Options are as follows:

- **Enable/Disable Spam Scanning**—Gives the administrator the ability to turn off spam processing temporarily.
- **Spam Score Levels**—To be considered spam, the message must exceed this score. Mark is the process of adding header information or modifying the subject line. Discard is the act of deleting or quarantining the message (see "Discard Options"). Scores map to the displayed levels as follows:

Name	Score
Never	<5
Low	5-10
Medium	10-15
High	>15

Selecting `Custom` gives the administrator the ability to set his or her own level.

- **Mark Options**—These settings control what SpamKiller does to the message in order to help the end user identify a spam message as such. The options are as follows:

  - Add Spam Score to Email X-Header—Adds the line `X-NAI-Spam-Score` to the headers of messages (on by default). For example:

    ```
    X-NAI-Spam-Score: 10000.60
    ```

    This header line indicates that SpamKiller assigned a score of 10000.60 to the message.
  - Add Abbreviated List of Spam Rules Triggered to the Email X-Header—Adds the header `X-NAI-Spam-Rules` indicating the list of spam rules broken in brief format (on by default). For example:

    ```
    X-NAI-Spam-Rules: 2 rules triggered GTUBE=1000.000, LINES_OF_YELLING=0.600
    ```

    This line indicates that the message triggered the `GTUBE` and `LINES_OF_YELLING` tests.
  - Add Verbose List of Spam Rules Triggered to the Email X-Header—Adds the header `X-NAI-Spam-Report` header indicating the spam rules that caused the message to be classified as spam in long format (off by default). For example:

    ```
    X-NAI-Spam-Report: 2 rules triggered        * 1000.000 -- GTUBE -- Generic Test \
    for Unsolicited Bulk Email         * 0.600 -- LINES_OF_YELLING -- A WHOLE LINE \
    OF YELLING DETECTED
    ```

This header tells us what rules were triggered and provides a description of those rules along with their scores.

- Add Subject Prefix—Modifies the subject line to include the string indicated in the field below this line; defaults to `***SPAM***` (on by default).
  Note that the default SpamKiller setting of both adding the `X-Header` and performing subject modification is redundant. One or the other (depending on the email client's filtering capability) can be safely removed. Notes only supports subject modification, so unless the message is being forwarded to another server or being read by an email client other than Notes, the additional `X-Header` can be turned off.

- **Email Messages Forwarded To Addressee**—For the class of messages that are forwarded from another email account, the administrator can set two options:
  - Add Spam Score to Email X-Header—This adds the header `X-NAI-Spam-Score` to messages indicating their spam score (default is on).
  - Add Abbreviated List of Spam Rules Triggered to the Email X-Header—This setting adds the header `X-NAI-Spam-Rules` indicating the anti-spam rules that triggered the spam classification (default is on).

- **Discard Options**—This option determines whether messages identified as spam are to be truly discarded or sent to a holding area or quarantine (default is on). Depending on your policy, it may be better to quarantine messages (which may have been misidentified as spam) rather than deleting them outright.

- **Blacklist and Whitelist**—These settings control the SpamKiller "always block" list (blacklist) and "always accept" list. Logic within the application will not allow contradictory settings to be entered by the administrator. Fully qualified email addresses are entered, with the asterisk (`*`) as the wildcard character. For example, let's assume you wanted to allow all users to send email from the domain `friends.com` except for the user `spammer`. You would enter `*@friends.com` in the whitelist and `spammer@friends.com` in the blacklist.

Configure Update Schedule

The Configure Update Schedule screen (shown in Figure 11.8) allows the administrator to manage the update process for the anti-spam rulesets provided by McAfee, Inc.

The defaults for this screen should be acceptable for most installations. This screen allows the administrator to specify the following parameters:

- Enable/disable updates
- Change the date/time of the updates
- Whether to FTP from a remote machine or copy from a machine on the LAN
- Various parameters for the update process such as FTP proxy, local file location, and username/password to use

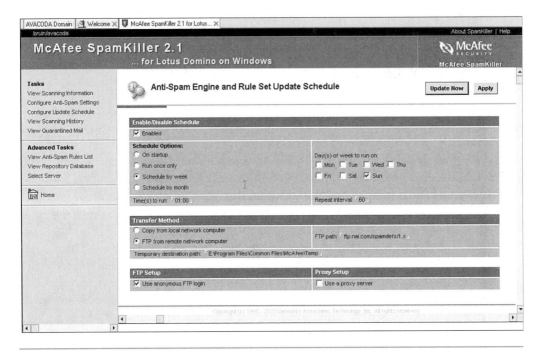

Figure 11.8 Configure Update Schedule screen.

View Scanning History

The view scanning history page is essentially a log of all of the messages that have been processed by SpamKiller. Figure 11.9 shows an example screen.
The attributes shown include

- Date and time
- Action performed by SpamKiller
- Subject of the message
- Sender of the message
- Score assigned by SpamKiller

This information can be used to help track down problems with scanning or for reporting or other requirements. For more detailed information on a logged message, right-clicking on the message and selecting Edit brings up a detailed screen where various actions can be taken on the message if it is quarantined (see the next section).

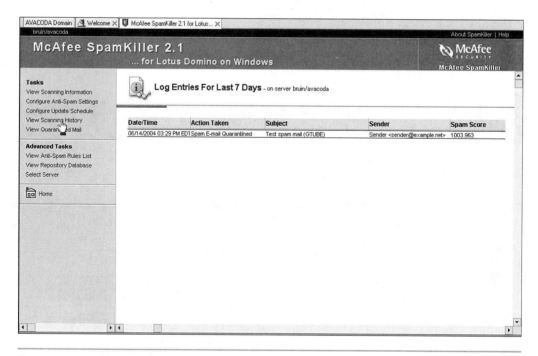

Figure 11.9 View Scanning History.

View Quarantined Mail

This screen shows all messages that have been redirected as spam and placed into the quarantine for disposition by the administrator. The screen is very similar to the scanning history, as the attributes displayed are

- Date and time
- Recipient of message
- Subject of message
- Score assigned by SpamKiller

Right-clicking on a message of interest and selecting the Open option brings up a screen similar to Figure 11.10.

This screen allows you to perform a number of functions, including

- View the original message
- Delete the message

- Release the message from quarantine
- Put the sender on whitelist/blacklist
- View detailed information on the rulesets triggered by this message

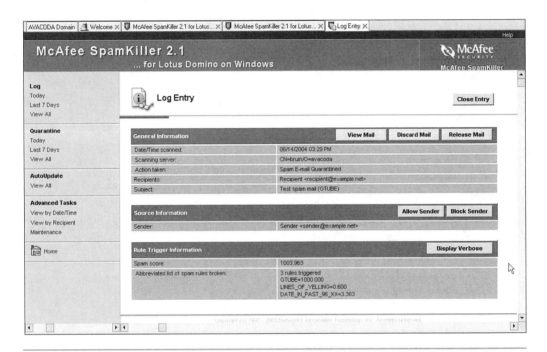

Figure 11.10 Quarantined Message Detail.

Use the Quarantined Message Detail screen to dispose of quarantined messages, either by deleting them or releasing them from quarantine so that they are delivered to the recipient. This should be performed on a regular basis so that any misclassified messages can be routed correctly and so that spam messages can be deleted.

View Anti-Spam Rules List

SpamKiller gives the administrator the ability to enable/disable rulesets. This functionality is available via the View Anti-Spam Rules List screen, as shown in Figure 11.11.

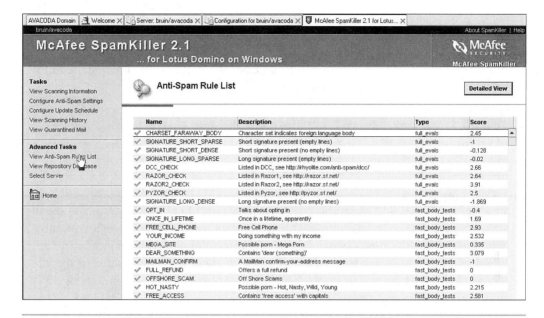

Figure 11.11 Rules List.

There are two buttons on the top right of the screen, marked Enable Rule and Disable Rule, which control the status of the rule. The rules as provided by McAfee can be turned off but cannot otherwise be modified. The rules screen shows the following information:

- Status of the Rule—Can be enabled (displayed as green check) or disabled (displayed as red X)
- Rule name
- Description
- Type
- Score

Right-clicking on a particular rule and selecting Open provides a detail screen that includes the actual rule text itself in addition to the other information available on the summary screen. For more information on rulesets, please refer to Chapter 3, "SpamAssassin."

View Repository Database

The View Repository Database screen contains several areas already covered, including

- Log-related activities
- Quarantine-related functions

However, there are a couple of areas not available elsewhere. These include the Auto Update and Advanced Tasks functions.

Auto Update
- **View All**—Clicking on the `View All` link under the Auto Update heading enables the administrator to see all of the ruleset updates that have occurred for the SpamKiller engine. This is useful for debugging problems with updating the software.

Advanced Tasks
- **View by Date/Time**—The View by Date/Time function allows administrators to see all logged messages sorted by date/time. This is useful for sorting through copious amounts of messages when the approximate date/time is known for a message of interest.
- **View by Recipient**—The View By Recipient screen enables administrators to sort the message logs by recipient. This is useful when the recipient is known and there is a large number of tagged messages to sort through.
- **Maintenance**—Clicking on the `Maintenance` link allows the administrator to turn on automatic deletion of logs and quarantine messages and to control the amount of time they are kept. Buttons marked Purge enable the administrator to run the purge function at any time desired. By default, the deletion of old messages must be performed by hand. If the system processes many spam messages, you should either turn on the auto purge function or remember to manually delete the information periodically.

Select Server

The Select Server screen enables those installations that run multiple SpamKiller instances to determine which server their changes should go against. Simply select the server desired, and all configuration, logs, and so on will be applied to that server.

SMTP AUTH AND STARTTLS

Domino has excellent support for SMTP AUTH and STARTTLS. The Domino configuration screens that control SMTP AUTH are on the same screens that control STARTTLS. The Lotus Domino server supports only the `LOGIN` SMTP AUTH protocol.

Because SMTP AUTH is simpler to set up, we'll start by covering SMTP AUTH, and then we'll move to STARTTLS. Our example for STARTTLS uses a self-signed certificate, which may be acceptable for certain applications. However, a "real" certificate can easily be configured for use with Domino. Please refer to Chapter 5 for more information on the topics of SMTP AUTH and STARTTLS.

SMTP AUTH

Enabling SMTP AUTH support is achieved by going to the main Lotus Domino tab screen and clicking on the following tabs: `Server==>All Server Documents==><select server, in our case bruin/avacoda>==>Edit Server==>Ports==>Internet Ports==>Mail` (see Figure 11.12).

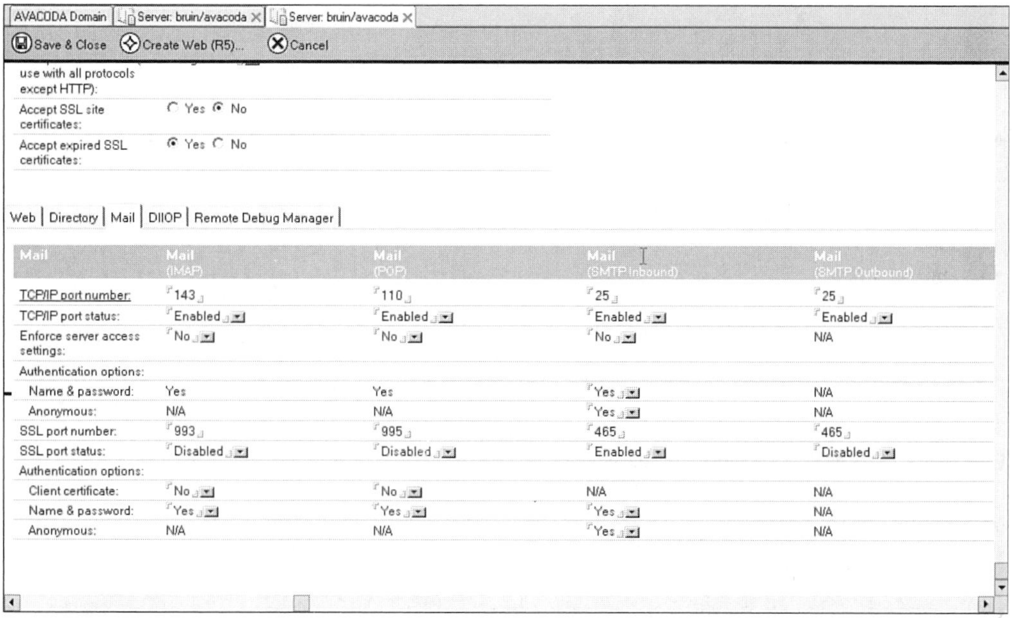

Figure 11.12 SSL Mail Certificate screen.

Ensure that `SSL port status for Mail (SMTP inbound)` is set to `Disabled` on this screen. Next, go back to the main Domain tab screen and follow this path: `Server==> Configurations==>(select server, in our case bruin/avacoda)==>Edit Configuration==>Router/SMTP==>Advanced==>Commands and Extensions` and be sure SSL negotiated over TCP port is set to Disabled (see Figure 11.13).

The Domino server is now configured to require SMTP AUTH when a client wants to relay SMTP messages through it.

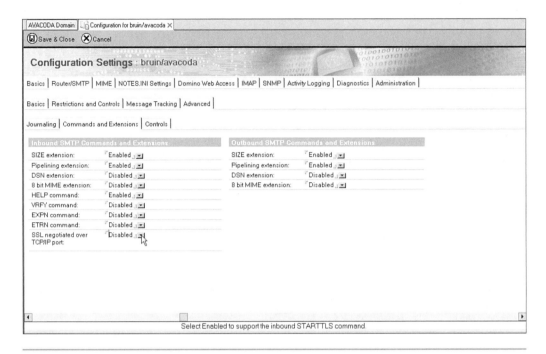

Figure 11.13 SMTP Commands and Extensions screen.

STARTTLS

STARTTLS is more difficult to install due to the requirement that a certificate be referred to by the server. However, having a certificate means that the SMTP connection from the relaying email client through the Domino server is encrypted (along with the authentication information). Note that this certificate does not encrypt email messages end-to-end (like PGP/GPG would).

To begin, start at the main Domino Domain tab screen and follow this path: `Server==>Configurations==>(select server, in our case bruin/avacoda)==>Edit Configuration==>Router/SMTP==>Advanced==Commands and Extensions` and be sure SSL Negotiated Over TCP Port is set to Enabled. Figure 11.12 from the previous section shows an example screen.

Next, the Server Certificate Administration screen needs to be accessed. This is achieved by going to `File==>Database==>Open==>Server==(select server name, in our example bruin/avacoda)==>Server Certificate Admin==>Open` (see Figure 11.14).

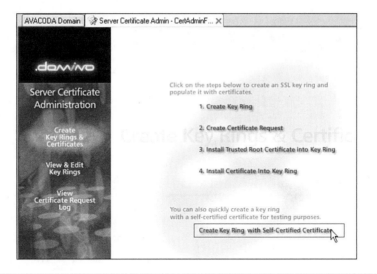

Figure 11.14 Server Certificate Administration.

From the Server Certificate Administration screen, click on Create Key Ring with Self-Certified Certificate button at the bottom of the screen, which brings up a screen similar to Figure 11.15.

Clicking on the Create Key Ring will bring up a similar screen where a real certificate signed by a known certificate authority can be entered.

After filling out the fields in the screen, click the Create Key Ring with Self-Certified Certificate button, and a dialog screen summarizing the key information is presented. Simply click the OK button to complete the generation of the self-signed certificate.

The certificate files must be copied to the correct location in Domino. This is accomplished by copying `selfcert.crt` and `selfcert.sth` from `\Program Files\lotus\notes\data to \Lotus\Domino\Data`.

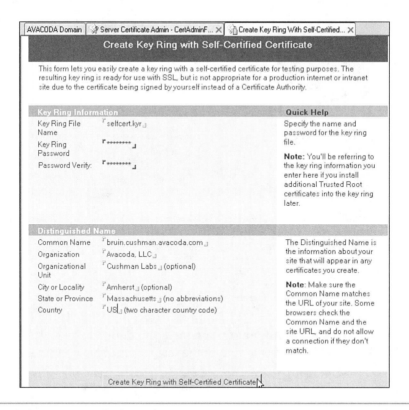

Figure 11.15 Create Key Ring (self signed).

Next, the SSL certificate must be enabled within Domino. This is achieved by going to the main Lotus Domino tab screen and clicking on the following tabs: `Server==>All Server Documents==>`*(select server, in our case bruin/avacoda)*`==>Edit Server==>Ports==>Internet Ports`. Under the SSL Settings heading, enter the name of the certificate in the SSL Key File Name field (see Figure 11.16).

Finally, SSL support must be activated for the Domino SMTP server to complete the STARTTLS installation. This is accomplished by clicking on the Mail tab when the Internet Ports tab is selected. Under Mail (SMTP Inbound), ensure that the SSL Port Status is set to Enabled and the Name and Password fields are set to Yes in both places. Figure 11.12 (previously) shows this screen.

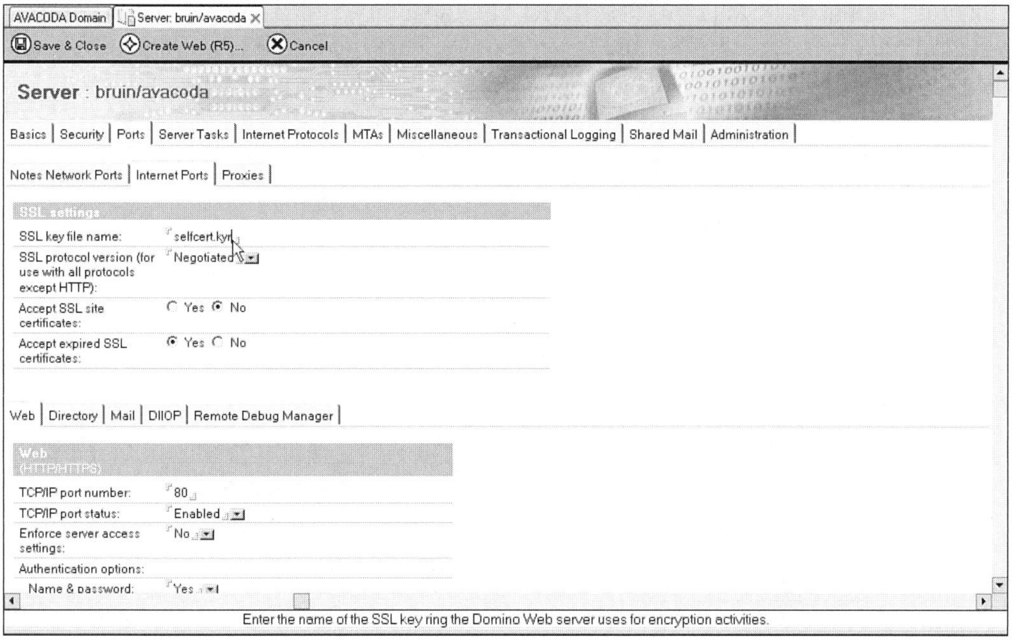

Figure 11.16 SSL settings.

CONCLUSION

Lotus Domino has all of the usual anti-spam features found in a modern MTA, which are covered in this chapter. One feature not found in most other MTAs is the ability to filter messages at the server level. Having this capability makes it much easier for administrators to deal with spam before it hits the user's mailbox. We also covered how to filter messages, blacklists, and other anti-spam features with Notes, the email client associated with Domino.

Because most modern MTAs don't include all of the needed anti-spam features, we chose to cover McAfee SpamKiller for Lotus Domino 2.1. SpamKiller implements the SpamAssassin content scoring and Bayesian analysis functionality. However, the administrator doesn't have much control over the anti-spam rules and scoring within SpamKiller, except that he or she can disable rules. SpamKiller's rules are updated by McAfee about once a quarter by default, although this ability can be adjusted by the administrator.

Lotus Domino has SMTP AUTH/STARTTLS capability, which can be used to control who can relay messages through the server. Both unencrypted (SMTP AUTH only) and encrypted (STARTLS) transmissions are available within Lotus Domino.

Sender Verification 12

In this chapter, we look at the area of sender verification. Sender verification systems are methods by which an email recipient requires the sender to perform some sort of action to prove that the message he or she is sending is legitimate. The fact that spammers usually forge their return addresses means that verification of the fake From: address will fail and the spam message will be blocked.

The areas of positive response and sender verification are very closely related, with positive response being a specific type of sender verification. The term "positive response" implies a response *after* the message is sent. However, sender verification can happen before or after the message is sent. For the purposes of our discussion, though, we consider them to be the same.

Some email sender validation processes that have been invented are particularly creative. Some sender verification methods include

- Visual captcha
- Haiku
- Sender compute

One of the more interesting verification systems is the use of a technique called visual captcha. Captcha is an acronym that stands for "completely automated public Turing test to tell computers and humans apart." This technique requires the sender to type in a character string that represents a visual pattern that is difficult for an automated system to process and turn into a string that could be input. This pattern might be a series of letters on a colored background, for example. Figure 12.1 illustrates a simple example of a captcha.

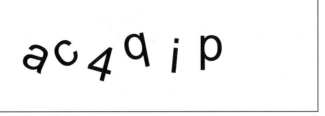

Figure 12.1 A simple visual captcha.

The Haiku method requires special headers in the message, which the Haiku anti-spam service provider subsequently uses to "warrant" that the message isn't spam. Sender compute requires the sender to calculate a known algorithm and accept the result before the sender's message is accepted by the recipient.

The email sender verification method is one of the more controversial areas in the fight against spam. Many people don't like these methods due to the chicken-and-egg problem: if both sender and recipient are using it, the message is guaranteed to not get through. Nonetheless, we cover positive response solutions here because there are open source systems available that implement it (though the technique is not widely used).

SENDER VERIFICATION BACKGROUND

There are many different types of sender verification methods to cover. For the purposes of this book, we cover the sender compute and challenge/response system types.

Sender Compute

In a native sender compute setup, the recipient of the email message requires the sender to calculate the result of a certain non-trivial algorithm. The result of the computation is placed into the message headers so that the recipient can know the sender is legitimate and so that the email server will allow the message to be passed. Sender compute systems contain whitelists of addresses the recipient has already communicated with, making the process for previous correspondents less burdensome.

The issue with this approach is that it is essentially a new protocol, although it is a backward-compatible extension to the existing mail protocols. Many of the shortcomings can be dealt with by using proxy software on both the email server and clients to make installation and use easier. However, these take time and effort on the administrator's part to implement.

Challenge/Response

Challenge/response is a system where the email recipient requires a sender to prove that he or she is a "real" person and not an automated email (spam) sending system. For correspondents who have not communicated with the recipient before, this is accomplished by the recipient's email system automatically sending a request for response to the sender, unless the sender is already on a whitelist. The message is "sidelined" while the confirmation process takes place. After the sender acknowledges the request, the message is "released" from the holding area and delivered to the recipient.

Although challenge/response does work, many email senders don't respond to challenge/response requests from recipients who require them. This is probably the biggest issue with challenge/response systems.

Sender Verification Systems Covered

We cover the following open source sender verification systems:

- Camram
- Active Spam Killer (ASK)
- Tagged Message Delivery Agent (TMDA)

Camram is a sender-compute (or proof of work) type system with CRM114 Bayesian filtering and a nice graphical user interface for CRM114 integrated into it. Camram uses the Hashcash algorithm that senders must calculate in order to fulfill the computation requirement or be subject to CRM114 filtering. The presence of a Hashcash sum associated with an acceptable address for the recipient will allow the message to pass without having to go through the CRM114 filter.

ASK uses the well-known "reply to this email message" method, where a special MD5 hash is generated for each outbound message. The sender must reply to this message in order for the recipient to see the original message. When authenticated, the sender can be whitelisted to automatically allow future messages without having to go through the authentication process needlessly. ASK employs whitelists and blacklists as part of its solution.

TMDA is very similar to ASK, except for a couple of functions. Most importantly, TMDA uses special reply addresses (such as `user-83ac943@isp.com`) rather than an MD5 hash, which ASK uses. Also, TMDA has optional support for the sender-compute idea built in, enabling further functionality if desired.

INSTALLING PYTHON

Python is a high-level scripting language comparable to Tcl, Perl, Scheme, and JavaScript. It is used by a number of packages in this chapter and is included in most Linux and BSD derivatives. However, many Unix flavors don't include it, so we show you how to install it here.

Download the most recent version of Python (currently 2.3.4) from here: *http://www.python.org/download/*. Copy the tar file to /usr/local/src and install like this:

```
bash$ cd /usr/local/src
bash$ gzip -d python-2.3.4.tar.gz
bash$ tar xvf python-2.3.4.tar
bash$ cd Python-2.3.4
bash$ ./configure
bash$ make
bash$ sudo make install
```

You should now have a running Python installation.

CAMRAM

The reason for Camram's original implementation was as a reference implementation for a sender compute system, namely Hashcash. Although this is still a large part of the goal, Camram has tight integration with the CRM114 spam classifier. It also contains a graphical user interface to manage itself and the CRM114 application as well. Camram is worth implementing just for the ease of use it provides in managing CRM114.

Camram can be set up as an invisible proxy between your existing MTA and email systems that want to send your users email. This eliminates the need to run Camram on your existing (perhaps overly loaded) email systems. Camram refers to this setup as the *interception* method.

You should be aware that Camram is still a work in progress. Some of the functionality doesn't work precisely as expected, but it should be suitable for most situations. Be sure to check the Camram web site often for code updates.

Inbound Messages

You can deploy Camram in two different ways in your inbound email infrastructure. The first way is by using `procmail` to redirect incoming messages, in a setup where Camram is run on the same machine as the end user mailboxes. This is the setup we cover here.

The second method that can be used is interception. This method "intercepts" the SMTP port 25 connection and redirects it to the Camram server, which processes the message and sends it to the mailbox. The interception method is used in a situation where your organization's email system is distributed into machines that perform the email relay function and servers that house mailboxes.

Another case is when your primary server is Exchange/Domino, where you cannot run Camram directly on the mail server. Implementing an anti-spam solution such as Camram on a separate system helps to distribute the load on machines outside of your regular mail machines.

In either case, the actual processing of messages is the same, regardless of whether the procmail or interception methods are used. Figure 12.2 shows the flow of messages through the Camram system.

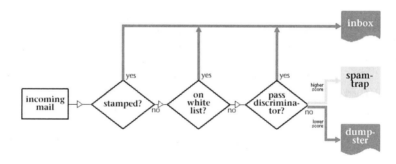

Figure 12.2 Camram inbound message flow. (From *http://www.camram.org*; courtesy of Keith Dawson, dawson@world.std.com; Used with permission.)

Outbound

Messages leaving the Camram system must be stamped to show that they have been processed through the Hashcash computational system (see Figure 12.3). This is done as a proxy, using the EmailRelay software. The message is reinjected into the MTA on port 30025.

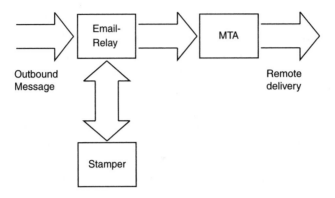

Figure 12.3 Camram outbound message flow.

INSTALLATION

Camram can be downloaded from *http://www.camram.org/download.html*. We cover Camram version 0.3.25 here. The build script downloads all of the needed components, including

- **TRE**—Regular Expression matching library required by CRM114
- **CRM114**—The Controlled Regular Expression Mutilator covered in Chapter 8, "Bayesian Filtering"
- **Hashcash**—This implements the sender compute algorithms required by Camram
- **EmailRelay**—MTA used by Camram to implement its message stamper functionality
- **normalizemime**—Used by CRM114 to convert MIME-encoded text

These are external packages that Camram requires for operation. Camram will download and install Python if it is not available on the system or if it is not at the correct version level when you run the `buildit.sh` script (shown next).

After downloading, become root, extract the files, add the Camram group and user, and run the build script like this (the downloaded installation is assumed to be `/usr/local/src/raging_dormouse-0.3.25.tar.gz`):

```
bash$ sudo su
# mkdir /usr/local/src/camram-0.3.25
# cd /usr/local/src/camram-0.3.25
# groupadd camram
# useradd -g camram -m -d /usr/local/camram camram
# tar xzvf ../raging_dormouse-0.3.25.tar.gz
# mv raging_dormouse-0.3.25/* .
# bash buildit.sh
```

You may need to restart the download script if a download error takes place. The raging_dormouse release will exit the build process if there is a checksum error in one of the components. The build script will make sure that the appropriate third-party applications have been downloaded before continuing on.

After the initial setup script has been run, several additional steps need to take place. These actions include

- Setting up the Camram GUI for use under Apache
- Setting up the MTA (Sendmail) to work with Camram
- Configuring a Procmail recipe for use with Camram

Apache Installation

Next, install the Camram hooks for the Apache web server. The installer attempts to copy the configuration to the Apache configuration directory on some Linux distributions, namely /etc/httpd/conf. If this is not how Apache is set up on your system (for example, Debian), then copy the configuration file manually to the Apache configuration directory and restart Apache like this:

```
# cp -p /usr/local/camram/ancillary/camram.conf/etc/apache/camram.conf
# /etc/init.d/apache restart
```

Sendmail (MTA) Integration

Integrating Camram with Sendmail requires setting up Sendmail to listen on three IP addresses and ports: we use 127.0.0.1 port 25, 127.0.0.1 port 30025, and the publicly available inbound interface. Any available IP and port combination can be used, but these are what Camram recommends, so they are the ones we use.

If you set up Sendmail per our examples in other parts of this book, sendmail.mc is located in /usr/local/src/sendmail-8.12.11/cf/cf/. If your current configuration is sendmail.cf, then edit your sendmail.mc file and add the following three lines, replacing 192.168.16.9 with the public IP address of your Camram machine that accepts email from the Internet:

```
DAEMON_OPTIONS(`Port=smtp,Addr=192.168.16.9, Name=MTA')dnl
DAEMON_OPTIONS(`Port=smtp,Addr=127.0.0.1, Name=MTA')dnl
DAEMON_OPTIONS(`Port=30025,Addr=127.0.0.1, Name=MTA')dnl
```

These lines tell Sendmail to listen to port 25 on its public IP address and localhost address (127.0.0.1) as well as 30025 on localhost for reinjecting messages into the MTA. Then rebuild sendmail.cf, install it (saving the old one), and restart Sendmail:

```
bash$ sudo su
# cd /usr/local/src/sendmail-8.12.11/cf/cf/
# make sendmail.cf
# cp /etc/mail/sendmail.cf /etc/mail/sendmail.cf.old
# cp sendmail.cf /etc/mail/sendmail.cf
# /etc/init.d/sendmail restart
```

Camram is now integrated into your Sendmail installation for all users on the system.

Procmail Integration

Figure 12.4 illustrates a procmail recipe showing Camram integration. This can be specified on a per-user basis by placing the recipe in each user's .procmailrc file or in a system-wide /etc/procmailrc file.

```
MAILDIR=$HOME/Maildir
DEFAULT=$MAILDIR/
ORGMAIL=$MAILDIR/

# Directory for storing procmail configuration and log files
PMDIR=/var/log/procmail

# Put ## before LOGFILE if you want no logging (not recommended)
LOGFILE=$PMDIR/log

# Set to yes when debugging
VERBOSE=no

# Remove ## when debugging; set to no if you want minimal logging
## LOGABSTRACT=all

# Replace $HOME/Msgs with your message directory
# Mutt and elm use $HOME/Mail
# Pine uses $HOME/mail
# Netscape Messenger uses $HOME/nsmail
# Some NNTP clients, such as slrn & nn, use $HOME/News
# Mailboxes in maildir format are often put in $HOME/Maildir
#MAILDIR=/var/spool/spamtrap       # Make sure this directory exists!

##INCLUDERC=$PMDIR/testing.rc
##INCLUDERC=$PMDIR/lists.rc

:0fw
| /usr/local/camram/bin/procmail_filter

:0
* < 2
/dev/null
```

Figure 12.4 Procmail recipe for use with Camram.

If you are not using Maildir-formatted mailboxes, you should change the lines that read

```
DEFAULT=$MAILDIR/
ORGMAIL=$MAILDIR/
```

to be

```
DEFAULT=
ORGMAIL=
```

CAMRAM CONFIGURATION

Besides the `procmail` recipe provided in Figure 12.4, Camram has three files that can be changed to adjust its behavior:

- `/usr/local/camram/ancillary/global_configuration`—Default values; we do not make any changes to this file
- `/var/spool/camram/configuration`—Where most site-specific changes are made to adjust Camram's functions
- `/usr/local/camram/ancillary/camram.local`—The email relay script used to control the parameters when sending messages from Camram

We also cover how to set up appropriate cron jobs and Camram users at the end of this section.

/var/spool/camram/configuration

The valid parameters in the `configuration` file are the same ones that are valid in the `global_configuration` file. The configuration file is broken down into the following sections:

```
core
spam analysis
spam storage
filter configuration
user e-mail addresses
```

All of the changes we list next are confined to the [core] section. Besides the ones we cover here, some of the parameters you should consider adjusting include any keyword involving a path or any of the CRM114 scoring thresholds. A default file with just the section headers (listed previously) is created at Camram install time. You might want to make a copy of this file before making changes to it. At a minimum, the following parameters should be defined under the [core] section in order to change from their default values:

```
authorized_users = comma-list:root,esj,dale
```

This should be a comma-separated list of privileged users who can manage the server via the GUI.

```
challenge_URL_base=string:http://mydomain.com/camram/pdgen.cgi
```

This is the parameter indicating the URL address for the challenge web page. Change mydomain.com to be the address of your web server.

```
correction_URL =string:http://mydomain.com/camram/correct.cgi
```

This is the URL where users enter corrections for messages misclassified as spam or ham.

```
reinjection_SMTP_port = string:30025
```

This is the port where Camram sends messages back to the MTA. If you used our example, leave this at 30025.

```
central_administration = boolean:0
```

This controls whether end users have access to the CRM114 retraining (0) or only the administrator has access to retraining (1). We recommend setting this to 0 so that end users can train their own filters.

```
password_key=string:notswordfish
```

This is the key used for the private password mechanism. Be sure to change it!

```
log_level=integer:1
```

The default logging level is 1. This value can be anything from 0 to 9, where 0 is no output and 9 is very verbose. Unless you are troubleshooting a problem, 1 should be acceptable. Messages are logged in /var/log/messages.

/usr/local/camram/ancillary/camram.local

The camram.local file is the script that starts up the email forwarder program, EmailRelay. A few changes need to be made in this file, but before going through those, be sure to make a copy of the file as it was initially distributed:

```
# cd /usr/local/camram/ancillary
# cp -p camram.local camram.local.orig
```

This makes a backup copy of `camram.local` as `camram.local.orig`.

This script is automatically read each time Camram is run, so there is no need to perform any steps to make changes to this file active.

You should consider making the following changes to the parameters in this file:

```
camram_architecture=procmail
```

If you are running Camram on the same machine as the email boxes (as we are in our example), this should be `procmail`; otherwise, it should be set to `intercept`.

```
stamper_interface=ip address
```

This is the IP address of the interface that stamped messages should be accepted on. `ip address` should be set to the internal IP address, which accepts email from users on your local network. Do *not* set this to any externally available IP address, or you could stamp messages for spammers!

```
filter_interface=ip address
```

This defines the interface of the server where email from the Internet originates. `ip address` should be set to an externally accessible interface that the MX record for your domain is set to, or a host that accepts mail for your domain.

```
local_smart_host=ip address
```

This is the machine that knows how to route email from your server/domain, or if your Camram machine is behind a firewall. If your Camram machine is the smart host gateway, then set this to `127.0.0.1`.

After changes are made to this file, the script must be invoked. Figure 12.5 shows a sample startup/shutdown script that can be installed in `/etc/init.d` for Redhat/Fedora systems.

Executing the script `/etc/init.d/camram.local start` will start the script on many Linux systems.

```
#! /bin/sh

case $1 in
  start)
    /usr/local/camram/ancillary/camram.local
    echo -n "Starting up camram.local"
    ;;

  stop)
      # Stop daemons.
      echo -n "Shutting down camram.local: "
      killproc emailrelay
      ;;
  restart)
      $0 stop
      $0 start
      ;;
  *)
      echo "Usage: $0 {start|stop|restart}"
      exit 1
esac

exit 0
```

Figure 12.5 `camram.local` startup script.

Cron Jobs

There are three cron jobs that need to be set up to perform various tasks. Camram distributes suggested cron entries for each.

`/usr/local/camram/ancillary/sweepup.py`

This script deletes messages in the Camram dumpster. Be sure to run this often enough so that directory lookups don't get too slow when too many files are present.

`/usr/local/camram/ancillary/clean_mail_queue.py`

This script forwards feedback to the end user and should be run very often. Camram's example cron job runs every minute.

`/usr/local/camram/ancillary/mbox2spamtrap.py`

This script automatically scans the `missed_spam_box` folder for messages incorrectly classified by CRM114 and retrains it accordingly.

Setting Up Camram Users

Each user who is going to have email (we assume all users) will need to have the appropriate directory and files set up on the system. This is accomplished by running the following script for every user on the system:

```
# /usr/local/camram/ancillary/clean_configuration.py -u username
```

You need to change *username* to be the user you want to set up on the system. If you are running Camram in intercept mode (without delivery to mailboxes on the machine Camram is running on), you need to create those accounts with the following command:

```
# /usr/local/camram/ancillary/new_account.py -u username
```

If you are running in procmail mode (like we are in our example), the accounts already exist as "real" Unix users, so this step must be skipped.

After setting up your users, you must run the edit_config_cgi script to create user accounts and set up the database by going to the following URL:

```
http://mydomain.com/camram/edit_config.cgi
```

Change mydomain.com to be the name of the Camram server you set previously. See the next section for using this screen.

USING CAMRAM

Camram classifies messages into three possible categories:

- **Red**—Definitely spam; delivered to junk email folder
- **Yellow**—Possibly spam, possibly non-spam; delivered to spamtrap (possibly spam) folder
- **Green**—Definitely not spam; delivered to inbox

This results in an accurate classification system of messages, and it requires users to look in their spamtrap folder. Camram has a web interface for accessing many functions. If you have followed our previous examples, the following screens are available at the listed URLs:

```
http://mydomain.com/camram/edit_config.cgi
```

The `edit_config` screen allows the administrator to edit the default settings for each user and should be run after adding each user to perform initial setup.

```
http://mydomain.com/camram/correct.cgi
```

This screen allows the user to correct CRM114 misclassifications via a web browser.

```
http://mydomain.com/camram/recover.cgi
```

The recover screen allows user access to the junk email folder (Camram calls it the `dumpster`) from a web browser.

Preferences

The parameters in the `edit_prefs.cgi` screen are stored in each user's home directory, in `~user/.camram/configuration`. However, the parameters should be changed only by the `preferences` web interface and not directly via editing the file, as changes will likely get overwritten. The parameters listed here are the same ones that are defined by the `global_configuration` file shown previously (see Figure 12.6).

The defaults here are reasonable. The field labeled `my_email_addresses` should be updated with all aliases for each user. These addresses represent the addresses for which Camram will accept Hashcash stamps for this account.

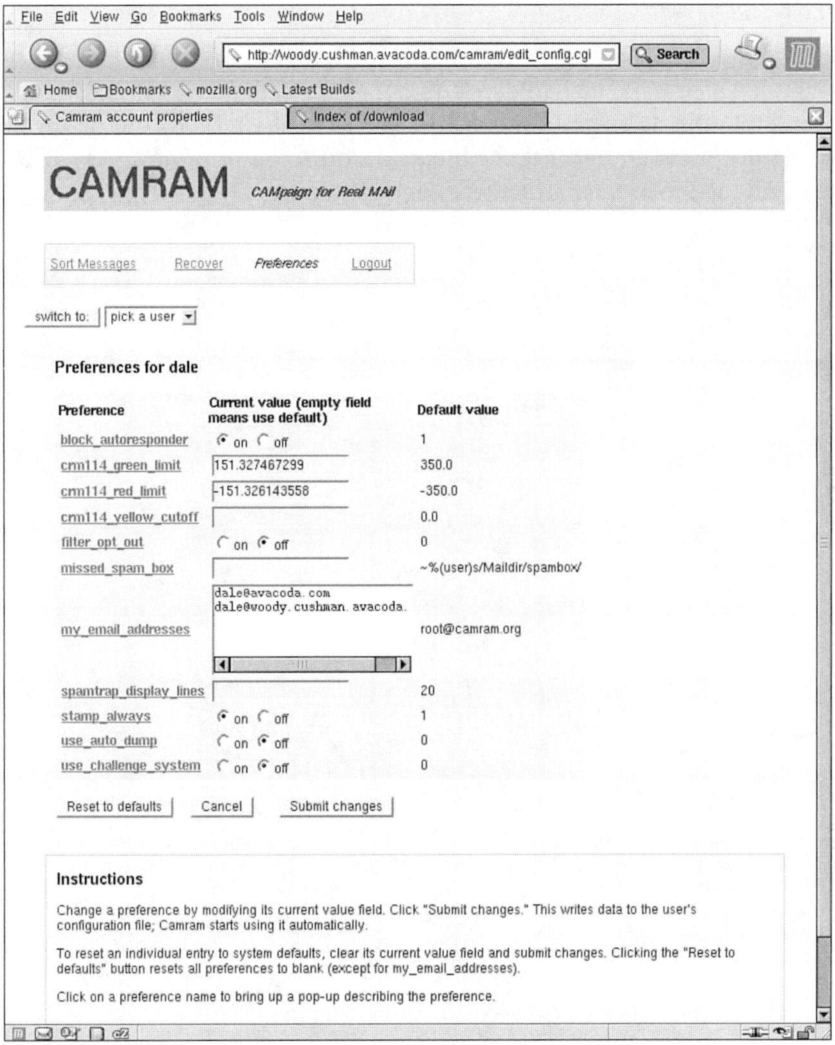

File Edit View Go Bookmarks Tools Window Help

http://woody.cushman.avacoda.com/camram/edit_config.cgi   Search

Home   Bookmarks   mozilla.org   Latest Builds

Camram account properties   Index of /download

CAMRAM   *CAMpaign for Real MAil*

Sort Messages   Recover   *Preferences*   Logout

switch to: | pick a user |

Preferences for dale

Preference	Current value (empty field means use default)	Default value
block_autoresponder	⦿ on ○ off	1
crm114_green_limit	151.327467299	350.0
crm114_red_limit	-151.326143558	-350.0
crm114_yellow_cutoff		0.0
filter_opt_out	○ on ⦿ off	0
missed_spam_box		~%(user)s/Maildir/spambox/
my_email_addresses	dale@avacoda.com dale@woody.cushman.avacoda.	root@camram.org
spamtrap_display_lines		20
stamp_always	⦿ on ○ off	1
use_auto_dump	○ on ⦿ off	0
use_challenge_system	○ on ⦿ off	0

Reset to defaults   Cancel   Submit changes

Instructions

Change a preference by modifying its current value field. Click "Submit changes." This writes data to the user's configuration file; Camram starts using it automatically.

To reset an individual entry to system defaults, clear its current value field and submit changes. Clicking the "Reset to defaults" button resets all preferences to blank (except for my_email_addresses).

Click on a preference name to bring up a pop-up describing the preference.

Figure 12.6 Preferences screen.

Spamtrap

The correct.cgi screen (see Figure 12.7) allows each user to manage their spamtrap (yellow messages), which is the mail folder containing messages that Camram was unsure about when it ran the classifier on them. Simply check the checkbox on the left side for each misclassified message and click the Process button, and your messages will be sent to your inbox and the Bayesian classifier will be retrained.

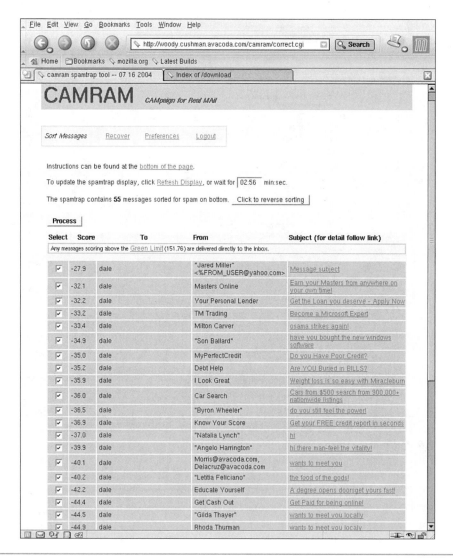

Figure 12.7 Spamtrap screen.

Recover

The recover.cgi screen (see Figure 12.8) lists all messages in the dumpster and inbox. This screen allows you to pull false positive messages out of the dumpster and into the Spamtrap for reclassification. Copies of all messages processed and classified as spam or not spam will end up in the dumpster. Do not be alarmed by the presence of non-spam emails. It is unfortunate that the dumpster contains more than just rejected spam messages because you can't just browse it quickly to identify false positives.

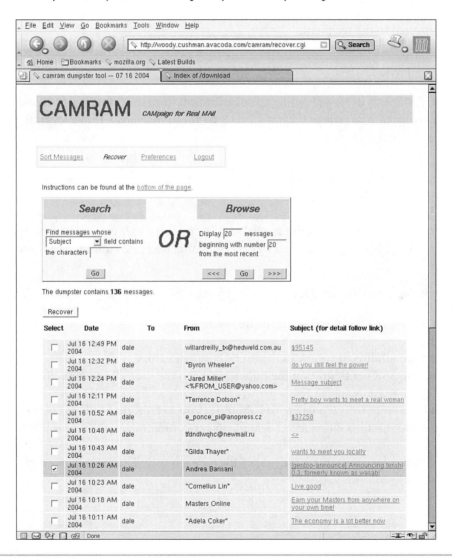

Figure 12.8 Recover screen.

Active Spam Killer

Active Spam Killer (ASK) is a challenge/response system that encrypts information in MD5 fields within the message's Subject: line. A sender who is not already whitelisted goes through a short confirmation process. The mail system of the recipient of the original message sends a challenge to the sender. The sender of the original message simply replies to the challenge, and the subsequent message is processed by the recipient's email system. The MD5 header is analyzed, and the message is released from the holding area and is delivered to the recipient.

Installation

To install ASK, start by downloading the distribution from the Sourceforge repository, *http://prdownloads.sourceforge.net/a-s-k/ask-2.4.1.tar.gz?download*, into a location such as /usr/local. Then unpack as follows:

```
bash$ cd /usr/local
bash$ gzip -d ask-2.4.1.tar.gz
bash$ tar xvf ask.2.4.1.tar
```

You must run a configure script to enable ASK for every user on your system who wants to run it. This is accomplished by becoming that user and running the asksetup.py like this:

```
bash$ sudo -u user -H /usr/local/ask-2.4.1/asksetup.py
```

The asksetup.py script performs the following steps:

- Creates the subdirectory .ask in the user's home directory
- Creates the ASK configuration file called .askrc in the user's home directory

If you have more than ten users, you should set up a script that calls asksetup.py for every user and installs a customized default .askrc configuration file (shown later) for each user.

The next step is to customize the .askrc file for each user. The most important settings to change are as follows:

`rc_mymails`

Set this to the comma-separated list of usernames from which you receive email. For example, if you have mail forwarded from your email addresses at `myaccount@company.com` and `otheracct@isp.net` to this account, you would use the following line:

`rc_myemails = myaccount@company.com,otheracct@isp.net`

`rc_mymailbox`

This setting specifies where your email box is located. If you use mbox format, this is often `/var/mail/username`. If you use Maildir format, the setting might be `/home/username/Maildir/`. Note that the trailing slash indicates Maildir; otherwise, the format is assumed to be mbox.

`rc_mailkey`

Set `rc_mailkey` to be any unique string in your signature without spaces. A phone number or URL would probably be a good choice.

`rc_md5_key`

This should be changed from the default string in the file.

It is recommended after changing these settings that you send yourself an email to be sure that your `rc_mailkey` setting is correct.

CONFIGURATION

ASK uses three files for managing username lists in the directory specified by the `rc_askdir` directory (usually `~/.ask`):

- `whitelist.txt`—Message gets delivered.
- `blacklist.txt`—Message is silently discarded.
- `ignorelist.txt`—Message is discarded, and a message is sent to the sender to indicate this fact.

Keywords in these files are as follows:

- `to`—A string in the To: line is matched.
- `from`—Tells ASK to match the line in the From: line.
- `subject`—ASK matches the Subject: line.
- `header`—Any header line of the message matches.

If the line doesn't contain one of the keywords, ASK assumes it is from. The matching uses the usual Regular Expression rules, a summary of which appears here.

- Special characters are preceded with \.
- ^ matches the beginning of a line.
- $ matches the end of a line.
- Be careful using unqualified string matches—they can match more than you think.

For example:

- The string .com$ matches user@isp.com but not user@div.company.com.
- The string ^com matches company@isp.com but not user@isp.com.

ASK never sends confirmation email messages to mailing lists. ASK uses the Precedence: Bulk header to determine what is a mailing list message.

The software also comes with a program called asksenders.py, which can be used to read in an mbox-formatted mailbox and generate a whitelist.txt file from the messages. This may reduce the learning curve you would otherwise have to go through with the application.

INTEGRATION WITH MTAs

The following section shows how to integrate ASK with Sendmail, Postfix, and qmail.

Sendmail and Postfix (without procmail)

The easiest way to integrate ASK with Sendmail and Postfix is to create a file named $HOME/.forward that contains the following:

```
"|/ask_path/ask.py --loglevel=5 --logfile=/home_dir/ask.log --home=/home_dir"
```

Be sure you substitute the proper paths for *home_dir* and *ask-path*. Due to security concerns, make sure the file permissions on the .forward file are 600 as follows:

```
bash$ chmod 600 home_dir/.forward
```

qmail

If you're using qmail, edit the .qmail file under your home directory and add the following line:

```
| preline /ask_path/ask.py --loglevel=5 --logfile=/home_dir/ask.log
```

Be sure you substitute the proper paths for *home_dir* and *ask_path*. Due to security concerns, make sure the file permissions on the `.qmail` file are 600 as follows:

```
bash$ chmod 600 home_dir/.qmail
```

Procmail

Procmail can be used to integrate ASK into your mail infrastructure. ASK provides a `-procmail` switch for direct support of `procmail`. Using the `-procmail` switch, ASK works as a mail filter and returns an error code telling `procmail` whether to deliver a message.

To use ASK in this fashion, your `procmail` recipe should be as follows:

```
:0 fW
|/ask_path/ask.py --procmail --loglevel=5 --logfile=/home_dir/ask.log

:0 e
/dev/null
```

Any rules coming after the first block will receive email processed by ASK.

The second rule in this example instructs `procmail` to delete the message if ASK returns a fail code. If you don't trust ASK to do the right thing, you can save the messages to a file by replacing /dev/null with the path and filename.

MTA Integration Discussion

The preceding configurations direct ASK to monitor your emails and generate log messages to a file named `ask.log` under your home directory. Messages are stored in */home_dir/*.ask/queue until acted upon by the sender or by you, the recipient (see the next section, "Queue Management").

To test your setup, send yourself some emails and ask friends to do the same. Confirm with your email correspondents who are not on your whitelist that they receive the confirmation message. Have them reply to the confirmation message and verify that their email addresses appear in your whitelist.

Ensure confirmation messages are not being sent to mailing lists or other places where they shouldn't be. This can be accomplished by checking the logfile for your account, by default `~/ask.log`. When you are satisfied with ASK's operation, reduce the logging level by setting the `--loglevel=1` parameter in the `.forward`, `.qmailforward`, or `.procmail` files.

QUEUE MANAGEMENT

ASK gives you the ability to manage the messages awaiting action by senders. ASK stores the original message under the `~/.ask/queue` directory. The message stays queued until the sender replies or the recipient deletes it.

Each user who has activated ASK should check the contents of the queue periodically, removing old messages and delivering any messages that may have not been responded to. Sending yourself a message with ASK PROCESS QUEUE in the subject line will cause ASK to reply with all the queued files. With the response, you will be able to act on queued messages:

- Delete messages
- Add the message sender to one of your lists
- Dequeue messages

If you're using HTML mode (by setting rc_remote_cmd_htmlmail=yes) and are using an HTML-aware mail client, you can click on specified links inside the email to process the messages. Text mode users need to reply to the message and edit it before sending it back to ASK for processing.

It is also possible to edit the lists (white, ignore, and blacklist) via email. To manage the lists, just send yourself a message with the command ASK EDIT *listname*, where *listname* is one of WHITELIST, IGNORELIST, or BLACKLIST. ASK will send you back an email with the contents of your list and instructions on how to manipulate the lists.

TAGGED MESSAGE DELIVERY AGENT

TMDA is a challenge/response system that has a number of interesting features, some of which include:

- Optional auto-whitelisting of senders
- A web interface (separately available from *http://tmda.net/tmda-cgi/*)
- Responds "smartly" to automated messages from mailing lists, etc.
- Support for client-side From: address generation for "mangled" addresses

Although the focus of TMDA appears to be qmail, TMDA has good support for other MTAs as well, including the two we cover in this book (Postfix and Sendmail) and Exim. TMDA has whitelisting and blacklisting support, as every challenge/response system must have. TMDA utilizes the Hashed Method Authentication Codes (HMAC) defined by RFC2104, which are encoded in the To: line to ensure a basic level of authentication.

INSTALLATION

The first step is to download the latest version of the TMDA software, tmda-1.0.2. The URL to download the latest version is *http://www.us.tmda.net/releases/stable/tmda.tgz*. When downloaded, move it to /usr/local and unpack and compile it as follows:

```
bash$ gunzip tmda-1.02.tar.gz
bash$ tar xvf tmda-1.02.tar
bash$ cd tmda-1.0.2
bash$ sudo su
# ./compileall
```

TMDA is run directly out of its source directory, /usr/local/tmda-1.0.2. The various MTA hooks will point directly at that directory to run the individual TMDA components.

CONFIGURATION

First we cover how to configure TMDA with Sendmail, Postfix, and qmail. (It is assumed that the mail delivery agent (MDA) is Procmail if you are using either Postfix or Sendmail.) Also, we assume you are using Maildir-formatted mailboxes. If this is not the case, you would replace ~/Maildir/ with the path to the user mailbox, usually something like /var/spool/mail/*user*.

The first step, no matter which MTA is used, is to create the directories and run the keygen program. Do this by performing the following steps:

```
bash$ ./tmda-keygen
Generating a unique, 160-bit private key, please wait a moment..

80f200a6ed3a80db1f4a21171b9e90a9d9cdd243

Now paste the above key into ~/.tmda/crypt_key
and make sure to keep your key secret! (chmod 600 ~/.tmda/crypt_key)
```

Then simply copy the generated key into the crypt_key file in ~/.tmda and make it readable only to you by executing the chmod command as indicated in the program output.

Config File

There are two configuration files with TMDA: a system one located by default in /etc/tmdarc and a per-user one located by default in ~/.tmda/config. Settings in the per-user config file override the system attributes if there are duplicates. Not all of the possible settings are covered here; please check the TMDA web site section called "Configuration Variables" (*http://www.us.tmda.net/config-vars.html*) for a complete list of possible settings.

qmail

The setup is performed on a per-user basis, so each user must have her own TMDA setup in order for TMDA to work correctly. The first step is to initialize the TMDA configuration file in ~username/.tmda/config:

```
MAIL_TRANSFER_AGENT = "qmail"
RECIPIENT_DELIMITER = "-"
DELIVERY = "~/Mailbox"
CONFIRM_APPEND = os.path.expanduser("~/.tmda/lists/confirmed")
LOGFILE_DEBUG = os.path.expanduser("~/.tmda/logs/debug")
LOGFILE_INCOMING = os.path.expanduser("~/.tmda/logs/incoming")
LOGFILE_OUTGOING = os.path.expanduser("~/.tmda/logs/outgoing")
```

These settings tell TMDA to use the qmail MTA, how to parse the recipient address, the delivery folder, and locations of the confirmed addresses (email address that has gone through the confirmation process) and logfile locations.

Next, you must set up your .qmail* files. An in-depth discussion of .qmail functionality is beyond the scope of this book, but here is a short description of how to set up .qmail files for use with TMDA.

The first step is to decide how you want mail to be processed. Do you want everything to go through TMDA? Or only certain aliases? The example here assumes that only email addressed to user-filtered@isp.net goes through the filter, but you can set up TMDA on your default account, on specific accounts, or as a default "last resort" delivery attempt.

In the user's home directory, you want to set up a file called .qmail-filtered. In this file, you place the following two lines:

```
| preline /usr/local/bin/tmda-filter
./Mailbox
```

This directs every mail message that has a To: line of user-filtered to TMDA. If you want all of your mail to go through TMDA, simply name the file .qmail instead of .qmail-filter.

Postfix

Make sure Postfix has the following variable set in `/etc/postfix/main.cf`:

```
export_environment = TZ MAIL_CONFIG RECIPIENT SENDER
```

If the `export_environment` is not set as shown here, set it and reload Postfix by issuing the `postfix reload` command as root.

Set the following variables in the TMDA configuration file `~username/.tmda/config` to work with Postfix:

```
MAIL_TRANSFER_AGENT = "postfix"
RECIPIENT_DELIMITER = "+"
DELIVERY = "~/Maildir/"
CONFIRM_APPEND = os.path.expanduser("~/.tmda/lists/confirmed")
LOGFILE_DEBUG = os.path.expanduser("~/.tmda/logs/debug")
LOGFILE_INCOMING = os.path.expanduser("~/.tmda/logs/incoming")
LOGFILE_OUTGOING = os.path.expanduser("~/.tmda/logs/outgoing")
```

These settings tell TMDA to use Sendmail as the MTA, define the username separator as "+", set the delivery format as Maildir, and set the confirmation and log file locations.

Next, modify your `~/.forward` file to send everything through TMDA:

```
| /path/to/bin/tmda-filter
```

If you receive the error `env: python: No such file or directory`, it means the path to python must be specified as follows:

```
|/usr/local/bin/python /usr/local/bin/tmda-filter
```

Alternatively, if you want to use `procmail` to invoke TMDA, use the following steps. First, set up `~/.forward` to call `procmail` with the `-p` option:

```
|/path/to/bin/procmail -p
```

Then simply tack the following code onto the end of your `.procmailrc` file:

```
# Run the message through tmda-filter.
:0 w
| /path/to/bin/tmda-filter

# Take the exit code from TMDA.
EXITCODE=$?

# TMDA takes care of final delivery
DEFAULT=/dev/null
```

This `procmail` recipe will run every message through the `tmda-filter` program, which will handle final delivery of the message.

Sendmail

Sendmail requires the use of Procmail. First, set the following variables in the TMDA configuration file `~username/.tmda/config` to work with Sendmail:

```
MAIL_TRANSFER_AGENT = "sendmail"
RECIPIENT_DELIMITER = "+"
DELIVERY = "~/Maildir/"
CONFIRM_APPEND = os.path.expanduser("~/.tmda/lists/confirmed")
LOGFILE_DEBUG = os.path.expanduser("~/.tmda/logs/debug")
LOGFILE_INCOMING = os.path.expanduser("~/.tmda/logs/incoming")
LOGFILE_OUTGOING = os.path.expanduser("~/.tmda/logs/outgoing")
```

The Sendmail configuration settings are identical to the Postfix settings, except for the MTA, which is Sendmail.

Finally, set the appropriate variables and invoke `tmda-filter` by adding the following code to the end of your `~/.procmailrc` or system-wide `/etc/procmailrc` file:

```
# Uncomment this for users without valid shells.
# SHELL=/bin/sh

# Set the necessary environment variables.
EXTENSION="$1"
:0
* EXTENSION ?? .
{
  DELIMITER="+"
}
RECIPIENT="$LOGNAME$DELIMITER$EXTENSION@$HOST"
SENDER=`formail -x Return-Path | sed 's/[<>]//g;s/^[ ]*//'`

# Run the message through tmda-filter.
:0 w
| /path/to/bin/tmda-filter

# Take the exit code from TMDA.
EXITCODE=$?

# TMDA takes care of final delivery
DEFAULT=/dev/null
```

This Procmail recipe processes each message through `tmda-filter` after setting the delimter to +.

CLI Mail Client

TMDA can send email messages with enhanced `From:` lines that are cryptographically encoded, making them difficult to fake. This functionality can be used for creating addresses that are valid for a specified

- number of days
- sender
- keyword address

A time-limited address can be used for mailing list postings and the like. A sender-specific address can be used for correspondence with automated mailing list signups and similar tasks. A keyword address might be used for corresponding with an online merchant that you don't want to have a time-limited address for but can revoke at any time.

This functionality is very easy to use for command line mail clients such as mutt. The sendmail-tmda wrapper must be used to generate the proper mail headers for sending these messages. The only change is to the respective configuration file so that the mail client knows where to find the sendmail-tmda wrapper. Figure 12.9 lists the mail client and associated setting that must be made to support this functionality.

Mail/mailx .mailrc set sendmail="/path/to/tmda/bin/tmda-sendmail"

Pine .pinerc file: sendmail-path="/path/to/tmda/bin/tmda-sendmail"

Mutt .muttrc set sendmail="/path/to/tmda/bin/tmda-sendmail"
and make sure sendmail_wait is not set to -1.

VM .vm (setq sendmail-program "/path/to/tmda/bin/tmda-sendmail")

Gnus .gnus (setq sendmail-program "/path/to/tmda/bin/tmda-sendmail")

For Sylpheed, Configuration --> Common Preferences --> Send --> External
  Program
Check Use external program for sending
In the Program path box, enter /path/to/tmda/bin/tmda-sendmail

For Mahogany, Edit --> Preferences --> Network
Check Use local mail transfer agent
In the Local MTA command box, enter /path/to/tmda/bin/tmda-sendmail

For XFMail, Misc --> Config Accounts+Misc --> Send
Check Sendmail under Send method
In the Sendmail Path box, enter /path/to/tmda/bin/tmda-sendmail

For SqWebMail,
Replace /usr/local/share/sqwebmail/sendit.sh with contrib/sendit.sh from the
  TMDA distribution.
sendit.sh automatically works with SqWebMail + vpopmail + TMDA, or just
  SqWebMail + vpopmail.

For KMail (KDE Mail), Settings --> Configure KMail --> Network --> Sending Mail
Check Sendmail
In the Location box, enter /path/to/tmda/bin/tmda-sendmail

Figure 12.9 Email client setting for sending mail command. (From the TMDA website, *http://tmda.net.*)

Non-CLI Mail Client

For non-CLI-based mail clients—for example, Mozilla (even run from Unix) or Outlook Express—to support this functionality, you must run what essentially amounts to a mail proxy on the server. This program is called `tmda-ofmipd`, and it supports a minimal SMTP server and SMTP authentication via RFC2554. You *must* authenticate to use the server in this fashion; otherwise, it is accessible to spammers. `tmda-ofmipd` is set up as follows.

The `tmda-ofmipd` program supports the following back-end authentication methods:

- A TMDA-specific password file, by default in `/etc/tofmipd`
- Checkpassword-compatible utility such as checkpassword-pam available at *http://checkpasswd-pam.sourceforge.net/*
- Using a POP3, IMAP, or LDAP server in conjunction with `tmda-ofmipd`'s -R flag

We will show the first way, utilizing a password file. First, create a user and group to run the `tmda-ofmipd` program as:

```
bash$ sudo groupadd tofmipd
bash$ sudo useradd tofmipd -g tofmipd -s /nonexistent
```

The `/etc/tofmipd` file consists of username/password pairs separated by colons like this:

```
bob:apassword
mary:abadpassword
```

The usernames should match the usernames on the system. This is not a requirement, but it makes support easier. The passwords should be different than other passwords on the system, but again they don't have to be. After the file is created and populated, be sure to change the privileges to 600 to ensure that the password information stays safe like this:

```
bash$ sudo chmod 600 /etc/tofmipd
```

By default, `tofmipd` listens on port 8025, which should be acceptable for most installations. This can be changed, however, using the -p flag. Please note that to use this functionality, the mail client user must change his client settings to reflect these changes, namely:

- SMTP authentication
- Port 8025 rather than the default port 25

Please refer to Chapters 5 and 9 for more information on setting up your mail client for use with SMTP authentication and alternate ports.

CONCLUSION

Many sender verification anti-spam systems are available. The most commonly used sender verification system is probably challenge/response, where a recipient requires a sender (who is not already whitelisted) to reply to a challenge message in order to verify that the sender's message is not spam. A variation on this is the sender compute method, where the recipient requires a sender (who is not whitelisted) to compute an algorithm to prove that he or she is not a bulk emailer.

We chose to cover Camram, which is a sender compute verification system, along with facilities for challenge/response and a very nice GUI for the CRM114 Bayesian filter. ASK is a traditional challenge/response system that implements verification via MD5 email message headers. We finished the chapter with coverage of TMDA, which is another challenge/response system with sender compute functionality as well as an available GUI.

Sender Policy Framework

Sender Policy Framework (SPF, formerly known as Sender Permitted From) is a method where domains list what IP addresses will originate email messages for the users in their domain. In this way, spammers won't be able to use a MAIL FROM address of any domain that uses SPF and any potential recipient who is enforcing SPF checks.

SPF can be very effective at reducing spam, although it is a relatively new concept and has not been widely adopted. At the very least, a domain can use SPF to run content filtering checks (such as Bayesian analysis) on email messages that weren't sent from SPF-verified domains. In this way, the expensive Bayesian and other such content checks can be run on messages that originate from possibly suspect senders.

HOW SPF WORKS

You can think of SPF as reverse mail exchange (MX) records for your domain. Because MX records define which machine should receive email for a given domain, reverse MX indicates which machines should be originating email for a given domain.

There are two pieces to Sender Policy Framework: the originating side and the enforcement side. The originating domain owner who wants to protect his or her domain from having spammers use it to forge MAIL FROM simply publishes the appropriate DNS TXT records in SPF format. Recipients who enforce SPF (in order to reduce the amount of spam coming into their users' mailboxes) look up those DNS TXT records.

The verification process goes like this. The IP address of the originating email server is checked against the SPF record for the domain in question. If the originating mail server was authorized to send messages for that domain, the message is allowed through. If not, the message can be rejected, sidelined, or subject to further checks (such as Bayesian or DCC) and delivered to the recipient.

PUBLISHING SPF RECORDS

Setting up your domain to support SPF records is as simple as setting up a DNS TXT record. Let's say you have the domain `mydomain.com`, and it originates all email from `mydomain.com` users from the netblock 1.2.3.4/24. The SPF TXT record for this domain is

```
mydomain.com    IN    TXT    "v=spf1 ip4:1.2.3.4/24 -all"
```

If the owner of `mydomain.com` has MX machines that originate messages but that are not in the 1.2.3.4 netblock, those can be added with the `mx` keyword. If the owner of `mydomain.com` wants to allow any host that ends in `mydomain.com` to be authorized to send email, then those can be added with the `ptr` keyword. The complete SPF record is

```
mydomain.com    IN    TXT    "v=spf1 mx ptr ip4:1.2.3.4/24 -all"
```

The SPF web site (*http://spf.pobox.com/*) has a nice wizard that generates SPF TXT records for you. It is available at *http://spf.pobox.com/wizard.html*. Figure A.1 is a screenshot of the SPF setup wizard.

The SPF records can be checked using an online tool for accuracy. Figure A.2 shows one such testing tool located at *http://spftools.net/check.php*.

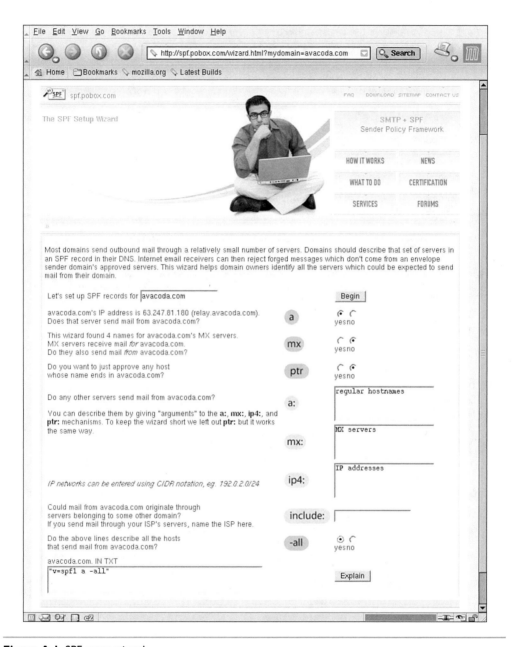

Figure A.1 SPF setup wizard.

File Edit View Go Bookmarks Tools Window Help

http://spftools.infinitepenguins.net/check.php?action=spfcheck   Search

Home   Bookmarks   mozilla.org   Latest Builds

SPF Tools at spfTools.net
Site FAQs | Test Records | Create Records | Adoption Roll & Validator | Email Header Checker | Login | SPF Wiki

SPF Check

SMTP client address (IPv4)	192.168.16.11	(eg 195.112.4.54)
SMTP HELO identifier	whammo.cushman.avacoda.com	(eg smtp.nildram.co.uk)
SMTP MAIL FROM address	dale@avacoda.com	(eg wechsler@spfmail.phase.org)

Submit Query

What's it mean?

Let's take the example that uses the values above. I send mail from my home machine (where my email address is wechsler@spfmail.phase.org) to an account on my server (eg wechsler@somewhere.org).
This message travels from my ISP's outgoing server at smtp.nildram.co.uk (195.112.4.54) to my server at mail.phase.org (212.13.198.241)

In this case, the SMTP client (the machine sending the mail) is 195.112.4.54, the HELO is 'smtp.nildram.net' and the FROM is wechsler@spfmail.phase.org
To perform an SPF check, mail.phase.org will check the SPF record for infinitepenguins.net and see if 195.112.4.54 is allowed to send mail from there. Click Here to see the result.

So where does the HELO come in? When an internet mail message is bounced or undelivered, the MAIL FROM data is empty. In this case, the server will use the HELO identifier to check permissions instead.

Let's suppose that something's gone wrong (eg my account on my server is full) and my server has to generate an error message. Then a message with a blank FROM field travels from mail.phase.org to smtp.nildram.co.uk. Click Here to see the result.

Now suppose that someone wants to pretend to be me. They can't send from any of the SMTP servers I've designated, because they're properly secured. So they try and send from a server at 11.22.33.44. Click Here to see the result.

In SMTP terms, smtp.nildram.net (acting as the client, and connecting from IP address 195.112.4.54) says:
HELO smtp.nildram.net
MAIL FROM: wechsler@spfmail.phase.org
This is followed by the to: address and the message of the data, but SPF has no interest in that.

The result

IP '192.168.16.11' HELO 'whammo.cushman.avacoda.com' SENDER 'dale@avacoda.com'

Testing record for avacoda.com (probably v=spf1 a -all)

Calling: /usr/local/bin/spfquery -ip=192.168.16.11 -sender=dale@avacoda.com

Response:
spfquery (reference implementation) says:

PHP spf1_parser says:

Received-SPF: fail (match default)

A service of libspf.org | Contact: webmaster@spftools.net
Please report all bugs (Product SPFTools)

Hosted by DCCNET High-Speed Cable Internet
DCCNET

Done

Figure A.2 SPF TXT record verification tool.

ENFORCING SPF RECORDS

In order to enforce SPF records, changes to the MTA that receives messages for your users must be made. SPF checks should occur on the (mail relay) machines, which receive messages from the Internet for your users. Otherwise, the envelope information is lost, and SPF enforcement is moot.

In our SPF enforcement example, we use Sendmail. The SPF downloads page (*http://spf.pobox.com/downloads.html*) contains links to various SPF enforcement implementations for a number of MTAs.

INSTALLING SPF-MILTER

spf-milter is an SPF implementation using milter for Sendmail written in Perl. It requires the following:

- Perl 5.8.x or higher, thread enabled (compiled with `-Duseithreads`)
- The following Perl modules:
  - POSIX
  - Sendmail::Milter
  - Socket
  - Net::CIDR
  - Mail::SPF::Query
  - Mail::SRS
  - Getopt
  - Errno
- Sendmail built for milter support

Install the Perl program somewhere on your system. (We assume that the location is `/usr/local/sbin/sendmail-milter-spf-1.41.pl` for the purposes of this example.)

Make the following changes to `sendmail.mc`:

```
define(`confMILTER_LOG_LEVEL',`9')dnl
define(`confMILTER_MACROS_HELO', confMILTER_MACROS_HELO`, {verify}')dnl
INPUT_MAIL_FILTER(`spf-milter', `S=local:/var/spf-milter/spf-milter.sock, F=T,
➥T=C:4m;S:4m;R:8m;E:10m')
```

Rebuild and install `sendmail.cf` by executing

```
# make sendmail.cf
# cp /etc/mail/sendmail.cf /etc/mail/sendmail.cf.orig
# cp sendmail.cf /etc/mail/sendmail.cf
```

Next, create the `spfmilter` user, start up `spf-milter`, and then start up Sendmail:

```
# useradd spfmilter
# /usr/local/bin/perl /usr/local/bin/sendmail-milter-spf-1.41.pl spfmilter
# /etc/init.d/sendmail restart
```

In this example, we run the `spf-milter` program as user `spfmilter`. Any valid system account will do, other than user `root`. The `spf-milter` creates a socket in the `/var/spf-milter` directory for communicating between Sendmail and SPF.

EXAMPLE REJECTION MESSAGE

Here is an example message where the server was enforcing SPF and a message was sent from an IP address not allowed from the SPF record:

```
Subject: Undelivered Mail Returned to Sender
From: MAILER-DAEMON@avacoda.com (Mail Delivery System)
Date: Mon, 23 Aug 2004 22:46:53 -0400 (EDT)
To: dale@avacoda.com

This is the Postfix program at host mail.avacoda.com.

I'm sorry to have to inform you that the message returned
below could not be delivered to one or more destinations.

For further assistance, please send mail to <postmaster>

If you do so, please include this problem report. You can
delete your own text from the message returned below.

                    The Postfix program

<dale@woody.cushman.avacoda.com>: host woody.cushman.avacoda.com[192.168.16.9]
    said: 550 5.7.1 <dale@avacoda.com>... Please see
    http://spf.pobox.com/why.html?sender=dale@avacoda.com&ip=
    ➥192.168.16.11&receiver=woody.cushman.avacoda.com
    (in reply to MAIL FROM command)

Reporting-MTA: dns; mail.avacoda.com
Arrival-Date: Mon, 23 Aug 2004 22:46:51 -0400 (EDT)

Final-Recipient: rfc822; dale@woody.cushman.avacoda.com
Action: failed
Status: 5.0.0
```

```
Diagnostic-Code: X-Postfix; host woody.cushman.avacoda.com[192.168.16.9] said:
    550 5.7.1 <dale@avacoda.com>... Please see
    http://spf.pobox.com/why.html?sender=dale@avacoda.com&ip=
    ➥192.168.16.11&receiver=woody.cushman.avacoda.com
    (in reply to MAIL FROM command)



Subject: testing
From: dale@avacoda.com (Dale Nielsen)
Date: Mon, 23 Aug 2004 22:46:51 -0400 (EDT)
To: dale@woody.cushman.avacoda.com

really!
```

The SPF enforcer places a link to where the sender can go to learn why the message was rejected and what the sender (or ISP) must do in order to communicate with that particular domain.

Reporting Spam

One of the oldest methods of dealing with spam is reporting it to the spammer's provider. More recently, however, spammers have begun using other people's resources to send their messages out, making spam reporting a difficult task. Many spammers have special contracts (often called "pink sheets") where the provider allows spammers to send their garbage with impunity. Reporting these types of spammers often does no good, unless additional investigation is performed, and the spammer's provider's "upstream" provider (or an organization such as the North American Network Operators Group) gets involved.

Some spammers have started taking revenge on people who report spam, making them victims of *joe job* (or other types of) attacks. A *joe job* attack is where a spammer uses an unsuspecting user (such as the person who originated a spam complaint) as the From: email address in one of their spam emailings. This causes the unsuspecting user to receive numerous misdirected complaints, filling up their email box.

In this appendix, we cover the following topics:

- How to read an email header
- Sam Spade, a utility that assists you in reading email headers
- SpamCop, a popular service to help you read spam and report it to ISPs automatically

To the untrained eye, an email message header may seem confusing. However, to the spam fighting email administrator, a wealth of information is contained in the headers. Spammers often don't even bother to attempt to do a good job of hiding their tracks.

If they did, it would make finding the spammers much more difficult. Some tactics spammers use to hide themselves include

- Adding fake headers
- Forging time stamps
- Using open relays to send spam
- Using compromised machines to send spam
- Using backup MX machines

The best spammers fake their originating IP address, making them virtually impossible to track down. However, this is difficult to do and often requires the assistance of ISPs in order to successfully use this technique.

READING AN EMAIL HEADER

Unfortunately, reading an email header takes much practice and knowledge. In this section, we present an overview of reading email headers, starting with how to view the headers.

The steps are as follows:

1. View the headers from the message.
2. Analyze the headers.
3. Act on the information found.

VIEWING HEADERS

All major email clients today by default do not show the "full headers" required in order to track down a spammer's origin. This can be accomplished as follows.

Mozilla Messenger

Within Messenger, be sure the message whose headers you want to view is active. Then press `Ctrl-U` or go to `View==>Message Source`, which brings up a window showing you the headers for the message. The headers can be copied/pasted with the appropriate select/copy action.

Mozilla also has the `View==>Headers==>All` setting, which sometimes shows all headers of the current email message. However, there have been many bugs in this functionality, and it is difficult to copy/paste headers viewed in this manner, so the View==>Message Source method is preferable.

Microsoft Outlook Express

From the Outlook Express screen, select the message whose headers you want to view. Then go to File==>Properties==>Details tab. This brings up the headers in a small window from which you can copy information by right-clicking, selecting Select All, right-clicking again, and selecting Copy.

Microsoft Outlook

From the main Outlook screen, select the message whose full headers you want to view. Then right-click on that message and select Options. The Message Options window appears, and at the bottom of this window is a small box labeled Internet headers: in which the headers for the message appear. The header text may then be selected and copy/pasted as necessary.

ANALYZING HEADERS

When the header information has been obtained, the header can be analyzed. Often, the most straightforward way to do this is to look at an actual spam message's headers and analyze them.

Here is the example spam message header we will use:

```
From - Sat Aug 28 17:47:24 2004
X-UIDL: 1074279839.16240
X-Mozilla-Status: 0001
X-Mozilla-Status2: 00000000
Return-Path: <hejslbott@ccnt.com>
Received: from jupiter.cnetwork.com ([unix socket]) by jupiter (Cyrus v2.1.13) with
LMTP; Sat, 28 Aug 2004 17:45:33 -0400
X-Sieve: CMU Sieve 2.2
Received: from mars.cnetwork.com (mars.cnetwork.com [67.107.96.132]) by
jupiter.cnetwork.com (Postfix) with ESMTP id A0A7267F0E for
<someuser_cnetwork_com@jupiter.cnetwork.com>; Sat, 28 Aug 2004 17:45:33 -0400 (EDT)
Received: from localhost (localhost [127.0.0.1]) by mars.cnetwork.com (Postfix) with
ESMTP id 527F02E829 for <someuser_cnetwork_com@jupiter.cnetwork.com>; Sat, 28 Aug 2004
17:45:33 -0400 (EDT)
Received: from mars.cnetwork.com ([127.0.0.1]) by localhost (mars [127.0.0.1])
(amavisd-new, port 10024) with ESMTP id 11179-09 for
<someuser_cnetwork_com@jupiter.cnetwork.com>; Sat, 28 Aug 2004 17:45:13 -0400 (EDT)
```

```
Received: from stibitz.computer.org (unknown [206.99.235.25]) by mars.cnetwork.com
(Postfix) with ESMTP id E9AC92E833 for <someuser@cnetwork.com>; Sat, 28 Aug 2004
17:45:08 -0400 (EDT)
Received: from cm61-10-30-47.hkcable.com.hk (cm61-10-30-47.hkcable.com.hk
[61.10.30.47]) by stibitz.computer.org (Switch-2.2.8/Switch-2.2.4) with SMTP id
W7SL314M00001634; Sat, 28 Aug 2004 17:37:40 -0400
X-Message-Info: POBTnBF00gQXv/dGlNIavToFj2xiPi4U
Received: from peugeot-x22.cheesecloth.aol.com ([66.30.88.216]) by xk6-
z34.hotmail.com with Microsoft SMTPSVC(5.0.2195.6824);
      Sat, 28 Aug 2004 17:33:39 -0400
From: Ginger Jacobson <epezrilrr@daum.net>
To: xxxxxx@computer.org
Subject: registry rochester
Date: Sun, 29 Aug 2004 01:36:39 +0400 EST
Message-ID: <24350179568703.72136.87869123@bash-y75.aol.com>
Mime-Version: 1.0
Content-Type: multipart/alternative;
      boundary="--=====7974805806777=_"
X-Virus-Scanned: by amavisd-new at cnetwork.com
X-Spam-Status: No, hits=4.7 tagged_above=0.1 required=6.3 tests=HTML_20_30,
 HTML_MESSAGE, INVALID_DATE, MIME_HTML_NO_CHARSET, MIME_HTML_ONLY, OFFER,
 ONLY_COST, ROUND_THE_WORLD_LOCAL
X-Spam-Level: ****
X-Text-Classification: spam
X-POPFile-Link: http://127.0.0.1:8080/jump_to_message?view=popfile13852=1.msg
```

The best way to read message headers is from the bottom up, so that is what we will do here. The goal is to follow the chain of (nonforged) Received: headers, which leads to our mail server. The first (bottom to top) nonforged Received: header in the chain is the originating IP address.

The headers that begin with X- indicate supplemental information, added by various applications.

X-POPFile-Link

Generated by POPFile, this allows the user to click on the header to easily reclassify the message.

X-Text-Classification

This header is generated by POPFile, with the tag spam indicating that POPFile correctly identified this message as spam.

X-Spam-Level

This is generated by SpamAssassin, and it shows that the message received a score of 4, indicated by the 4 asterisks. Interestingly, this score falls just below the default Spam-Assassin threshold of 5, so the spammer probably tuned the message specifically to achieve a score below the default threshold.

X-Spam-Status

This shows the SpamAssassin results from scoring the message.

X-Virus-Scanned

This header is added by the virus scanner in use, amavisd-new.

When we are past the X- headers, we get into the headers that are actually defined by the SMTP protocol. These are often abused by spammers.

Mime-Version
Content-Type

These are normal headers.

Message-ID: <24350179568703.72136.87869123@bash-y75.aol.com>

This header is faked, as the spammer tries to obfuscate his tracks by using the @bash-y75.aol.com at the end of the value (more on this later).

Date: Sun, 29 Aug 2004 01:36:39 +0400 EST

Spammers and spamming software often tamper with the date field, as in this message. In this case, EST is indicated as +0400, but EST is in fact -0400, not +0400 from GMT. Spammers do this to make it harder for ISPs to find their dial-in records in their logs.

Subject: registry rochester

The subject line used here is an attempt to get past Bayesian classifiers. Unfortunately for the spammer, the recipient doesn't get many messages with registry rochester as the subject line, making spam easier to spot.

To: xxxxxx@computer.org
From: Ginger Jacobson <epezrilrr@daum.net>

These are fairly normal headers. The To is probably a legitimate email address (changed here for privacy reasons), and the From may or may not be. Not much help here.

The next lines are where things get really interesting. The trick here is to find the first "real" `Received` header, as that will tell us the source IP address of the message. More often than not, the first "real" received header will be some compromised machine that is difficult or impossible to track down. It may also be an open email relay machine whose owner is unaware of or doesn't care about its status as such.

```
Received: from peugeot-x22.cheesecloth.aol.com ([66.30.88.216])
by xk6-z34.hotmail.com with Microsoft SMTPSVC(5.0.2195.6824);
     Sat, 28 Aug 2004 17:33:39 -0400
```

This is another attempt at a faked header. You can tell by doing a WHOIS and reverse DNS lookups on the IP address (`66.30.88.216`) and name (`peugeot-x22.cheesecloth.aol.com`), confirming that they don't match. In fact, the IP address `66.30.88.216` is owned by Comcast. Comcast would not have a hostname that ends in `aol.com`, as Comcast and AOL are competitors!

```
X-Message-Info: POBTnBF00gQXv/dGlNIavToFj2xiPi4U
```

This header normally indicates that the message was sent from a Hotmail account. Due to the fact that this message was not sent from a Hotmail account (see the following), this is yet another attempt at a faked header.

```
Received: from cm61-10-30-47.hkcable.com.hk (cm61-10-30-47.hkcable.com.hk
[61.10.30.47]) by stibitz.computer.org (Switch-2.2.8/Switch-2.2.4) with SMTP id
W7SL314M00001634; Sat, 28 Aug 2004 17:37:40 -0400
```

This looks like the first "real" `Received` header, though we won't know for sure until we check the next `Received` header in the chain. This header indicates that the message originated from `61.10.30.47` and was received by `stibitz.computer.org`.

```
Received: from stibitz.computer.org (unknown [206.99.235.25]) by mars.cnetwork.com
(Postfix) with ESMTP id E9AC92E833 for <someuser@cnetwork.com>; Sat, 28 Aug 2004
17:45:08 -0400 (EDT)
```

This header indicates that `stibitz.computer.org` sent the message to `mars.cnetwork.com`. The presence of `stibitz.computer.org` as the originator corresponds to the sender in the previous `Received` header. As a result, we know that the originating IP address in the previous `Received` header (namely `61.10.30.47`) is indeed the originating IP address of the message.

The originating IP address (in our case, `61.10.30.47`) can be analyzed a number of ways:

- Whose network is it on?
- What provider(s) are upstream of that network?
- Where is the machine located geographically?
- Is the machine on any known spammer list?
- What type of machine is it?

If we want to report the message, the most important question is the first one—Whose network is it on? When we know the network the IP address comes from, the spam report can be filed. The other information can be useful in certain cases, depending on the type of spammer. For example, if the spammer is colluding with an ISP who is condoning spamming, the other information could be used to pressure other large networks into blocking that ISP's traffic.

Using the DNSstuff tool (see the following), a WHOIS lookup of the IP address in question (61.10.30.47) returns the following information:

```
WHOIS results for 61.10.30.47
Generated by www.DNSstuff.com

Country: HONG KONG

ARIN says that this IP belongs to APNIC; I'm looking it up there.


Using cached answer (or, you can get fresh results).
Hiding E-mail address (you can get results with the E-mail address).

% [whois.apnic.net node-1]
% Whois data copyright terms    http://www.apnic.net/db/dbcopyright.html

inetnum:       61.10.0.0 - 61.10.63.255
netname:       HKCABLE-HK
descr:         HK Cable TV Ltd
descr:         Cable Multi-Media Services
country:       HK
admin-c:       AD23-AP
tech-c:        AD23-AP
mnt-by:        APNIC-HM
mnt-lower:     MAINT-HK-ICABLE
changed:       **********@apnic.net 20000127
status:        ALLOCATED PORTABLE
source:        APNIC
```

```
person:        administrator dns
address:       12/F., Cable TV Tower,
address:       9 Hoi Shing Road,
address:       Tsuen Wan,
address:       N.T.,
address:       HK
country:       HK
phone:         +852-2112-7516
fax-no:        +852-2112-7977
e-mail:        *********@cms.hkcable.com
nic-hdl:       AD23-AP
mnt-by:        MAINT-HK-ICABLE
changed:       *********@cms.hkcable.com 20000811
source:        APNIC
```

A link is available on DNSstuff that displays the email address for reporting the message, if desired.

Occasionally, the message body contains information that might be useful in reporting. For example, any valid URL that is contained in the message itself can be analyzed and reported. SpamCop automatically identifies and reports (if you desire) URLs that are referenced in spam messages. In our example case, the referenced URLs were not valid, so there is no way to report them.

TOOLS

In order to perform the preceding analysis of who is responsible for the spamming IP address, it is helpful to have network lookup tools at your disposal. These tools are available either as web sites or as applications that run under Windows or Linux workstations.

You might wonder why one type of tool might be better than the other. Workstation-based tools are usually better because they cannot be stopped by denial of service attacks, web site outages, or similar types of interruptions. However, web site tools can be updated more often and may be easier to use than workstation-based tools.

Workstation Tool

An excellent Windows-based network lookup tool is called SamSpade. It enables all of the utilities you might require for spam fighting:

- WHOIS
- DNS
- traceroute

It has many other functions as well. It is available for download here: *http://www.samspade.org/ssw/download.html.*

Online Tool

An excellent web-based tool is available at *http://www.dnsstuff.com/*. The DNSstuff main page has all of the functions you might require for fighting spam. There are many other online utilities that can help in the fight against spam.

SpamCop

SpamCop can help to automate the analysis of email headers. It is available at *http://www.spamcop.net*. Although SpamCop is useful, it does have some limitations. Like any automated solution, SpamCop will occasionally fail to analyze a header correctly. In that case, you will need to analyze the message headers by hand in order to find the party to complain to. However, it can be very useful in the process of automating spam reporting.

SpamCop has free services and services you must pay for. The difference is that the non-free service works faster and doesn't have a nag screen.

With the free service, you have two choices regarding how you can submit spam, namely via email or via a web site to which you can copy/paste the message. Continuing our example, the SpamCop result is as follows:

```
Please make sure this email IS spam:
From: Ginger Jacobson <epezrilrr@daum.net> (registry rochester )
 ----=====7974805806777=_
 Content-Type: text/html;
View full message

Report Spam to:

Re: 61.10.30.47 (Administrator of network where email originates)
To: abuse@cms.hkcable.com (Notes)

Re: 61.10.30.47 (Third party interested in email source)
To: Cyveillance spam collection (Notes)

Re: 67.107.96.132 (Automated open-relay testing system(s))
To: Internal spamcop handling: (relays) (Notes)

Re: http://excellent.agidgkf.info/?sh.xudytk0zressr... (Administrator of network
hosting website referenced in spam)
To: postmaster@epnetworks.co.kr (Notes)
To: spamcop@kisa.or.kr (Notes)
To: abuse@epnetworks.co.kr (Notes)
```

```
Re: http://splendid.ahhdjkb.info/excellence?olknq3o... (Administrator of network
hosting website referenced in spam)
To: postmaster@epnetworks.co.kr (Notes)
To: spamcop@kisa.or.kr (Notes)
To: abuse@epnetworks.co.kr (Notes)
```

Each To: line indicates a spam report message that SpamCop will send if you click the
Send Spam Report(s) Now button while the appropriate checkboxes are on. As you can
see in this example, SpamCop analyzed the message and identified the same IP address as
we did in our manual analysis. In addition, it analyzed the message for additional email
addresses to send the message to, including URLs referenced. In our case, the referenced
URLs that are most likely bogus are

```
http://splendid.ahhdjkb.info
http://splendid.ahhdjkb.info
```

Because the URLs are not valid, there is no need to have SpamCop report them. Simply
uncheck the appropriate boxes before clicking the Send button.

Default SpamAssassin Ruleset

This appendix contains the description of the list of rules distributed as part of SpamAssassin 2.63. The table is taken from the SpamAssassin web site, *http://spamassassin.apache.org/tests.html*.

There are five columns in this table:

1. Area Tested
2. Locale
3. Description of Test
4. Test Name
5. Default Scores

Each is covered in the sections that follow.

AREA TESTED

This attribute specifies the location within the message that is tested. The four possible values are

1. `full`

    Indicates the test is active for the entire message, including header and body

2. `body`

    Indicates the test is active for only the body of the message

3. `rawbody`

   Indicates text, including all textual parts decoded from base64 or quoted-printable encoding, leaving HTML tags and line breaks intact

4. `header`

   Indicates the test is active for the header (envelope) part of the message

5. `uri`

   Any part of the message that is identified as a universal resource indicator such as `http://` or `ftp://`

LOCALE

Specifies the language the test expects. Defaults to `en`. The only language locale in the default ruleset as of version 2.63 other than `en` is `es` (Spanish).

DESCRIPTION OF TEST

This is a plain language explanation of the test.

TEST NAME

This is the name given to the test. It can be used to reassign scores to a given test; see the next section, "Default Scores Assigned."

DEFAULT SCORES ASSIGNED

Scores can be positive or negative, and can be real numbers. There are four possible values here:

1. `local`

   Purely local tests, such as header and heuristic checks

2. `net`

   Network tests (DCC, Pyzor, Vipul Razor, MX/DNS verification, etc.)

3. `with bayes`

   Integrated SpamAssassin Bayesian tests

4. `bayes+net`

Bayesian and network tests

In cases where there is only one score listed, it is used for all four values. Scores can be overridden by using the `score` keyword in the `local_prefs` file. For example, the following would change the value of the `CHARSET_FARAWAY` test assigned from the default of 3.2 to 4.2:

```
score CHARSET_FARAWAY      4.2
```

In a case where there are all four scores, but you want to change only one of the scores, simply repeat the other three scores, and change the score that needs changing. For example, to change the rule named `MIME_BASE64_TEXT` `bayes+net` score to be 0.498, you would place an entry in your `local_prefs` file like this:

```
score MIME_BASE64_TEXT     1.780 0.110 1.403 0.498
```

The preceding line changes the `bayes+net` score to be 0.498, leaving the other three scores the same.

SAMPLE RULES

The full list of rules that are distributed as part of SpamAssassin 2.63 is available from the SpamAssassin web site, *http://spamassassin.apache.org/tests.html*. The following table is an excerpt from that list.

AREA TESTED	LOCALE	DESCRIPTION OF TEST	TEST NAME	DEFAULT SCORES (local, net, with bayes, with bayes+net)			
body		Generic Test for Unsolicited Bulk Email	GTUBE	1000.000			
full		Listed in Razor2 (http://razor.sf.net/)	RAZOR2_CHECK	0	0.150	0	1.511
body		Razor2 gives confidence level above 50%	RAZOR2_CF_RANGE_51_100	0	1.485	0	0.056
full		Listed in DCC (http://rhyolite.com/anti-spam/dcc/)	DCC_CHECK	0	1.373	0	2.169
full		Listed in Pyzor (http://pyzor.sf.net/)	PYZOR_CHECK	0	2.041	0	3.451
body		Incorporates a tracking ID number	TRACKER_ID	1.825	1.064	1.818	0.555
body		Weird repeated double-quotation marks	WEIRD_QUOTING	1.353	1.966	1.774	2.000
rawbody		Extra blank lines in base64 encoding	MIME_BASE64_BLANKS	0.693	0.819	1.391	1.469
rawbody		base64 attachment does not have a file name	MIME_BASE64_NO_NAME	0.022	0	0.017	0.000
rawbody		Message text disguised using base64 encoding	MIME_BASE64_TEXT	1.780	0.110	1.403	0.298
rawbody		MIME section missing boundary	MIME_MISSING_BOUNDARY	0	0.247	0.224	0
body		Multipart message mostly text/html MIME	MIME_HTML_MOSTLY	1.540	0.285	0.713	1.023
body		Message only has text/html MIME parts	MIME_HTML_ONLY	1.204	1.158	1.156	0.177
rawbody		Quoted-printable line longer than 76 chars	MIME_QP_LONG_LINE	0	0.000	0.105	0.039
rawbody		MIME filename does not match content	MIME_SUSPECT_NAME	0.100			
body		HTML and text parts are different	MPART_ALT_DIFF	1.837	1.505	1.823	0.066
body		Character set indicates a foreign language	CHARSET_FARAWAY	3.200			

SpamAssassin Command Line Interface Reference

This appendix contains a complete list of command options for SpamAssassin version 2.63. The command descriptions in this appendix are based on the SpamAssassin website: *http://spamassassin.apache.org*. The commands covered here are as follows:

```
spamassassin
spamd
spamc
sa-learn
```

SPAMASSASSIN COMMAND OPTIONS

The flags listed in this section are available to the spamassassin command. spamassassin commands are broken down into the following categories:

- **General**—Options that deal with how spamassassin runs, such as checks, filenames, debugging, etc.
- **Configuration File**—Flags that define actions associated with the various configuration files
- **Blacklisting/Whitelisting**—Options that manage spamassassin's integrated blacklist and whitelist functionality
- **Reporting**—Command options that tell spamassassin how to manage reporting of spam back to Vipul's Razor, DCC, Pyzor, and the internal SpamAssassin Bayesian engine

General

```
-P, --pipe                      Deliver to STDOUT (now default)
```

The program now delivers output to standard out by default. This option is deprecated and should not be used.

```
-L, --local                     Local tests only (no online tests)
```

Only perform header and body checks—no distributed checksum or DNS testing.

```
-e, --exit-code
```

Exit with a non-zero exit code if the tested message was spam.

```
-l filename, --log-to-mbox=filename Log messages to a mbox file
```

Log all messages that pass through the filter to an mbox-formatted file named "file." This is useful for reporting spamtrap messages.

```
-t, --test-mode
```

Pipe message through and add extra report to the bottom.

```
-D, --debug [area=n,...]         Print debugging messages
```

The area(s) of code and levels (n) that can be debugged.

```
-V, --version
```

Print version information.

```
-h, --help
```

Print usage message.

Configuration File

```
-C path, --configpath=path, --config-file=path   Path to standard configuration dir
```

Set an alternate location for the distributed configuration files directory (defaults to /usr/share/spamassassin).

```
-p prefs, --prefspath=file, --prefs-file=file    Set user preferences file
```

Set an alternate location for user score preferences (defaults to
`~/.spamassassin/user_prefs`).

```
--siteconfigpath=path              Path for site configs
```

Set alternate location for site-specific configuration files directory (defaults to
`/etc/mail/spamassassin`).

```
-x, --nocreate-prefs               Don't create user preferences file
```

Disable creation of user preference file.

```
--lint                             Lint the rule set: report syntax errors
```

Check the configuration files for syntax errors and report accordingly.

Blacklisting/Whitelisting

```
-W, --add-to-whitelist             Add addresses in mail to whitelist
                                   (Auto White List or AWL)
```

Add all email addresses in body and text of message to automatic whitelist. Note that you
must use this with the -a option.

```
--add-to-blacklist                 Add addresses in mail to blacklist (AWL)
```

Add all email addresses in headers and text of message to blacklist. Note that this must be
used with the -a option.

```
-R, --remove-from-whitelist        Remove all addresses found in mail from whitelist
(AWL)
```

Remove all email addresses in message from whitelist. Note that this must be used with
the -a option.

```
--add-addr-to-whitelist=addr       Add addr to whitelist (AWL)
```

Add named email address to whitelist. This must be used with the -a option.

```
--add-addr-to-blacklist=addr       Add addr to blacklist (AWL)
```

Add named email address to blacklist. This option must be used with the -a option.

`--remove-addr-from-whitelist=`*addr* Remove *addr* from whitelist (AWL)

Remove the named address from whitelist. You must use this with the -a option.

Reporting

`-r, --report`   `Report message as spam`

Report this message as spam to various checksum services, Vipul Razor, DCC, Pyzor, and the internal Bayesian processor. In order to only report to the internal Bayesian engine, use the sa-learn command instead.

`-k, --revoke`   `Revoke message as spam`

Tell the Vipul Razor clearinghouse that the message is not spam. DCC and Pyzor do not support this functionality.

`-w `*addr*`, --warning-from=`*addr*   `Send a warning mail to sender from addr`

Set the From: address for reporting trapped spam. Only useful with the -r option.

`-d, --remove-markup`   `Remove spam reports from a message`

Remove the headers added by SpamAssassin.

SPAMD

The spamd program is a daemonized version of spamassassin. Therefore, several of the options are the same as spamassassin. The options for spamd are as follows, broken down by function:

General

`-d, --daemonize`   `Daemonize`

Detach from terminal and run in the background.

`-h, --help`

Print usage message.

`-r pidfile, --pidfile`   `Write the process id to pidfile`

The name for the spamd process id file.

```
-m num, --max-children num          Allow maximum num children
```

Specifies the maximum number of children spamd can spawn. Note that this can vary, depending upon underlying Unix implementation. If the maximum is reached, additional incoming connections will be queued.

```
-D, --debug
```

Print debugging messages.

Configuration File

```
-c, --create-prefs                  Create user preferences files
```

Create user preference files. The default action is not to create them.

```
-C path, --configpath=path          Path for default config files
```

Set an alternate location for the distributed configuration files directory (defaults to /usr/share/spamassassin).

```
--siteconfigpath=path               Path for site configs
```

Set alternate location for site specific configuration files directory (defaults to /etc/mail/spamassassin).

Virtual Users

```
-V, --virtual-config=dir            Enable Virtual configs
```

Specifies where virtual users configuration files can be found. Requires -x option.

```
--virtual-config-dir=dir            Enable pattern based Virtual configs
```

Enables per-domain lookup of virtual user configurations. The following patterns are recognized:

- %u   The current user string as sent by spamc
- %l   The string to the left side of the @, e.g., equal to joe if current user is joe@isp.net
- %d   The string to the right of the @, e.g., equal to isp.net if current user is joe@isp.net

Example:

If the setting is `--virtual-config-dir=/home/virtual/%d/%l/spam` and the current user string is `joe@isp.net`, the virtual configuration used for that invocation is `/home/virtual/isp.net/joe/spam`.

```
-v, --vpopmail                 Enable vpopmail config
```

Enables support for the vpopmail suite (*http://www.inter7.com/vpopmail.html*).

```
-x, --nouser-config            Disable user config files
```

Turns off the per-user config files; `-x` is required for activating the virtual processing parts of the server.

SSL

```
--ssl                          Run an SSL server
```

Only accept SSL connections; the Perl IO::Socket::SSL library is required.

```
--server-key keyfile           Specify an SSL keyfile
```

The location for the SSL keyfile.

```
--server-cert certfile         Specify an SSL certificate
```

The location for the SSL certificate.

Syslog

```
-s facility, --syslog=facility   Specify the syslog facility
```

Defines the syslog facility that `spamd` should use; defaults to `mail`.

```
--syslog-socket=type           How to connect to syslogd
```

Specifies how `spamd` sends messages to syslog. Options are `unix` (default), `inet`, or `none`.

MySQL

```
-q, --sql-config               Enable SQL config
```

Activates SQL lookups even when disabled with `-x`. Useful for virtual host setups where user home directories are on a remote server.

```
-Q, --setuid-with-sql            Enable SQL config
```

Activates SQL lookups even when disabled with -x. This is useful for virtual host setups that want to support automatic whitelists (-a) and helper home directories (-H).

Network/Access Control

```
-i ipaddr, --listen-ip=ipaddr1, ipaddr2, ...  Listen on the IP ipaddr
```

Listens on specified IP addresses. Defaults to 127.0.0.1.

```
-p port, --port                  Listen on specified port
```

Causes spamd to listen on specified port. If not specified, defaults to 783.

```
--socketpath=path                Listen on given UNIX domain socket
```

Have spamd listen on the given domain socket path.

```
-A hostA, hostB, ..., --allowed-ips=ipaddr1, ipaddr2, ...   Limit ip addresses which
can connect
```

Specify hosts that can connect to this instance of spamd. Defaults to 127.0.0.1. Addresses can be specified in CIDR format (192.168.1.0/24) or ranges (192.168.1 would allow 192.168.1.1 through 192.168.1.255, inclusive).

Ident

```
--auth-ident                     Use ident to authenticate spamc user
```

Turns on identification protocol (IDENT) support for requests coming from spamc.

```
--ident-timeout=timeout          Timeout for ident connections
```

Time in seconds spamd will wait for an IDENT response. Default is 5 seconds. 0 or less will disable timeout, which is strongly discouraged.

Processing/User

```
-P, --paranoid                   Die upon user errors
```

Rather than falling back to user nobody and using the default configuration, stop processing this request and skip to the next request.

```
-H dir                          Specify a different HOME directory, path optional
```

Require external program such as Razor or DCC to specify $HOME rather than inheriting $HOME variable from the spamd shell that spawned it. Specifying no argument for -H will cause the spamc $HOME variable to be used.

```
-L, --local                     Use local tests only (no DNS)
```

Same as for spamassassin; only perform header and body checks, no distributed checksum or DNS testing.

```
-u username, --username=username   Run as username
```

Run spamd as named user; if not specified, run as spamc user; setting username to "root" disables setuid() functionality and runs spamd as root.

SPAMC

spamc is the client side of the spamc/spamd pair. It is meant to be called by scripts, although there is no reason that it cannot be run manually. It is written in C and is meant for high performance. spamc reads from STDIN and then reads the results back from spamd and presents the output on STDOUT. The options it accepts are broken down by function in the next sections.

General

```
-B                              BSMTP mode
```

Treat input as an SMTP-formatted message.

```
-c                              check only
```

Print score/threshold and set exit code to 0 if message is not spam or 1 if it is spam.

```
-r                              report if spam
```

Print report for spam messages.

```
-R
```

Print report for all messages.

-y

Output spam test names that are executed.

-d *host*

Specify host to connect to spamd on; defaults to 127.0.0.1.

-e *command [args]*

Command to output to instead of STDOUT. Must be the last option.

-f   fallback safely

In case of communications error, dump original message changes instead of setting exit code.

-h

Print usage message.

-p *port*   specify port for connection

Specifies port to connect to spamd on; defaults to 783.

-s *size*   specify max message size

Any message larger than size will not be processed; the default value is 250k.

-u *username*

Username under which spamd should process this message.

-x   don't fallback safely

Upon error, exit with a temporary failure error code as follows:

```
EX_USAGE        64  command line usage error
EX_DATAERR      65  data format error
EX_NOINPUT      66  cannot open input
EX_NOUSER       67  addressee unknown
EX_NOHOST       68  host name unknown
EX_UNAVAILABLE  69  service unavailable
EX_SOFTWARE     70  internal software error
EX_OSERR        71  system error (e.g., can't fork)
EX_OSFILE       72  critical OS file missing
```

```
EX_CANTCREAT    73  can't create (user) output file
EX_IOERR        74  input/output error
EX_TEMPFAIL     75  temp failure; user is invited to retry
EX_PROTOCOL     76  remote error in protocol
EX_NOPERM       77  permission denied
EX_CONFIG       78  configuration error
```

`-t`   `spamd timeout`

Timeout in seconds to read from `spamd`; the default is 600; 0 disables.

`-H`   `hostname randomization`

Randomize the IP addresses in the looked-up hostname.

`-U path`   `use UNIX domain socket with path`

Have `spamc` listen on the given domain socket path.

sa-learn

`sa-learn` is SpamAssassin's command line interface to the Bayesian retrainer. It should be used when the SpamAssassin Bayesian engine misclassifies a message, and you read your messages via a command line email client such as `mutt`.

`--ham`

Learn the input message(s) as ham.

`--spam`

Learn the input message(s) as spam.

`--folders=filename, -f filename`

`sa-learn` reads in the list of folders from the specified file, reading one folder per line in the file. If the folder is prefixed with "ham:" or "spam:", `sa-learn` learns that folder appropriately; otherwise the folders are assumed to be of the type specified by `--ham` or `--spam`.

`--use-ignore`

Don't learn the message if a `From` address matches configuration file item `bayes_ignore_from` or a `To` address matches `bayes_ignore_to`.

`--sync`

Synchronize the journal and databases. Upon successfully syncing the database with the entries in the journal, the journal file is removed.

`--force-expire`

Forces an expiry attempt, regardless of whether it is necessary. Note that this doesn't mean any tokens will actually expire. Note: `--force-expire` also causes the journal data to be synchronized into the Bayes databases.

`--forget`

Forget a previously learned message.

`--dbpath`

Allows a command-line override of the `bayes_path` configuration option.

`--dump <magic|data|all>`

Display the contents of the Bayes database. Without an option or with the `all` option, all magic tokens and data tokens are displayed. `magic` displays only magic tokens, and `data` only displays the data tokens. The `--regexp` option can also be used to specify which tokens to display based on a regular expression.

`--clear`

Clear an existing Bayes database by removing all traces of the database.
WARNING: This is destructive and should be used with care.

`--backup`

Performs a dump of the Bayes database in machine/human readable format. The dump includes token and seen data; use the `--restore` command to input data back into the database.

`--restore=filename`

Performs a restore of the Bayes database defined by the filename.
WARNING: This is a destructive operation—all previous Bayes data will be wiped out.

`-h, --help`

Print help message and exit.

`-C /path/to/config_file, --configpath=/config/path, --config-file=file_name`

Use the specified path for locating the distributed configuration files. Ignore the default location, `/usr/share/spamassassin`.

`--siteconfigpath=path`

Use the specified path for locating site-specific configuration files. Ignore the default directories (usually `/etc/mail/spamassassin` or similar).

`-p /path/to/prefs_file, --prefspath=/some/path, --prefs-file=prefs_file_name`

Read user score preferences from prefs; overrides the default of `$HOME/.spamassassin/user_prefs`.

`-item B<-D>, B<--debug-level>`

Produce diagnostic output.

`--no-sync`

Skip the slow synchronization step, which normally takes place after changing database entries.

`--import`

If you previously used SpamAssassin's Bayesian learner without the `DB_File` module installed, it will have created files in other formats, such as `GDBM_File`, `NDBM_File`, or `SDBM_File`. This switch allows you to migrate that old data into the `DB_File` format. It will overwrite any data currently in the `DB_File`.

SpamAssassin Configuration File

This appendix covers the various pieces of the SpamAssassin configuration file, breaking it down by function for clarity's sake. Portions of this appendix are taken from the Spam-Assassin web site, *http://spamassassin.apache.org/doc/Mail_SpamAssassin_Conf.html*.

There are a large number of configuration parameters. For the purpose of discussion here, we have broken them down into the following top-level categories:

- General
- Whitelist/Blacklist
- Bayesian
- Network Tests
- Ruleset/Scoring
- Tags

The General parameters are global settings for basic SpamAssassin functionality such as versions, reporting, etc. Whitelist/Blacklist settings control the action of the always-allow and always-deny lists, including the automatic whitelisting support. Bayesian is the set of keywords that control how SpamAssassin's integrated Bayesian analyzer works.

Network tags control how the tests for Pyzor, Vipul Razor, DCC, DNS, and IP filtering are handled. The Ruleset consists of the settings by which SpamAssassin rules can be changed or added. The Tags section contains some additional parameters that control various settings.

Each type of rule has as many as three classifications:

- Globally changeable by anyone (User Settable)
- Changeable only with permission of the administrator (Privileged, discussed in the next section)
- Changeable only by the administrator (Admin Only)

PRIVILEGED SETTINGS

Privileged settings are enabled by the administrator. Only the following user classes may change privileged settings:

- Users running the spamassassin executable from procmailrc or .forward files
- Users editing a system-wide file in the configuration directory (i.e., /etc/mail/spamassassin)

Privileged Settings Under spamd

spamd users are allowed to change these values if allow_user_rules is set to 0 (see the allow_user_rules description next). Also, please note that configuration commands on blacklisting and other areas are covered elsewhere in this appendix for the commands indicated.

allow_user_rules (0 | 1) (default: 0)

This setting allows users to create rules (and only rules) in their user_prefs files for use with spamd. It defaults to off (0) because it may be possible for users to gain root-level access if spamd is run as root.

Notes:

- Don't use this option unless you are certain you know what you are doing.
- This option causes spamassassin to recompile all the tests each time it processes a message for a user with a rule in his/her user_prefs file, which could have a *significant* effect on server load.

Note that it is not currently possible to use allow_user_rules to modify an existing system rule from user_prefs with spamd.

GENERAL SETTINGS

The General options are broken down into the following categories:

Version
Scoring
Message Tagging
Language

USER SETTABLE

The following categories can be changed by any user.

Version

The version-related keywords enable you to manage your configuration files. For example, you can ensure that all of your mail relays are running the same config file version by using these options.

```
require_version n.nn
```

This requires SpamAssassin to read in a configuration file with the required version set. If SpamAssassin tries to read in a different version (newer or older), it will output a warning and ignore the configuration file.

```
version_tag string
```

`string` is reported as the version of the configuration file. This should be used if you plan on distributing your own SpamAssassin rulesets.

Scoring Threshold

Assigning scores to inbound email is the basis of SpamAssassin. The `require_hits` option enables you to define the score at which SpamAssassin should consider a message to be spam.

```
required_hits n.nn (default 5)
```

This parameter sets the number of hits before a message is considered spam. If this is a single-user setup, 5 is an acceptable value. If this is a system-wide setup, then set this number much higher. Also, if you are deleting messages based on the score (which is not recommended), this number should be set very high. Otherwise, it is very likely you *will* lose (what you probably consider to be) non-spam messages.

Message Tagging

These options help you control how SpamAssassin manipulates headers and how it reports spam.

```
rewrite_subject { 0 | 1 } (default 0)
```

The default is to not rewrite subject lines of messages processed by SpamAssassin. Setting this value to 1 enables subject lines to indicate that the message has been processed.

```
fold_headers { 0 | 1 } (default: 1)
```

By default, headers added by SpamAssassin will be broken up into multiple lines, and each subsequent line (broken up after the first) will have a tabulator character prepended to it. Note that this is set to "on" by default; if disabled, this can cause very long subject lines to be generated.

```
add_header { spam | ham | all } header name string
```

This option adds the customized header to the indicated message type (spam, ham [not spam], all). All headers begin with X-Spam- and end with *header name*. For example, a message with a *header name* of MyCheck will result in a header of X-Spam-MyCheck.
Notes:

- *string* can contain tags as explained previously in the tags section. You can also use \n and \t in the header to add new lines and tabulators as desired. A backslash must be written as \\; any other escaped characters will be silently removed.
- Manually adding new lines via \n disables any further automatic wrapping (i.e., long header lines are possible). The lines will be properly folded (marked as continuing), however.
- All headers will be folded if fold_headers is set to 1.
- For backward compatibility, some headers are (still) added by default. You can customize existing/default headers with add_header. (Only the specified subset of messages will be changed.)

By default, this version of SpamAssassin executes the following add_header checks:

```
add_header spam Flag _YESNOCAPS_
add_header all Status _YESNO_, hits=_HITS_ required=_REQD_ tests=_TESTS_
➥ autolearn=_AUTOLEARN_ version=_VERSION_
add_header all Level _STARS(*)_
add_header all Checker-Version SpamAssassin _VERSION_ (_SUBVERSION_) on _HOSTNAME_
```

See the clear_headers and remove_headers description for information on removing headers.

```
remove_header { spam | ham | all } header name
```

The headers added by add_header can be removed by specifying remove_header. This is useful for a system-wide local.cf to change SpamAssassin default values, or for a user to change system-wide or SpamAssassin defaults by modifying his or her user_prefs file appropriately. Note that the X-Spam-Checker-Version header, added by SpamAssassin, is not removable.

```
clear_headers
```

This option clears all headers added by SpamAssassin. Note that the X-Spam-Checker-Version header, added by SpamAssassin, is not removed.

```
report_safe_copy_headers header_nameA, header_nameB, ...
```

When specifying report_safe, the following headers from the original message are copied into the wrapper header by default:

- From
- To
- Cc
- Subject
- Date

If you want to have additional headers saved outside of the defaults, they are added using the report_safe_copy_headers option. Multiple headers can be added on the same line (separated by spaces) or by using additional report_safe_copy_headers lines.

```
subject_tag string (default: *****SPAM*****)
```

If rewrite_subject is 1, subject_tag sets the verbiage added to the Subject line of emails that are considered spam. Tags can be used here as with the add_header option. If report_safe is not used (see the following), you may only use the _HITS_ and _REQD_ tags, or SpamAssassin will not be able to remove this markup from your message.

report_safe { 0 | 1 | 2 } (default 1)

If report_safe is set to 1:

If an incoming message is tagged as spam, instead of modifying the original message, SpamAssassin will create a new report message and attach the original message as a message/rfc822 MIME part (ensuring the original message is completely preserved, not easily opened, and easier to recover).

If report_safe is set to 2:

The original messages will be attached with a content type of text/plain instead of message/rfc822. This setting may be required for safety reasons on certain broken mail clients that automatically load attachments without any action by the user. This setting may also make it somewhat more difficult to extract or view the original message.

If report_safe is set to 0:

Incoming spam is only modified by adding some X-Spam- headers, and no changes will be made to the body. In addition, a header named X-Spam-Report will be added to spam. You can use the remove_header option to remove the X-Spam-Report header after setting report_safe to 0.

report_charset CHARSET (default: unset)

Set the MIME Content-Type charset used for the text/plain report that is attached to spam mail messages.

report string

Set the report template that is attached to spam mail messages. See the 10_misc.cf configuration file in /usr/share/spamassassin for an example.

Notes:

- If you change this, try to keep it under 78 columns.
- Each report line appends to the existing template, so use clear_report_template to restart.
- Tags can be included as shown in the tags section.

clear_report_template

This clears the report template.

report_contact string

Set what _CONTACTADDRESS_ is replaced with in the report text. By default, this is "the administrator of that system" because the hostname of the system on which the scanner is running is also included.

`unsafe_report` *some text for a report*

Set the report template that is attached to spam mail messages that contain a non-text/plain part. See the 10_misc.cf configuration file in /usr/share/spamassassin for an example. Notes:

- Each unsafe-report line appends to the existing template, so use clear_unsafe_report_template to restart.
- Tags can be used in this template (see the tags section for details).

`clear_unsafe_report_template`

Clears the unsafe_report template.

`spamtrap` *string*

A template for spamtrap responses. If the first few lines begin with *Xxxxxx: yyy* where *Xxxxxx* is a mail header and *yyy* is some text, they'll be used as headers. See the 10_misc.cf configuration file in /usr/share/spamassassin for an example. Note: Tags cannot be used with this option.

`clear_spamtrap_template`

Clears the spamtrap template.

`describe` *test name string*

Gives `test name` the description indicated in `string`. This text is shown to users in the detailed report.
Notes:

- Test names that begin with '__' are reserved for meta-match sub-rules.
- Test names that begin with '__' are not scored or listed in the 'tests hit' reports.
- By convention, rule descriptions should be limited in length to no more than 50 characters.

Language

The language-related options enable you to specify the languages in which you expect to receive mail and associated scoring penalties.

```
ok_languages xx [ yy zz ... ] (default: all)
```

This option is used to specify which languages are considered OK for incoming mail so that they will not be penalized in the resulting score. SpamAssassin will try to detect the language used in the message text, though this is not always possible. The rule UNWANTED_LANGUAGE_BODY is triggered based on how ok_languages is set.
Notes:

- If the language cannot be recognized with sufficient confidence, no points will be assigned.
- The two- or three-letter language specifier in lowercase.
- Use all (the default) if a desired language is not listed or if you want to allow any language.
- If multiple ok_languages lines exist in a configuration, only the last one is used.

Examples:

```
ok_languages en          (only allow English)
ok_languages en ja zh    (allow English and Japanese)
```

Select the languages to allow from the following list:

af - Afrikaans	*ga* - Irish Gaelic	*pl* - Polish
am - Amharic	*gd* - Scottish Gaelic	*pt* - Portuguese
ar - Arabic	*he* - Hebrew	*qu* - Quechua
be - Byelorussian	*hi* - Hindi	*rm* - Rhaeto-Romance
bg - Bulgarian	*hr* - Croatian	*ro* - Romanian
bs - Bosnian	*hu* - Hungarian	*ru* - Russian
ca - Catalan	*hy* - Armenian	*sa* - Sanskrit
cs - Czech	*id* - Indonesian	*sco* - Scots
cy - Welsh	*is* - Icelandic	*sk* - Slovak
da - Danish	*it* - Italian	*sl* - Slovenian
de - German	*ja* - Japanese	*sq* - Albanian
el - Greek	*ka* - Georgian	*sr* - Serbian
en - English	*ko* - Korean	*sv* - Swedish
eo - Esperanto	*la* - Latin	*sw* - Swahili
es - Spanish	*lt* - Lithuanian	*ta* - Tamil
et - Estonian	*lv* - Latvian	*th* - Thai
eu - Basque	*mr* - Marathi	*tl* - Tagalog
fa - Persian	*ms* - Malay	*tr* - Turkish
fi - Finnish	*ne* - Nepali	*uk* - Ukrainian
fr - French	*nl* - Dutch	*vi* - Vietnamese
fy - Frisian	*no* - Norwegian	*yi* - Yiddish
		zh - Chinese

```
ok_locales xx [ yy zz ... ] (default: all)
```

This option is used to specify which locales (country codes) are considered OK for incoming mail without triggering a scoring penalty. Mail using character sets used by languages in these countries will not be marked as possibly being spam in a foreign language. If you receive lots of spam in foreign languages and never get any non-spam in these languages, this may help.
Notes:

- All ISO-8859-* character sets and Windows code page character sets are always permitted by default.
- Set this to all (default setting) to allow all character sets.
- The rules CHARSET_FARAWAY, CHARSET_FARAWAY_BODY, and CHARSET_FARAWAY_HEADERS are triggered based on how this is set.
- If there are multiple ok_locales lines in a configuration, only the last one is used.

Examples:

```
ok_locales en          (only allow English)
ok_locales en ja zh    (allow English, Japanese, and Chinese)
```

Select the locales to allow from the following list:

en - Western character sets in general

ja - Japanese character sets

ko - Korean character sets

ru - Cyrillic character sets

th - Thai character sets

zh - Chinese (both simplified and traditional) character sets

WHITELIST/BLACKLIST OPTIONS

The whitelist/blacklist options control the ability for users to always allow or disallow email from certain senders. These options are all global options, available to anyone.

```
whitelist_from sender
```

Enables mail from *sender* to always make it through the filters. This option is useful for identifying email from certain senders that send messages often misidentified by

SpamAssassin. Strings are parsed in glob format but with "*" and "?" as the only allowable metacharacters. Multiple matching patterns are allowed per line (separated by spaces), and multiple instances of whitelist_from are allowed in the file.

The Resent-From header is checked, if available. If not, all of the following headers are checked:

Envelope-Sender
Resent-Sender
X-Envelope-From
From

Examples:

```
whitelist_from friend@enemies.com *@friends.com
whitelist_from ?@enemies.com *@?.enemies.com
```

The first line would allow friend@enemies.com and anyone from the domain friends.com through the filters. The second line would allow any one-letter email accounts from the domain enemies.com and any one-letter subdomains in the enemies.com domain through the filters.

```
unwhitelist_from sender
```

Overrides whitelist_from setting as long as whitelist_from string(s) match exactly. This is useful for an individual's user_prefs file to override system-wide settings. Syntax is identical to whitelist_from.

```
whitelist_from_rcvd sender string
```

This will perform a reverse DNS lookup of the machine that sent *sender*'s email to your system and will compare it to *string*. The *string* can be a fully qualified name, or it can be only the domain. The trusted_networks must be set up properly for this to work.
Examples:

```
whitelist_from_rcvd *@friends.com mail.friends.com
whitelist_from_rcvd *@buddies.com buddies.com
```

The first line would allow any mail from anyone at friends.com, as long as the machine that sent the mail resolved to mail.friends.com. The second line would allow anyone from buddies.com to send mail, as long as the domain of the MX host sending the mail resolved to something within the buddies.com domain.

```
def_whitelist_from_rcvd sender string
```

Same as `whitelist_from_rcvd`, except that it uses the list of domains that ships with SpamAssassin.

```
unwhitelist_from_rcvd sender
```

Used to reverse the `whitelist_from_rcvd` setting. Useful in the `local.cf` to override the SpamAssassin-distributed whitelists and in the `user_pref` files for overriding system (local.cf) and SpamAssassin-distributed whitelists. Syntax is the same as `whitelist_from_received`. The *sender* values listed in this must match those in `whitelist_from_received` in order to activate.

```
blacklist_from sender
```

Used to tag messages from *sender* incorrectly identified as non-spam. For usage, see `whitelist_from`.

BAYESIAN

The Bayesian-related parameters that control SpamAssassin's handling of the internal Bayesian analyzer are covered in this section. The Bayesian-related settings are available for all three classifications of keywords (nonprivileged, allowed by administrator, and administrator only).

USER SETTABLE

The following Bayesian-related parameters are not considered privileged and can be set by anyone:

```
bayes_auto_learn { 0 | 1 } (default: 1)
```

This parameter specifies whether SpamAssassin should automatically feed high-scoring mails (or low-scoring mails for non-spam) into its learning systems. The only learning system supported currently is a naive Bayesian-style classifier.

Please note that the following tests are ignored when determining whether a message should be trained:

- Auto-whitelist (AWL)
- Rules with tflags set to 'learn' (the Bayesian rules)
- Rules with tflags set to 'userconf' (user white/blacklisting rules, etc.)

Also note that auto-training occurs by using scores from score set 0 or 1, depending on what score set is used during message check. It is likely that the message check and auto-train scores will be different.

`bayes_auto_learn_threshold_nonspam n.nn (default: 0.1)`

If a message scores below this number, then it is fed into SpamAssassin's learning systems automatically as a ham (non-spam) message.

`bayes_auto_learn_threshold_spam n.nn (default: 12.0)`

If a message scores above this score, then it is fed into SpamAssassin's learning system automatically as a spam message.

Note: SpamAssassin requires at least 3 points from the header and 3 points from the body to auto-learn as spam. Therefore, the minimum working value for this option is 6.

`bayes_ignore_header header name`

If you receive mail filtered by upstream mail systems, these headers may provide inappropriate cues to the Bayesian classifier, causing classification errors. To avoid this, use this keyword to list the headers added by your provider.

For example:

```
bayes_ignore_header X-Upstream-Spamfilter
bayes_ignore_header X-Upstream-SomethingElse
```

`bayes_min_ham_num n (Default: 200)`

`bayes_min_spam_num n (Default: 200)`

The Bayesian classification system does not activate until a certain number of ham (non-spam) and spam have been "learned."

`bayes_learn_during_report {0|1} (Default: 1)`

The Bayesian classification system will, by default, learn any reported messages (spamassassin -r) as spam. If you do not want to allow reported messages to be learned as spam, set this option to 0.

ADMINISTRATOR ONLY

No Bayesian-related SpamAssassin parameters are "privileged." However, the following parameters are available to the administrator:

`bayes_path` */path/to/file* (default: ~.spamassassin/bayes)

This keyword specifies the path for the Bayesian probabilities databases. Several database files will be created, with this parameter as the base. Depending on the type of database, certain keywords are appended. For example, if this setting were left as the default `~/.spamassassin/bayes`:

- `~/.spamassassin/bayes_toks` would be the token database.
- `~/.spamassassin/bayes_seen` would be the seen database.

By default, each user has her own database in her `~/.spamassassin` directory with mode 0700/0600. For system-wide SpamAssassin use, you may want to reduce disk space usage by sharing database files across all users. (However, it should be noted that Bayesian filtering can be more effective with an individual database for each user.)

`bayes_file_mode` *mode* (default: 0700)

This setting specifies the file mode bits used for the Bayesian filtering database files. Make sure you specify this using the 'x' mode bits set because it may also be used to create directories. However, if a file is created, the resulting file will not have any execute bits set (i.e., the umask is set to 111).

`bayes_use_hapaxes` {0|1} (default: 1)

This setting enables the Bayesian classifier to use hapaxes (words/tokens that occur only once) when classifying messages. Utilizing hapaxes produces significantly better hit rates but increases database size by a factor of 8 to 10.

`bayes_use_chi2_combining` {0|1} (default: 1)

This determines whether the Bayesian classifier uses chi-squared combining instead of Robinson/Graham-style naive Bayesian combining. Chi-squared produces more 'extreme' output results but may be more resistant to changes in corpus size and the like.

`bayes_journal_max_size` *n* (default: 102400)

SpamAssassin will opportunistically synchronize the journal and the database. It will do so at least once a day, but it can also synchronize if the file size goes above this setting in bytes. If it's set to 0, the journal sync will only occur once a day.

`bayes_expiry_max_db_size` *n* (default: 150000)

This determines the maximum size of the Bayes tokens database. When expiration occurs, the Bayes system will keep either 75% of the maximum value or 100,000 tokens, whichever is larger. 150,000 tokens is roughly equivalent to an 8Mb database file.

`bayes_auto_expire` {0|1} (default: 1)

If enabled, the Bayes system will try to automatically expire old tokens from the database. Auto-expiry occurs when the number of tokens in the database surpasses the `bayes_expiry_max_db_`size value.

`bayes_learn_to_journal` {0|1} (default: 0)

If this option is set, whenever SpamAssassin does Bayes learning, it will put the information into the journal instead of directly into the database. This lowers contention for locking the database to execute an update, but it will also cause more access to the journal and create a delay before the updates are actually committed to the Bayesian filtering database.

MySQL-Related

`user_scores_dsn` *DBI:databasetype:databasename:hostname:port*

If you load user scores from an SQL database, this will set the DSN (data source name) used to connect.

For example, the value

`DBI:mysql:spamassassin:localhost:3309`

would translate to the command: "Attach to the MySQL database named `spamassassin`, located on machine `localhost` port 3309."

`user_scores_sql_username` *username*

The authorized username to connect to the referenced DSN.

`user_scores_sql_password` *password*

The password for the database username for the above DSN.

`user_scores_sql_table` *tablename*

The table in which user preferences are stored for the above DSN.

`user_scores_sql_field_username` *field_username* (Default: `username`)

The field in which the username whose preferences you're looking up is stored.

`user_scores_sql_field_preference` *field_preference* (Default: `preference`)

The name of the preference for which you're looking.

`user_scores_sql_field_value` *field_value* (Default: `value`)

The name of the SQL field value for which you're looking.

`user_scores_sql_field_scope` *field_scope* (Default: `spamassassin`)

The scope field. In Horde, this makes the preference a single-module preference or a global preference.

NETWORK TESTS

Perhaps the easiest method to incorporate the DCC and Razor systems into your mail architecture is via SpamAssassin. This section covers the SpamAssassin-related configuration settings as they relate to DCC, Vipul's Razor, and Pyzor. Please note that no privileged class SpamAssassin configuration commands are available with respect to DCC and Razor.

By default, SpamAssassin ships with DCC, Razor, and Pyzor active, if available. As a result, if you want to use the features available with these distributed checksum facilities, you don't have to do anything because they will be activated automatically if they're available. If you do need to tweak the default settings, the following sections explain each option.

USER SETTABLE

The following user preference options are available for SpamAssassin. Recall that these setup files can be activated system-wide (normally in `/etc/mail/spamassassin`) or for individual users (`local_prefs` file in a user's home directory in the `.spamassassin` subdirectory).

`use_dcc { 0 | 1 }` (default: 1)

Whether to use (1) or not use (0) the DCC scores in SpamAssassin.

`dcc_timeout` *seconds* (default: 10)

How many seconds to wait for DCC to complete before continuing without results.

`dcc_body_max` *count* (Default: 999999 for all)
`dcc_fuz1_max` *count*
`dcc_fuz2_max` *count*

This option sets how often a message's body/fuz1/fuz2 checksum score must have been reported to the DCC server before SpamAssassin will consider the DCC check as matched. Because nearly all DCC clients auto-report these checksums, you should set this to a relatively high value, such as 999999 (this is DCC's MANY count).

`use_pyzor { 0 | 1 }` (default: 1)

Whether to use Pyzor (1) or not (0), if it is available.

`pyzor_timeout` *seconds* (default: 10)

How many seconds to wait for Pyzor to complete before continuing.

`pyzor_max` *number* (default 5)

This option sets how often a message's body checksum must have been reported to the Pyzor server before SpamAssassin will consider the Pyzor check as matched.

`pyzor_options` *options*

Specify options to the pyzor command. Please note that only [A-Za-z0-9 -/] are allowed (for security).

`use_razor2 { 0 | 1 }` (default: 1)

This option indicates whether (1) or not (0) to use Razor version 2, if it is available.

`razor_timeout` *seconds* (default: 10)

How many seconds you wait for the Razor server to answer before continuing on without the results.

`trusted_networks` ipaddr1 ... (default: none)

Which networks or hosts are trusted in your setup. "Trusted" in terms of SpamAssassin means that hosts on these networks are known to not be

- Operated by spammers
- Open relays
- Open proxies
- Zombies (hijacked machines running spamming software unknown to their owners)

DNS blacklist checks will never query for hosts on these networks. If a /mask is specified, it's considered a CIDR-style netmask, specified in bits. If it is not specified, but less than 4 octets are specified with a trailing dot, that's considered a mask to allow all addresses in the remaining octets. If a mask is not specified, and there is no trailing dot, then just the single IP address specified is used as if the mask were set to /32.

This operates additively, so a `trusted_networks` line after another one will result in all those networks becoming trusted. To clear out the existing entries, use `clear_trusted_networks`.

If you're running with DNS checks enabled, SpamAssassin includes code to infer your trusted networks on-the-fly, so the `trusted_networks` may not be necessary. This inference works as follows. If any of these cases is true, then the address is considered trusted:

- The 'from' IP address is on the same /16 network as the top Received line's 'by' host
- The address of the 'from' host is in a reserved network range
- Any addresses of the 'by' host are in a reserved network range

Examples:

```
trusted_networks 192.168/16 127/8    # all in 192.168.*.* and 127.*.*.*
trusted_networks 212.17.35.15        # just that host
trusted_networks 127.                # all in 127.*.*.*

clear_trusted_networks
```

Empty the list of trusted networks.

```
check_mx_attempts number (default: 2)
```

By default, SpamAssassin checks the From: address for a valid MX this many times, waiting 2 seconds each time.

`check_mx_delay` *seconds* (default: 5)

How many seconds to wait before retrying an MX check.

`dns_available { yes | test[:` *server1 server2 ...*`] | no }` (default: test)

By default, SpamAssassin will query three of its internal 13 default DNS servers to attempt to check if DNS is working or not. However, this check can be problematic because DNS servers can and do go down. You can specify your own list of DNS servers to query in the following manner using the test argument:

`dns_available test:` *server1.tld server2.tld server3.tld*

Note that the DNS test queries for MX records. If you specify your own list of servers, make sure to choose a set of servers that have associated MX records.

Administrator Only

The following administrator-only options are available:

`razor_config` *filename*

Define the filename used to store Razor's configuration settings.

`pyzor_path` *string*

This option tells SpamAssassin specifically where to find the `pyzor` client instead of relying on SpamAssassin to find it in the current `PATH`.

`dcc_home` *string*

This option tells SpamAssassin specifically where to find the DCC homedir. If `dcc_path` is not specified, it will default to looking in `dcc_home/bin` for DCC client instead of relying on SpamAssassin to find it in the current `PATH`. If it isn't found there, it will look in the current `PATH`. If a `dccifd` socket is found in `dcc_home`, it will use that interface that instead of `dccproc`.

`dcc_dccifd_path` *string*

This option tells SpamAssassin specifically where to find the `dccifd` socket. If `dcc_dccifd_path` is not specified, it will default to looking in `dcc_home`. If a `dccifd` socket is found, it will use it instead of `dccproc`.

dcc_path *string*

This option tells SpamAssassin specifically where to find the dccproc client instead of relying on SpamAssassin to find it in the current PATH. Note that if taint mode is enabled in the Perl interpreter, you should use this because the current PATH will have been cleared.

dcc_options *options* (default: "-R")

Specify additional options to the dccproc(8) command. Please note that only the upper- and lowercase alphabetic characters and the "-" character are allowed.

RULESET AND SCORING

The following settings control adding and modifying SpamAssassin scoring rules.

USER SETTABLE

score *test name score* [*score score score*]

Assign scores (the number of points for a hit) to a given test. Scores can be positive or negative real numbers or integers. *test name* is the symbolic name used by SpamAssassin for that test; for example, FROM_ENDS_IN_NUMS. If only one valid score is listed, then that score is always used for a test. Setting a rule's score to 0 will disable that rule from running.
   Notes:

- Test names that begin with __ are reserved for meta-match sub-rules and are not scored or listed in the 'tests hit' reports.
- If no score is given for a test, the default score is 1.0, or 0.01 for tests whose names begin with T_ (indicates a rule in testing).
- By convention, rule names should be all uppercase and should have a length of no more than 22 characters.

Up to four scores can be listed. The order determines how they are used:

- The first score is used when both Bayes and network tests are disabled.
- The second score is used when Bayes is disabled but network tests are enabled.
- The third score is used when Bayes is enabled and network tests are disabled.
- The fourth score is used when Bayes is enabled and network tests are enabled.

PRIVILEGED

```
header test_name header operation /pattern/modifiers [if-unset: string]
```

The `header` command defines a test against the headers of a message. Arguments are as follows:

- *test_name* is a symbolic test name, such as FROM_ENDS_IN_NUMS
- *header* is the name of a mail header, such as Subject:, To:, etc.
  - ALL can be used to mean the text of all the message's headers.
  - ToCc can be used to mean the contents of both the To: and Cc: headers.
  - MESSAGEID is a symbol meaning all Message-Id's found in the message; some mailing list software moves the real Message-Id to Resent-Message-Id or X-Message-Id and then uses its own one in the Message-Id header. The value returned for this symbol is the text from all three headers, separated by newlines.
- op is either =~ (contains regular expression) or !~ (does not contain regular expression), and `pattern` is a valid Perl regular expression, with modifiers as regexp modifiers in the usual style. Note that multiline rules are not supported, even if you use x as a modifier.
- If the optional if-unset: *string* tag is present, then *string* will be used if the header is not found in the mail message.

Notes:

- Test names should not start with a number.
- Test names must contain only alphanumeric characters and underscores.
- By convention, lowercase characters should not be used.
- Dashes (-) are not allowed.
- Test names that begin with __ are reserved for meta-match sub-rules and are not scored or listed in the tests hit reports.
- Test names that begin with T_ are reserved for tests that are undergoing testing, and these are given a very low score.
- If you add or modify a test, please be sure to run a sanity check afterward by running `spamassassin --lint`. This will avoid confusing error messages or other tests being skipped as a side effect.

```
header test_name exists:name_of_header
```

Defines a test for the existence of a header. *name_of_header* is the name of a header to test for existence. This is just a very simple version of the header tests (as shown previously).

```
header test_name eval:name_of_eval_method([arguments])
```

Defines a header evaluation test from the SpamAssassin libraries. *name_of_eval_method* is the name of a method on the Mail::SpamAssassin::EvalTests object. arguments are optional arguments to the function call.

```
header test_name eval:check_rbl(set, zone)
```

Check a DNSBL (a DNS blacklist or whitelist). This will retrieve Received: headers from the message, extract the IP addresses, select which ones are untrusted based on the trusted_networks logic, and query that DNSBL zone.

```
header test_name eval:check_rbl_txt(set, zone)
```

Same as check_rbl, except querying using IN TXT instead of IN A records.

```
header test_name eval:check_rbl_sub(set, sub-test)
```

Create a sub-test for the named set. If you want to look up a multi-meaning zone (for example, relays.osirusoft.com), you can then query the results from that zone using the zone ID from the original query.

```
body test_name /pattern/modifiers
```

Define a test against the body of the mail message. The string /pattern/modifiers is a Perl regular expression. The 'body' in this case is the textual parts of the message body.
  Notes:

- Any non-text MIME parts are stripped from the body.
- The message is decoded from Quoted-Printable or Base-64-encoded format if necessary.
- The Subject header is considered part of the body and becomes the first paragraph when running the rules.
- All HTML tags and line breaks will be removed before matching.

```
body test_name eval:name_of_eval_method([args])
```

Defines a header evaluation test from the SpamAssassin libraries. See the header eval command previously.

```
uri test_name /pattern/modifiers
```

Define a test for the URI (for example *http://www.yahoo.com*). `/pattern/modifiers` is a Perl regular expression. The 'uri' in this case is a list of all the URIs in the body of the email, and the test will be run on each and every one of those URIs, adjusting the score if a match is found. Use this test instead of one of the body tests when you need to match a URI because it is more accurately bound to the start/end points of the URI and will also be faster.

```
rawbody test_name /pattern/modifiers
```

Define a test for a raw-body pattern. `pattern` is a Perl regular expression. The 'raw body' of a message is the text, including all textual parts.
 Notes:

- The text will be decoded from base64 or quoted-printable encoding.
- HTML tags and line breaks will be present.

```
rawbody test_name eval:name_of_eval_method([args])
```

Define a test for raw-body eval. See the eval tests for `header eval` previously.

```
full test_name /pattern/modifiers
```

Define a test for a full-body pattern. `/pattern/modifiers` is a Perl regular expression.
 The 'full body' of a message is the undecoded text, including all parts (such as images or other attachments). SpamAssassin no longer runs full tests against decoded text; use rawbody for that.

```
full test_name eval:name_of_eval_method([args])
```

Define a test for full-body eval. See the eval test for `header eval` previously.

```
meta test_name boolean_symbol
```

Define a boolean expression test in terms of other tests that have been hit or not hit. Boolean symbols are as follows:

&&   Logical AND
|| Logical OR
!   Logical NOT (negation)

For example, say the following tests had the given values:

```
TEST1=1
TEST2=0
TEST3=0
```

When this expression is run

```
meta META1 TEST1 && !(TEST2 || TEST3)
```

it evaluates to 1.

Notes:

- English language operators (AND, OR) will be treated as rule names.
- There is no XOR operator.

```
meta test_name boolean_arithmetic_expression
```

A boolean arithmetic expression can be expressed in terms of other tests, with a hit test having the value 1 and an unhit test having the value 0.

Notes:

- Perl built-in functions, like abs(), can't be used and will be treated as rule names.
- If you do not want individual sub-rules to count towards the final score unless the entire meta-rule matches, give the sub-rules names that start with __ (two underscores). SpamAssassin will ignore these rule results for scoring.

Example:

Assume the following values:

```
TEST1=0
TEST2=1
```

When the following is evaluated, the expression

```
meta META2 (3 * TEST1 - 2 * TEST2) > 0
```

returns 0.

```
tflags test_name [ ( net | nice | learn | userconf ) ... ]
```

The tflags keyword is used to set flags on a test. These flags are used in the score-determination back-end system for details of the test's behavior. The following flags can be set:

`net`

The test is a network test and will not be run in the mass checking system or if `-L` is used; therefore its score should not be modified.

`nice`

The test is intended to compensate for common false positives and should be assigned a negative score.

`userconf`

The test requires user configuration before it can be used (for example, language-specific tests).

`learn`

The test requires training before it can be used.

ADMINISTRATOR ONLY

`test test_name (ok|fail) string`

Define a regression testing string. You can have more than one regression test string per symbolic test name. Simply specify a string that you want the test to match.

These tests are only run as part of the test suite—they should not affect the general running of SpamAssassin.

TAGS

The following configuration strings (tags) have special meaning for certain SpamAssassin configuration options (noted after the following code strings):

```
_YESNOCAPS_     "YES"/"NO" for is/isn't spam
_YESNO_         "Yes"/"No" for is/isn't spam
_HITS_          message score
_REQD_          message threshold
_VERSION_       version (eg. 2.55)
_SUBVERSION_    sub-version (eg. 1.187-2003-05-15-exp)
_HOSTNAME_      hostname
_BAYES_         bayes score
_AWL_           AWL modifier
```

```
_DATE_               rfc-2822 date of scan
_STARS(*)_           one * (use any character) for each score point (50 at most)
_RELAYSTRUSTED_      relays used and deemed to be trusted
_RELAYSUNTRUSTED_    relays used that can not be trusted
_AUTOLEARN_          autolearn status ("ham", "no", "spam")
_TESTS(,)_           tests hit separated by , (or other separator)
_TESTSSCORES(,)_     as above, except with scores appended (eg. AWL=-3.0,...)
_DCCB_               DCC's "Brand"
_DCCR_               DCC's results
_PYZOR_              Pyzor results
_RBL_                full results for positive RBL queries in DNS URI format
_LANGUAGES_          possible languages of mail
_PREVIEW_            content preview
_REPORT_             terse report of tests hits (for header reports)
_SUMMARY_            summary of tests hit for standard report (for body reports)
_CONTACTADDRESS_     contents of the 'report_contact' setting
```

The tags listed here can be used by the following SpamAssassin configuration options:

```
add_header
subject_tag
report
unsafe_report
```

Outside of these options, the tags have no effect.

DSPAM

DSPAM (as in de-spam, or to eliminate spam) is a high-performance and highly accurate Bayesian-style classifier designed for large installations. It contains many of the features present in other leading Bayesian classifiers, including

- Per-user spam corpus
- Easy filter retraining
- Graphical user interface
- Proxy/MDA masquerade support for easy installation
- Integration with all major MTAs
- Support for all users or per-user integration

It also has features that are relatively unique to DSPAM:

- Designed expressly for large-scale deployments and efficiency
- Can be configured to be run as a POP3 proxy, making installation/configuration easier
- Supports multiple types of back-end databases for storing data, including
  - SQLite
  - Berkeley DB3
  - Berkeley DB4
  - MySQL
  - PostgrSQL
  - Oracle

- Ability to choose Bayesian algorithm(s) to use, including
  - Graham-Bayesian
  - Burton-Bayesian
  - Robinson's Geometric Mean
  - Fisher-Robinson's Chi-Square
- Bayesian algorithms can be combined for increased accuracy

DSPAM is a good candidate for any large installation that needs a highly accurate Bayesian classifier. However, DSPAM doesn't have non-Bayesian functionality such as heuristics and distributed checksum filtering (such as DCC or Razor).

SIDELINING VERSUS TAGGING

By default, DSPAM is designed to perform message sidelining. That is, it places any message it determines as spam into a "quarantine" area, which requires the user to log in to the DSPAM cgi-bin management utility and view the quarantine in order to check for false positives. This is a good solution for some circumstances because it doesn't require changes on the end-user email client like tagging does.

Message Headers

The alternative is to filter the messages at the email client by using the tags added by DSPAM. Although it's more work to set up, it may be beneficial to do this in certain situations. Here is an example set of message headers added by DSPAM:

```
X-DSPAM-Result: Spam
X-DSPAM-Confidence: 0.9997
X-DSPAM-Probability: 1.0000
X-DSPAM-Signature: 410e6679221221187111503
X-DSPAM-User: dale
```

The meanings of the fields added by DSPAM are as follows:

```
X-DSPAM-Result:
```

Value can be Spam or Innocent.
Indicates whether DSPAM considers the message to be spam or not spam (Innocent).

```
X-DSPAM-Confidence:
```

Value is a real number, from 0.0000 to 1.0000 (inclusive).

Indicates how sure DSPAM is that the message score is correct.

`X-DSPAM-Probability:`

Value is a real number, from `0.0000` to `1.0000` (inclusive).
Indicates the spam score assigned by DSPAM.

`X-DSPAM-Signature:`

Value is a hex string.
Represents an identifier for the original message, used for retraining the filters.

`X-DSPAM-User:`

Value is the DSPAM user associated with the message.
Identifies the DSPAM user associated with this message, used when retraining filters.

IMPLEMENTATION PLANNING

At least three methods can be used to integrate DSPAM into your environment:

- POP3 proxy
- Per-user, by using `procmail`
- Server-wide, using DSPAM as the MDA

POP3 proxy requires the fewest changes to your environment. If you want a certain set of users to run DSPAM, or if you are performing initial testing of the software, you might use Procmail integration. In a large setup with thousands of users, you would probably use DSPAM as the MDA, which is the most efficient use of resources but is also the most difficult to set up.

You also need to consider the use of the quarantining feature. Specifically, you need to think about how to manage the authentication of users when accessing the DSPAM quarantine area. DSPAM uses Apache `.htaccess` files for authentication. Although static users can be set up by using an `.htpasswd` file, this is an unworkable solution in the case where there are thousands of end-user mailboxes.

INSTALLATION

In this example, we show how to install DSPAM under Sendmail using Procmail as the delivery agent. We assume a Linux installation here.

First, download the source tar file from the DSPAM web site: *http://www.nuclearelephant.com/projects/dspam/sources/dspam-3.0.0.tar.gz*. After downloading, move it to `/usr/local/src` and unpack and install it as follows:

```
bash$ tar xzvf dspam-3.0.0.tar.gz
bash$ cd dspam-3.0.0
bash$ ./configure --with-delivery-agent=/usr/bin/procmail \
--with-db4-includes=/usr/local/BerkeleyDB.4.2/include \
--with-db4-libraries=/usr/local/BerkeleyDB.4.2/lib
bash$ make
bash$ sudo make install
```

The `configure` statement in this example tells DSPAM to use `/usr/bin/procmail` as the delivery agent and to use Berkeley DB4 as the back-end database.

Post Installation Tasks

By default, the DSPAM installation process creates the DSPAM home directory as `/var/dspam`. Make sure permissions on the `/var/dspam` directory are set correctly so that cgi-bin and MTA users can write files in that directory. This enables the DSPAM web application to manage each user's quarantine directory, and it enables DSPAM to write spam messages there.

Next, create the file `trusted.users` in `/var/dspam`. It is a list, with one username per line, of the users who are allowed to make changes to the DSPAM system-wide parameters. We suggest placing the following users in the `trusted.users` file:

```
root
daemon
dspam
```

dspam is the cgi-bin user as configured in the Apache configuration file using `suexec`. daemon and root are used by the MTA in this example. This list will allow the appropriate users to change DSPAM settings.

Next, the `dspam` user and group need to be created and added to the `mail` group. Under Red Hat/FC, this is accomplished by running the `useradd` command:

```
# useradd -G mail -M dspam
```

This creates the user and group named `dspam` and adds them to the `mail` group without a home directory (`-M`).

When installed, you need to configure Sendmail to use dspam rather than procmail or another mail delivery agent. Add the following line to the cf/cf/sendmail.mc file:

```
FEATURE(local_procmail,`/usr/local/bin/dspam',`dspam -t -Y -a $h "--mode=teft"
➡"--feature=chained" "--deliver=innocent" --user $u -d %u',`SPfhn9')dnl
```

Then rebuild your sendmail.cf, save a copy of the old one, and restart Sendmail like this:

```
# make sendmail.cf
# cp /etc/mail/sendmail.cf /etc/mail/sendmail.cf.old
# cp sendmail.cf /etc/mail/sendmail.cf
# /etc/init.d/sendmail restart
```

DSPAM will now process your email.

APACHE SETUP

In order to enable end users to manage their quarantined email, several changes must be made to the Apache setup on the machine running DSPAM.

The web user interface requires Apache suexec functionality, which is best provided through a virtual host. For best results, we recommend setting up DSPAM as a virtual host under your main domain. In our example here, we use dspam.mydomain.com. Add the following lines to the Apache configuration file located in /etc/httpd/conf/httpd.conf:

```
<VirtualHost ip.ad.dr.es>
ServerName      dspam.mydomain.com
DocumentRoot    /var/www/dspam
User            dspam
Group           dspam
</VirtualHost>

<Directory "/var/www/dspam/">
    Order allow,deny
    Allow from all
    Options ExecCGI
    AddHandler cgi-script .cgi

    AuthType        Basic
    AuthName        dspam
    AuthGroupFile   group
    AuthUserFile    user
    Require         valid-user
</Directory>
```

Change *ip.ad.dr.es* to an IP address on the machine you want to run DSPAM. Also, change dspam.mydomain.com to the address you want your users to go to when checking their quarantined messages. We place the DSPAM web home directory under /var/www for suexec to work, which also happens to be the default DocumentRoot location for many Apache/Linux installations. The .htpasswd file is created and/or updated via the /usr/bin/htpasswd command.

Alias Setup

In order to retrain DSPAM on classification errors using email, DSPAM user aliases must be set up. This can be done in one of two ways:

- Single system-wide alias
- Per-user aliases, one for every DSPAM user

System-Wide Alias

Using this method, DSPAM will read the username submitting the retraining request from the email header. It requires a couple of things to be set up. First of all, DSPAM needs to be configured with the --enable-parse-to-header flag. Secondly, a wildcard domain (such as spam.mydomain.com) must be set up to forward all messages to a user, which we will call spamtrainer.

The following /etc/mail/aliases entry will be defined:

```
spamuser:    "|/usr/local/bin/dspam --class=spam --source=error --mode=toe"
```

This alias forwards all mail to the dspam program, using the listed command line options. End users would forward their misclassified spam messages to the email address spam-*<username>*@spam.mydomain.com, where *<username>* is the email account of the user. For example, let's say the user joe wanted to have DSPAM reclassify a misclassified spam message. He would forward the message to spam-joe@spam.mydomain.com, and the message would be reclassified as spam.

If you are delivering spam messages rather than quarantining them, you need another alias for false positives. In that case, you use the dspam flag --deliver=innocent to specify a false positive rather than a false negative.

Per-User Aliases

This method is simpler, though it does require one alias per DSPAM user. Using per-user aliases, the user joe has the following /etc/mail/alias entry:

```
spam-joe:    "|/usr/local/bin/dspam --user bob --class=spam --source=error --mode=teft"
```

Then the user joe sends his misclassified spam messages to spam-joe@mydomain.com. If you are delivering spam messages rather than quarantining them, you need an alias for false positives defined for each user on the system. In that case, use the dspam flag --deliver=innocent to specify a false positive rather than a false negative.

OTHER SETUP

A couple of other items need to be set up. These include nightly cron jobs and notifications.

dspam_clean cron job

Each night, you should run the dspam_clean program, which cleans the database of unnecessary data. The user who runs the cron job needs to have read/write access to the DSPAM home directory (in our example, /var/dspam), so we use the dspam user. To run dspam_clean each night at 1:01 a.m., install the following cron job as user dspam:

```
0 0 * * * /usr/local/bin/dspam_clean
```

Include any necessary options at the end of this line.

Database Purge cron Job

If you are running the Berkeley DB back end, you probably will want to re-create your databases every week. Use the db_dump and db_load commands in a shell script to reclaim free space and make your installation run smoothly.

Notifications

DSPAM can send notification emails to users in the following cases:

- When the user receives the first message processed by DSPAM
- When the user receives the first spam message quarantined by DSPAM
- When the user's quarantine exceeds 2 MB

These notifications can be activated by copying the txt/ directory from the distribution into /var/dspam. You should modify these templates prior to installing them to reflect your organization's email addresses and URLs. This can be done by searching for the strings named configureme and yourdomain within the templates and changing them to your organization's specific settings.

Using DSPAM

After installation, the administrator doesn't need to do much. DSPAM includes a number of command line utilities intended for administrator use, as well as web-based GUI for user settings and user quarantine management.

Command Line Utilities

Some of the command line utilities that ship with DSPAM include

dspam_corpus

Used to populate a spam corpus with an existing mailbox-formatted file.

dspam_dump

Displays a DSPAM dictionary for a user.

dspam_clean

Cleans unneeded user data from databases.

dspam_stats

Displays spam stats for a particular user or all users on the system.

dspam_genaliases

Generates the DSPAM aliases required from the /etc/passwd file.

dspam_merge

Combines multiple users' dictionaries into a single dictionary.

DSPAM Graphical User Interface

The DSPAM package includes a web-based graphical user interface (GUI). If you used our example, you would access it by going to the following URL: *http://dspam.mydomain.com* (changing *mydomain.com* to the name of your domain). There are six screens in the DSPAM user GUI. These include

Performance

Preferences

Alerts

Quarantine

Analysis

History

The Performance screen displays statistics regarding this user's DSPAM statistics, including

- Messages processed
- Spam messages identified
- Spam ratio
- Accuracy
- False positives

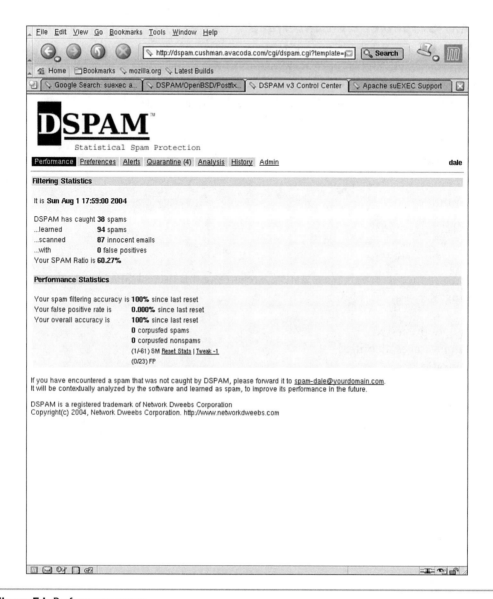

Figure F.1 Performance screen.

The Preferences screen includes some basic system settings that can be changed by the administrator, including

- Training mode
- Action to take when identifying a message as spam
- Training sensitivity
- Features

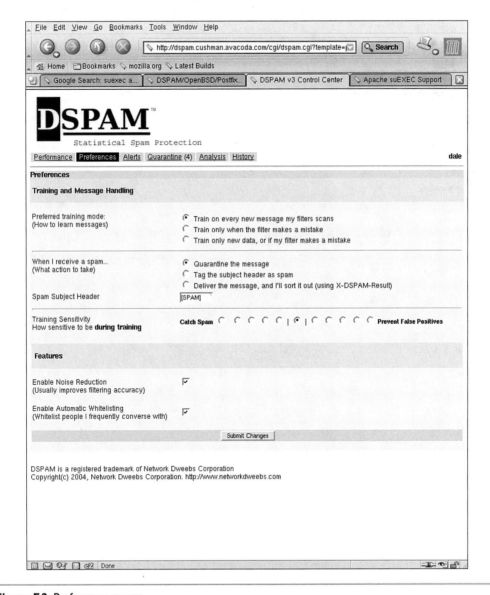

Figure F.2 Preferences screen.

The Alerts screen gives the user the ability to highlight quarantined messages with the given attributes, making identification of potential false positives easier.

Figure F.3 Alerts screen.

The Quarantine screen lists the messages sitting in the user's quarantine. There are buttons for deleting confirmed spam and delivering misclassified non-spam messages.

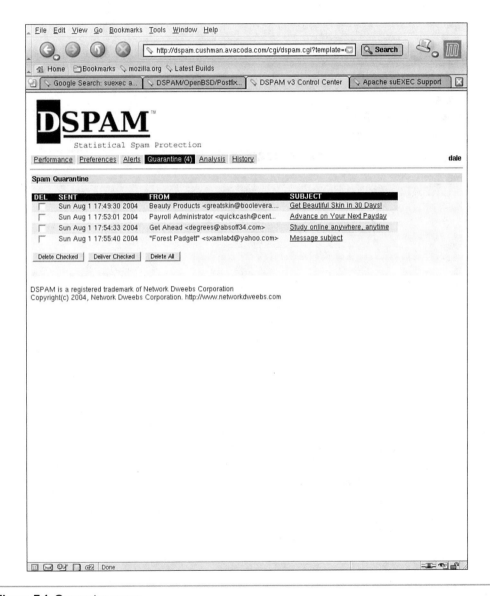

Figure F.4 Quarantine screen.

The Analysis screen shows a nice summary graphs of the past 24 hours and past 14 days of DSPAM activity.

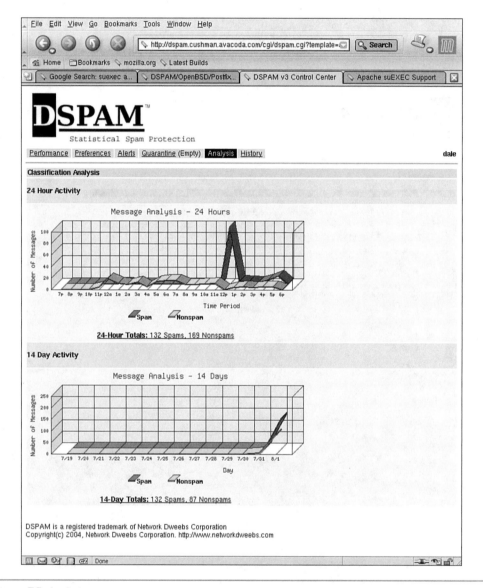

Figure F.5 Analysis screen.

The History screen lists all messages processed by DSPAM and how they were classified.

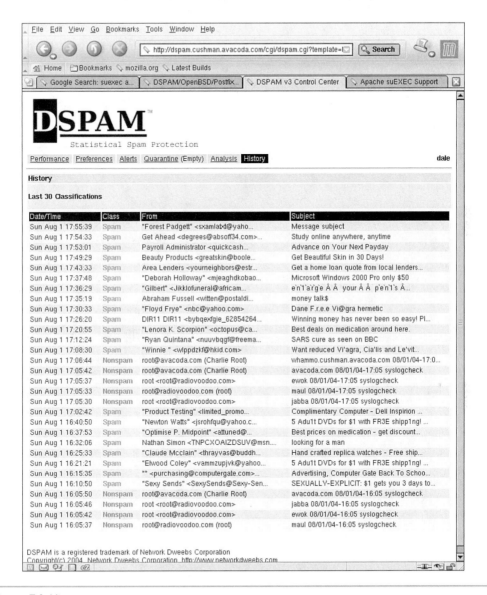

Figure F.6 History screen.

TROUBLESHOOTING

After starting DSPAM, the following log files can be examined for any errors that might occur:

```
/var/dspam/dspam.debug
/var/dspam/system.log
```

References

The references are arranged by chapter/appendix. The "Tools" section contains references related to the building of the anti-spam utilities covered in this book. The "Miscellaneous" section contains references not specific to a chapter.

Be sure to visit the web site for *Slamming Spam*, at *http://slammingspam.com*. It contains a complete list of URLs referenced, errata and other important information for the administrator battling spam.

INTRODUCTION (CHAPTER 1)

Ciphertrust Ironmail
http://www.ciphertrust.com/ironmail/

Internet Message Format (RFC2822)
http://www.ietf.org/rfc/rfc2822.txt

McAfee System Protection
McAfee SpamKiller Appliances
http://www.networkassociates.com/us/products/mcafee/antispam/spk_appliances.htm

Mirapoint anti-spam firewall
http://www.mirapoint.com/

Postini
http://www.postini.com/

Simple Mail Transfer Protocol (RFC2821)
http://www.ietf.org/rfc/rfc2821.txt

Symantec Brightmail AntiSpam
http://enterprisesecurity.symantec.com/products/products.cfm?ProductID=642%20

PROCMAIL (CHAPTER 2)

Procmail home page
http://www.procmail.org

Thorough collection of Procmail resources
http://www.iki.fi/era/procmail/links.html

The SpamBouncer: All-in-one Procmail spam filter
http://www.spambouncer.org/

SPAMASSASSIN (CHAPTER 3)

SpamAssassin home
http://spamassassin.apache.org/

SpamAssassin wiki
http://wiki.apache.org/spamassassin/

MICROSOFT WINDOWS INTEGRATION

SpamAssassin with Win32
http://www.openhandhome.com/howtosa260.html

POSTFIX INTEGRATION

amavisd-new
http://www.ijs.si/software/amavisd/

amavisd reference page
http://www.ijs.si/software/amavisd

qmail Integration

maildrop
http://www.flounder.net/~mrsam/maildrop/

qmail-scanner
http://qmail-scanner.sourceforge.net/

Sendmail Integration

milter
http://www.milter.org/

MIMEDefang
http://www.mimedefang.org/

Native MTA Anti-Spam Features (Chapter 4)

Blackhole Listing Services

Declude's List of All Known DNS-based Spam Databases
http://www.declude.com/JunkMail/Support/ip4r.htm

Jeff Makey's Blacklists Compared
http://www.sdsc.edu/~jeff/spam/Blacklists_Compared.html

Kelkea Mail Abuse Prevention (MAPS)
http://www.mail-abuse.com/

Spam and Open Relay Blocking System (SORBS)
http://www.dnsbl.au.sorbs.net/

SpamCop Blocking list
http://www.spamcop.net/bl.shtml

Spamhaus Block List (SBL)
http://www.spamhaus.org/SBL/

Spamlink's listing
http://spamlinks.net/filter-dnsbl.htm

POSTFIX

Fairly-Secure Anti-SPAM Gateway
http://www.flakshack.com/anti-spam/

Jim Seymour's suggestions/examples for Postfix anti-UCE configuration
http://jimsun.linxnet.com/misc/postfix-anti-UCE.txt

Postfix home
http://www.postfix.org/

Postfix access file documentation
http://www.postfix.org/access.5.html

Postfix Configuration - UCE Controls
http://www.postfix.org/uce.html#additional

QMAIL

checkpassword
http://cr.yp.to/checkpwd/checkpassword-0.90.tar.gz

The author of qmail, Dan Bernstein's qmail home
http://cr.yp.to/qmail.html

Dave Sills' Life With qmail page
http://www.lifewithqmail.org/

flame.org (wrote another patch that performs various header checks and bounce/flagging functionality)
http://www.flame.org/qmail/

Incoming MAIL FROM: addresses are verified to be returnable by requiring an MX or A record for the host given
http://www.flame.org/qmail/

mailscanner home
http://www.flounder.net/~mrsam/maildrop

Nagy Balazs wrote a patch called mfchec that ensures the domain name on the envelope sender is a valid DNS name
http://js.hu/package/qmail/qmail-1.03-mfcheck.4.patch

Netqmail, a collection of patches to qmail
http://www.qmail.org/netqmail

netqmail-1.05 distribution
http://www.qmail.org/netqmail-1.05.tar.gz

qmail on the web
http://qmail.org/top.html

qmail Anti-Spam HOWTO
http://www.chrishardie.com/tech/qmail/qmail-antispam.html

qmail-scanner home page
http://qmail-scanner.sourceforge.net

qmailqueue patched version of qmail-1.03 prebuilt RPM
http://untroubled.org/qmail+patches/

Patch for implementing qmailqueue patch
http://www.qmail.org/qmailqueue-patch

rblsmtpd, the realtime blackhole listing facility for qmail
http://cr.yp.to/ucspi-tcp/rblsmtpd.html

Rejecting SMTP connections at the network level from hosts with bad DNS
http://www.chrishardie.com/tech/qmail/qmail-antispam.html

tcprules documentation
http://cr.yp.to/ucspi-tcp/tcprules.html

SENDMAIL

Collection of anti-spam features in Sendmail
http://www.sendmail.org/m4/anti_spam.html

m4 documentation
http://www.sendmail.org/m4/intro_m4.html

Sendmail home
http://www.sendmail.org/

SMTP AUTH AND STARTTLS (CHAPTER 5)

SMTP Service Extension for Authentication RFC
http://www.ietf.org/rfc/rfc2554.txt

SMTP Service Extension for Secure SMTP over TLS
http://www.ietf.org/rfc/rfc2487.txt

Stunnel home
http://www.stunnel.org/

POSTFIX INTEGRATION

Security Sage's SASL2 authentication and TLS encryption guide
http://www.securitysage.com/guides/postfix_sasltls.html

QMAIL INTEGRATION

qmail SMTP AUTH patch
http://shupp.org/patches/netqmail-1.05-tls-smtpauth-20040705.patch

SMTP Authentication [Tutorial]
http://www.fehcom.de/qmail/smtpauth.html

SENDMAIL INTEGRATION

Claus Aßmann's Compiling STARTTLS in sendmail
http://www.sendmail.org/~ca/email/tlscomp.html

Jon Fullmer's How to Set Up SMTP AUTH
http://www.jonfullmer.com/smtpauth

SMTP AUTH in sendmail 8.10-8.12
http://www.sendmail.org/~ca/email/auth.html

DISTRIBUTED CHECKSUM FILTERING (CHAPTER 6)

Distributed Checksum Clearinghouse home
http://www.rhyolite.com/anti-spam/dcc/

Vipul's Razor home
http://razor.sourceforge.net/

Vipul's Razor documentation
http://razor.sourceforge.net/docs/

INTRODUCTION TO BAYESIAN FILTERING (CHAPTER 7)

Bogofilter Calculations: Comparing Geometric Mean with Fisher's Method for Combining Probabilities
http://www.bgl.nu/bogofilter/fisher.html

Paul Graham's essay titled "A Plan for Spam"
http://www.paulgraham.com/spam.html

Paul Graham's essay titled "Better Bayesian Filtering"
http://www.paulgraham.com/better.html

Paul Graham's essay, "So Far, So Good"
http://www.paulgraham.com/sofar.html

Patrick Pantel and Lin, Dekang, "SpamCop—A Spam Classification & Organization Program." Proceedings of AAAI-98 Workshop on Learning for Text Categorization

Gary Robinson, "A Statistical Approach to the Spam Problem"
http://www.linuxjournal.com/article.php?sid=6467

The Wabe: Bayesian Filtering: Part II
http://www.the-wabe.com/log/?entry=76

Yerazunis, Bill, "Sparse binary Polynomial Hash Message Filtering and the Crm114 Discriminator." Proceedings of the 2003 Spam Conference

BAYESIAN FILTERING (CHAPTER 8)

Anti-Spam Server Proxy
http://assp.sourceforge.net

bogofilter
http://bogofilter.sourceforge.net

CRM114
http://crm114.sourceforge.net/

EMAIL CLIENT FILTERING (CHAPTER 9)

K9, another interface to POPFile for MS Outlook
http://www.keir.net/k9.html

Microsoft Outlook Express home
http://www.microsoft.com/windows/oe/

Microsoft Outlook web page
http://www.microsoft.com/outlook/

Mozilla Suite (including Messenger)
http://www.mozilla.org/products/mozilla1.x/

Outclass, a POPFile plugin for MS Outlook
http://www.vargonsoft.com/Outclass/

POPFile, a Bayesian Classifier for any POP3 email client
http://popfile.sourceforge.net

Spamihilator, a Bayesian Classifier for any POP3 client
http://www.spamihilator.com/

MICROSOFT EXCHANGE (CHAPTER 10)

IMF Archive Manager to view SCL scores in the UceArchive folder
http://www.gotdotnet.com/Community/Workspaces/workspace.aspx?id=e8728572-3a4e-425a-9b26-a3fda0d06fee

IMF primer
http://www.msexchange.org/tutorials/Microsoft-Exchange-Intelligent-Message-Filter.html

Viewing IMF SCL scores in Outlook
http://blogs.msdn.com/exchange/archive/2004/05/26/142607.aspx

McAfee SpamKiller for Mail Servers
http://www.mcafeesecurity.com/us/products/mcafee/antispam/spk_mailserver.htm

Microsoft Exchange
http://www.microsoft.com/exchange/

MSExchange.org's anti-spam section
http://antispam.msexchange.org/

LOTUS DOMINO AND LOTUS NOTES (CHAPTER 11)

IBM Lotus Notes/Domino
http://www.lotus.com/products/product4.nsf/wdocs/dominohomepage

McAfee SpamKiller for Mail Servers
http://www.mcafeesecurity.com/us/products/mcafee/antispam/spk_mailserver.htm

SENDER VERIFICATION (CHAPTER 12)

Active Spam Killer (ASK)
http://ask.thinkhost.com/

Camram, proof of work, electronic signature, CRM114 interface
http://www.camram.org/

checkpassword-pam, an implementation of checkpassword-compatible authentication program
http://checkpasswd-pam.sourceforge.net/

EmailRelay SMTP proxy and store-and-forward MTA
http://emailrelay.sourceforge.net/

Hashcash Proof of work web site
http://www.hashcash.org/

NormalizeMIME, a MIME email message parser
http://hyvatti.iki.fi/~jaakko/spam/

Python language home
http://www.python.org

Tagged Message Delivery Agent (TMDA) home
http://tmda.net

TMDA Web interface
http://tmda.net/tmda-cgi

TRE regular expression matching library
http://laurikari.net/tre/

SENDER POLICY FRAMEWORK (APPENDIX A)

Sender Policy Framework (SPF) home
http://spf.pobox.com

SPF online wizard setup tool
http://spf.pobox.com/wizard.html

SPF online record check tool
http://spftools.net/check.php

Reporting Spam (Appendix B)

Online tool for help in analyzing spam messages
http://www.dnsstuff.com/

Reading email headers
http://www.stopspam.org/email/headers.html

SamSpade tool for analyzing spam messages
http://www.samspade.org/ssw/download.html

SpamCop online service for analyzing spam headers and reporting spam
http://www.spamcop.net

DSPAM (Appendix F)

DSPAM home
http://www.nuclearelephant.com/projects/dspam/

Tools

GNU gcc
http://gcc.gnu.org/

GNU make
http://www.gnu.org/software/make/

GNU wget
http://www.gnu.org/software/wget/wget.html

MISCELLANEOUS

A good starting point for fighting spam
http://spam.abuse.net/

Apache web server home
http://httpd.apache.org/

Coalition Against Unsolicited Commercial Email (CAUCE)
http://www.cauce.org/

Comprehensive Perl Archive Network (CPAN)
http://www.cpan.org

Internet Mail Consortium
http://www.imc.org/

Maildir home
http://cr.yp.to/proto/maildir.html

mutt command line email client
http://www.mutt.org/

SpamLinks
http://spamlinks.net/

Index

B

E

Register

Your Book

at www.awprofessional.com/register

You may be eligible to receive:

- Advance notice of forthcoming editions of the book
- Related book recommendations
- Chapter excerpts and supplements of forthcoming titles
- Information about special contests and promotions throughout the year
- Notices and reminders about author appearances, tradeshows, and online chats with special guests

Contact us

If you are interested in writing a book or reviewing manuscripts prior to publication, please write to us at:

Editorial Department
Addison-Wesley Professional
75 Arlington Street, Suite 300
Boston, MA 02116 USA
Email: AWPro@aw.com

Addison-Wesley

Visit us on the Web: http://www.awprofessional.com